WITH THE BEST OF INTENTIONS

WITH THE BEST OF INTENTIONS

Interreligious Missteps and Mistakes

EDITED BY

LUCINDA MOSHER, ELINOR J. PIERCE,
AND OR N. ROSE

ORBIS BOOKS
Maryknoll, New York 10545

ORBIS BOOKS
Maryknoll, New York 10545

Fathers and Brothers
MARYKNOLL.™

Founded in 1970, Orbis Books endeavors to publish works that enlighten the mind, nourish the spirit, and challenge the conscience. The publishing arm of the Maryknoll Fathers and Brothers, Orbis seeks to explore the global dimensions of the Christian faith and mission, to invite dialogue with diverse cultures and religious traditions, and to serve the cause of reconciliation and peace. The books published reflect the views of their authors and do not represent the official position of the Maryknoll Society. To learn more about Maryknoll and Orbis Books, please visit our website at www.orbisbooks.com

Library of Congress Cataloging-in-Publication Data

Names: Mosher, Lucinda, editor. | Pierce, Elinor J., editor. | Rose, Or N., editor.
Title: With the best of intentions : interreligious missteps and mistakes / Lucinda Mosher, Elinor J. Pierce, and Or N. Rose.
Description: Maryknoll, New York : Orbis, [2023] | Includes bibliographical references and index. | Summary: "Mistakes, missteps, and outright failures of the interreligious encounter are explored through personal essays"— Provided by publisher.
Identifiers: LCCN 2023012210 (print) | LCCN 2023012211 (ebook) | ISBN 9781626985452 (trade paperback) | ISBN 9798888660041 (epub)
Subjects: LCSH: Religions—Relations. | Intercultural communication—Religious aspects. | Psychology, Religious. | Miscommunication.
Classification: LCC BL410 .W58 2023 (print) | LCC BL410 (ebook) | DDC 201/.5—dc23/eng/20230801
LC record available at https://lccn.loc.gov/2023012210
LC ebook record available at https://lccn.loc.gov/2023012211

CONTENTS

Part II

Presumptions

Part III

Conversations

Part IV
Competing Values

Part V
Power Dynamics

PREFACE

Since missteps are inevitable in life, we do well to learn from them, even in matters of religious import. It is good that interfaith relations have progressed to the point where smaller and more intimate successes and failures are taking place, and where a book like *With the Best of Intentions* can be quickly populated with the reflections of so many experienced practitioners of interfaith relations who have learned by their mistakes as well as their successes.

It is only when people of different faith traditions are regularly in contact with one another that we can really learn the small courtesies that signal deeper familiarity with one another's living practices and slowly advance beyond the awkward politeness of strangers. As we become closer to one another and more intentionally live as neighbors whose lives regularly and normally intermingle, then missteps become more likely. Greater familiarity increases the possibility of slips and lapses in the more intimate courtesies that all of us in our communities presume. We may be surprised to learn others do not take our customs for granted. When problems arise, both outsiders and insiders should be able to start thinking anew about our ways of speaking, our customs when we gather for worship or meditation, and the truths we adhere to but never question until we see, perhaps for the first time, how such truths can appear to others.

Some courtesies and customs are, from the start, deep rooted— grounded in the scriptures or earliest generation of a tradition. Others come later, reflecting cultural differences that are only later on and by habit charged with religious significance. As many of the stories in *With the Best of Intentions* also show, some small differences end up having deeper philosophical and theological implications, and it is harder simply to accommodate those we meet. Several stories raise a case in point: can a man and a woman of different faiths and cultural backgrounds shake hands in public? Deference is definitely required; but over time, when greater mutual respect and trust have developed, further discussion about how men and women relate in public should be possible, with both sides learning. It is fitting that *With the Best of Intentions* takes note of these deeper, complicated tensions, finding a way into them not by theories but by negotiating how we act toward one another.

Reading through many of the stories gathered here prompted me to recollect my own experiences as well. About five years ago, I was near the center of one small, but not unimportant, religious misstep. I was hosting a regular monthly Catholic Mass at my Jesuit house in Cambridge, just off the Harvard campus. A group of thirty or more students, staff, and faculty had gathered for Mass and supper after it. As usual, the gathering attracted a few members of the Harvard Divinity community who were not Catholic or not Christian. On that particular evening, two Buddhist nuns from Asia walked in, clearly a little apprehensive about whether they should have come or would be welcomed. I was very glad to see them, and greeted them warmly. They asked if they could enter the chapel and share in the Mass. I told them that they could, but that it would be best that they did not receive Communion. They readily agreed, and all was set, I thought. But, at Communion, they did receive. Since the nuns were in their gray garb and had shaved heads, it was obvious that they were Buddhists. One Catholic student, a visitor from abroad, was visibly upset by the fact that the nuns had received Communion, and confronted me: why did I let that happen?

After the visiting student expressed her concern, I went over to clarify things with the nuns. I said that I hoped they had enjoyed the service. (They had.) I also said that I was curious why they received Communion when they had agreed not to. They explained that, when I had mentioned "receiving Communion," they did not know what that meant. Throughout the Mass, they simply did as the others did, including receiving the host. Ah, I had not explained even the basics! The disturbed Catholic student too eventually went over to talk with the Buddhist nuns. After a moment of similar explanation and regrets, they quickly found that, otherwise, they had much in common. Peace returned, and even an unexpected friendship became possible. It was a Mass to remember, since what was unheard of before was now becoming part of Catholic life in Cambridge, and we were finding our way. So, there is hope. Buddhist nuns at a Catholic Mass—it is a sign of hope when such events become common, and when the discussion is not about whether this should happen, but about how we—insiders and outsiders—should act when it does happen. *With the Best of Intentions* is full of such examples that show, again and again, that mistakes turn out to be real parts of a necessary longer learning process.

A bonus inherent in this book is that what we learn interreligiously will be beneficial at home, too. Even traditions in themselves and on their own are not free of disagreements about how to practice the faith. Among us Catholics, for instance: Genuflect or bow upon entering the church?

Prefer the vernacular or Latin as the language of worship? Kneel or stand during the Eucharistic Prayer? Perform the sign of peace as a wave, a handshake, an embrace, or, indeed, a holy kiss? Receive Communion in the hand or on the tongue? As we learn interreligiously, we might well gain wisdom that will help us to negotiate difficult issues at home too.

It is a great step forward, then, that we now have before us so fine a treasury of tales arising from the world of practice—wisdom by which we can critique and adjust our theories about one another, learning from what we do, and from how others do or don't understand what we are up to. Filled as it is with the learned wisdom of women and men committed to interreligious relations, cooperation, and friendships, *With the Best of Intentions* is required reading in the maturing world of interreligious protocols and courtesies.

Francis X. Clooney, SJ
Parkman Professor of Divinity
Harvard University

INTRODUCTION

It often begins with the best of intentions. So it was when Rabbi Or N. Rose asked his wife, a scholar-practitioner of Jewish feminism, to speak about intersectionality to participants in a leadership initiative. The session seemed to go well. "On the drive home, we talked about how pleased we were," Or recalls. But, then came a strongly worded email, expressing concern over the session's handling of the topic of "Zionism." In spite of good intention, says Or, "we had made a mistake. During the next few hours, we would need to figure out how to repair it. Then we would need to consider how to avoid similar missteps in the future." Incidents like this are at the foundation of *With the Best of Intentions*, a collection of stories exploring some of interfaith encounter's mistakes, missteps, and outright failures.

Concept

This book is the product of the merger of two creative impulses. The first came from Or, who with Jennifer Peace and Gregory Mobley edited *Our Neighbor's Faith: Stories of Interreligious Encounter, Growth, and Transformation* (Orbis Books, 2012). Most of its essays focused on positive transformations, which was appropriate at that moment in the emergence of the field of interreligious studies. Yet, contributor Frank Clooney was moved to ask: "What about when things go wrong?" The question grabbed Or's attention. Perhaps, one day, he might help to curate a follow-up volume. He already had a name for it: *With the Best of Intentions.*

The second impulse came from Elinor Pierce. She leads The Pluralism Project's case initiative, in which the dilemmas and disputes of our multireligious society serve as primary texts for understanding religious diversity and interfaith relations. Having concentrated for some time on decision-focused cases (which steer directly into the problems of a protagonist), she wanted to experiment with a new format: the failure case. The emphasis would still be on a mishap, but the focus would shift from the *other* to the *self*. We might document our own mistakes, missteps, or misunderstandings as a move toward building humility, self-reflexivity, and other capacities for interfaith encounter. A volume of essays about mistakes, she thought, would provide helpful examples for students, scholars, and practitioners.

In 2021, Or and Ellie—now aware of the symbiotic potential of their respective visions of a new interfaith resource—enlisted a third partner: Lucinda Mosher. Known for her particular skill as an editor of books and journal issues on multireligious concerns, she would act as catalyst, facilitating the merger of Or's and Ellie's impulses into a cohesive project highlighting accounts of specific, situated opportunities for considering alternative paths, means of repair, and improvements to interfaith efforts.

We three editors are no strangers to such phenomena. Many of Or's reflections on interfaith challenges arise from his work at Hebrew College. For Lucinda, the contexts have been classrooms, denominational and grassroots interfaith engagement, and involvement with an international Christian–Muslim dialogue. Ellie's perspective has been informed by case study interviews, but also by decades of field research and site visits. We recount challenges in an effort to engage others in a personal narrative that holds important lessons within it.

Approach

Our book's subtitle includes the term *interreligious*, an apt descriptor of interactions between people who differ in their orientation toward religion—whether that relationship be deeply committed or aloof; whether that attitude be positive and generative or negative and destructive. In actuality, we use *interreligious* and *interfaith* somewhat interchangeably—fully aware of the debates around which term is broader and cognizant that some may feel that a neologism such as *interbelief* or *interspiritual* might be more appropriate. Whichever of these terms is in play, our primary concern is with the prefix. *Inter-* implies difference.

Our concern is with the work that takes place between and among different faiths, religions, beliefs, worldviews, life stances, ethical systems, and value frameworks. That work is intersectional: it recognizes multiple, diverse categories of identity. The work is also fraught. Bridge-building efforts traverse vast fault lines: some chasms cannot be bridged; some obstacles cannot be overcome. The complexity of religious difference and the challenges of bridging it provide ongoing opportunity for learning, growth, and real transformation. Reflecting on our missteps is crucial for this sometimes sacred and often complicated work. We need more (self-) critical discussion of the times and places that interfaith efforts go awry. Why did a particular program, initiative, or relationship falter? What was our part in it? Could it have worked under different circumstances? Were the conditions just not right for such an undertaking? Were we able to regroup or salvage elements of what we hoped for? Did something unexpected emerge? What have we learned from these experiences?

Application

With the Best of Intentions foregrounds the lived experience of dealing with such questions. The reader hears from forty scholars, leaders, students, and activists whose stances vis-à-vis religion include Judaism, Christianity, Islam, Mormonism, the Bahá'í Faith, Buddhism, Hinduism, Ifá, Sikhism, Ruism, Humanism, multifaith, blended identity, and unaffiliated.[1] Through their essays, they promote a new form of religious literacy. As Marianne Moyaert has explained, interfaith literacy requires humility, self-reflexivity, curiosity, and open-mindedness.[2] These tales of mistakes, missteps, and conundrums encourage us to ponder: What are the limits of my knowledge or understanding? What prejudices am I bringing to the encounter? What impact might my missteps, however unintentional, have on others? How might I repair, reframe, or reimagine my role?

Hence, this book's chapters, which can be read in any order, are well suited to collegial reading and discussion. This makes *With the Best of Intentions* suitable not only for the classroom but as a resource for community organizations, book clubs, and youth groups. As Diana Eck has suggested, the mistakes examined in this book are more significant than a mere hole in one's sock, uncovered during the removal of shoes at a visit to another's place of worship. They are situations that can help us uncover holes in our understanding, reveal our own privilege, or discover our own failings. In some instances, the writer is subject to the mistakes of others—whether situational or structural. Some involve intractable issues. Some reveal fundamental threats to the purpose, or premise, of interreligious work. A few are genuinely funny. All are grounded in personal experience—with the potential to help readers reflect upon their own.

Overview

A preface by Francis X. Clooney, SJ—an acclaimed scholar of comparative theology—sets the tone of this volume. *Part I: First Impressions* offers seven considerations of mistakes made in initial encounters. Lexi Gewertz and Kathryn Lohre explain how minor mishaps can have major impact. David Grafton demonstrates the value in getting people's names right. Leadership lessons emerge as Hans Gustafson considers the cost of deflection. Aida Mansoor affirms the importance of asking questions—particularly in matters of food. On the matter of identity, Or Rose describes a moment of misinterpretation; Marcia Sietstra recounts missteps during a tour of a religious site; and Jon Sweeney details a misunderstanding.

Part II: Presumptions ponders interreligious misunderstandings in six diverse contexts. For Jack Gordon, a prayer at an interfaith event proves problematic; for Soren Hessler, the physical site chosen for interreligious engagement raises red flags. Wakoh Shannon Hickey offers a White Buddhist's perspective on religious and racial equity, while Rachel Mikva considers assumptions in faith-based coalitions. Hussein Rashid argues for authenticity in interreligious settings, and Heather Miller Rubens details how origin stories express organizational assumptions.

The six essays in *Part III: Conversations* explore difficult one-on-one encounters. Daniel Berman describes reflections that have led to greater understanding. Nancy Fuchs Kreimer discovers an intrafaith mistake. Jeffery Long recounts a contentious interreligious exchange. Nisa Muhammad considers her own bias. Anthony Cruz Pantojas explores radical interdependence. Nikky-Guninder Kaur Singh reflects on an interreligious tête-à-tête that she wishes had taken place.

Part IV: Competing Values examines seven examples of intractable interreligious divides. Preeta Banerjee argues for appreciation, rather than appropriation. Yehezkel Landau unpacks lessons from interreligious dialogue on Israel/Palestine, while Christopher Leighton describes how concert planning exacerbated longstanding interreligious tensions. Eboo Patel outlines competing concepts of justice in interfaith work. Jennifer Peace considers her boundaries in intra- and interfaith contexts. Bin Song details the challenges underlying the founding of a campus Confucian association. Jaxon Washburn reflects on mistakes in interfaith spaces— among them, his own family!

With eight diverse offerings, *Part V: Power Dynamics* steers directly into personal experiences of structural oppression. M. Ajisebo McElwaine Abimbola describes the impact of racism and colonialism on a global interreligious gathering. Bilal Ansari contends with religious and racial power structures while a chaplain. Danielle Buhuro (a Black clinical pastoral education supervisor) and Maggie Goldberger (through the lens of Gen Z) each question power structures in interreligious contexts. Chenxing Han and Andrew Housiaux respond to erasure of Asian American Buddhists by constructing an immersive educational experience. Cassandra Lawrence and Wendy Goldberg challenge male misconduct and create new pathways for women's leadership. Vrajvihari Sharan describes student experiences of classroom conversations gone awry. C. Denise Yarborough explores the power structures embedded in Israel/Palestine dialogue.

An *Afterword* by Mahan Mirza of the University of Notre Dame emphasizes the value of making mistakes.

Gratitudes

Any collaborative project succeeds only by virtue of the kindness of others. Our first round of gratitude belongs to each of this volume's contributing authors. We are thankful for their enthusiasm for our goals for *With the Best of Intentions* and their patience with our editorial process. We are grateful also for conversations with activists and scholars that did not yield book chapters but nevertheless informed our approach to exploring interreligious missteps.

Each of us editors is blessed to have had the support of family, friends, and colleagues throughout this project. Special mention is due to Barrie Mosher, Asheesh Gupta, and Judith Rosenbaum; to the staff of the *Journal of Interreligious Studies*; and to our respective colleagues at Hartford International University for Religion and Peace, The Pluralism Project at Harvard University, and Hebrew College. In addition, all three of us acknowledge the impact of Diana Eck on our lives as interfaith activists. And, of course, we thank Robert Ellsworth, Jon Sweeney, and everyone else at Orbis Books who enabled the publication of this volume.

With the Best of Intentions is informed by belief that unpacking our mistakes, failures, and misunderstandings—surfacing awkward, and sometimes painful, moments—can disrupt assumptions, promote reflection, and lead to deeper transformation. This volume of essays—accessible by a general audience yet appropriate for the classroom—invites further reflection upon interfaith mistakes, disappointments, and conundrums, with the goal of identifying fault lines, exploring means for repair, and finding new insights. We hope it will be a vital contribution to the expanding field of interreligious studies and helpful for those engaged in local and national interfaith efforts. Finally, please know that any errors herein are ours and that we will be grateful to have our attention called to them. In return, we will strive to offer not only a sincere apology but also a means for repair.

Notes

1. We recognize that our roster of contributors, while quite varied, certainly does not encompass the full range of religious diversity in the United States, nor all key voices and perspectives from our field.

2. Marianne Moyaert "Interreligious Hermeneutics, Prejudice, and the Problem of Testimonial Injustice," *Religious Education* 114, no. 5 (2019): 609–23.

Part I

FIRST IMPRESSIONS

Chapter 1

SWEATING THE SMALL STUFF
When Minor Missteps Have Major Impact

LEXI GEWERTZ AND KATHRYN LOHRE

Have you ever made a trivial mistake in your interreligious work when you focused more on preparation than on being present? Or have you ever made a small misstep because you were overthinking your encounter which prevented you from paying attention to the people in the moment? In this chapter, we coauthors each share a small mistake we have made in interreligious engagement over the years. We explore how such mistakes can serve as a mirror, showing us our bigger intentions and hopes for interreligious understanding—and can increase our capacity to cultivate interreligious spaces of grace where mistakes are expected.

The two of us met because of our interest in, and commitment to, interreligious relations. Both of us started as researchers at The Pluralism Project at Harvard University—an initiative by Diana Eck that studies and interprets the changing religious landscape of the United States. Eventually each of us served (in different years) as its assistant director. Our interreligious work, then and since, has helped us to grow in appreciation for what is at the heart of any transformative interfaith effort: real human relationships. After all, interreligious dialogue and cooperation take place among people, not traditions. At the same time, we have learned (sometimes the hard way) that whenever human beings are involved, mistakes are bound to be made. We have both made our fair share!

In the fifteen years since our meeting, we have seen each other grow from student researchers to professional interfaith leaders in various roles in the academy, in nonprofits, and within our religious communities. Yet no matter how much we have grown in our work, we have never completely outgrown making mistakes. We can make mistakes when we overthink the nature of difference in an interfaith encounter, and we can make mistakes when we fail to prepare ourselves for those differences, perhaps focusing too much on information and not enough on inter-personal interaction. Over the years, we have learned to stop striving for the impossibility of perfection and instead to recognize that our growth is tied directly to learning from our mistakes. The two examples we share below seek to illustrate this point. Our capacity to provide leadership that acknowledges, reflects upon, and learns from our mistakes can serve to cultivate grace for others to do the same.

Under Construction:
Lexi's "Should Have Known Better" Misstep

Growing up, I lovingly referred to myself as a religious mutt: I was the product of a culturally Jewish father who was not observant despite a traditional religious Jewish upbringing, and a formerly Catholic mother who attended only Catholic schools as a child but who no longer engaged with Catholicism beyond Christmas. Our home was not at all a religious one; we had a Christmas tree at home, and we made latkes in December, but the rest was for us to sort out ourselves.

Although I felt a deep connection to my Jewish heritage, had a close relationship with my Jewish grandparents, and had predominantly Jew-ish classmates and close friends, I never felt like I had a seat at the Jew-ish table, so to speak. I can see now that some part of my desire to study religion was to elbow my way in; I may not have been bat mitzvah-ed along with the rest of my friends in seventh grade, but maybe I could make up for this through intense academic study. I traveled to Israel on a group trip for young adults. In college, I participated in Jewish celebra-tions at the student center and immersed myself in the study of religion. I was encouraged by two mentor professors who helped me explore Juda-ism from an academic perspective and who cultivated an interest in also studying Islam. Upon graduating, I set out for Harvard Divinity School to deepen that knowledge.

Kathryn and I met when she interviewed me to be a summer intern at The Pluralism Project in 2007. I was excited to join an all-women cohort in researching the religious sites and communities of Greater Boston. It was the summer after my first year of graduate school, and I was eager to stop studying ancient religious histories in the library and start engag-ing with current-day religious traditions and the people who ascribed to them. By the time I started my internship, I was feeling overly confident in my growing expertise as a religion scholar.

As part of my internship, I took on the project of researching the fledgling Islamic Society of Boston Cultural Center (ISBCC), set to become New England's biggest mosque. The ISBCC community, like countless other Muslim communities around the country, faced backlash and objections when the group wanted to build and open a mosque. On the surface, these objections concerned parking and zoning; in the case of the ISBCC, the objections went further, questioning the source of funding for the mosque, causing many delays. When an exhaustive investigation revealed the baselessness of these concerns, construction finally began. By the time I started my internship, the building was almost complete. I familiarized myself with the community, then reached out to its leaders to have a brief conversation. I was impressed and a little intimidated to hear back from the imam himself. He offered not just to sit with me for a conversation but also to give me a tour. I eagerly accepted the invitation. A week later, on a sweltering August day, I boarded a subway train and headed to the ISBCC.

I was nervous! This was the first time I was going out as a researcher into the religious communities I studied, and I wanted to represent The Pluralism Project well. I tried to remind myself that I was well prepared and knowledgeable about Islam, despite being a (sort of?) Jewish girl from Chicago. I was proudly wearing my crisp new Pluralism Project t-shirt that depicted the American flag with religious symbols instead of stars. In order to respect the modesty expected in a mosque, I also carried a jacket and headscarf. When I got to the mosque, the huge tower—not yet capped as a minaret—was striking. I marveled at how the design blended the classic New England sturdiness of red brick with the curved lines of the arches, dome, and tower typically found in a mosque.

I donned my scarf, walked up the steps to the almost-complete building, and waited in the lobby. Soon the imam appeared, wearing a white cap, a white *thawb* (robe), and a big, welcoming smile. As he strode toward me with his hands clasped behind his back, I returned the smile and walked toward him with my hand outstretched. As I came closer, the imam made no effort to move his hands from behind his back. Being slow to understand what was happening, I left my hand out for a few seconds too long, and the imam made a kind and conciliatory nod of his head to acknowledge me and offer a welcome. My nervousness turned to pure embarrassment as I realized that the imam would not shake my hand! As in some Jewish communities, some observant Muslims will not touch or shake hands with a person of the opposite gender if they are not related. While this varies greatly across Muslim communities, it is a fairly safe assumption that an imam would follow this religious prohibition. Here I was, not just a fledgling religion scholar who studied Islam, but also a researcher for an organization built on interreligious relationships, and I made a glaring faux pas that I absolutely should have known better to avoid.

Remaining friendly and hospitable, the imam introduced himself and began to walk us around the building. I feebly attempted to ask him questions about the mosque and the community center, about the school they were planning to open, about the Muslim-owned stores they were going to host in part of the building—all of the questions I had prepared that I thought would carry me through the encounter. But, I was still stuck in my head about my gaffe. It eroded my sense of confidence. I stumbled over a few of my prepared questions. The imam could not have been more open or kind. He answered all my questions and was proud to show me how the ISBCC would bring people together in a way that had not previously been possible. Upon completion, it would be creating space—literally and figuratively—for worship and community.

On the subway ride home, my excitement over my first visit in Boston's religious communities was overshadowed by my embarrassment over the (nonexistent) handshake. While admittedly this was a small mistake, it hurt because I should have known better. My education, my prior experiences in mosques and in Muslim countries, my training at The Pluralism Project was such that I should have known to let the imam take the lead, so as to prevent either one of us from feeling awkward or uncomfortable. And there was something more complex here too; while my mistake undermined my sense of identity as a scholar of religion, more broadly it also eroded some of my confidence that I could study my way into a community. Small moments like this one with the imam—or when I once incorrectly translated into English the Hebrew name of a Jewish holiday while speaking in a small graduate seminar—could quickly undermine the work I put in to feel like I belonged, whether in the Jewish community or the interfaith community.

Fifteen years later, when I think of that moment with the imam, my cheeks still prickle with embarrassment. Even after all these years, that "I should have known better" feeling lingers. I remember how quickly my mind jumped to the conclusion that I was somehow not qualified or deserving of representing an interfaith center like The Pluralism Project. But, I also remember the imam's response: the kindness he showed through his willingness to still accept me and move on together in conversation without condemning me for my foible. Experiences like that have helped me work through uncomfortable situations. The imam's graciousness, and my desire to still engage and build a relationship with him and his community despite my mistake, confirmed for me that I could make a faux pas and still have a seat at the table.

That memory also continues to reassure me of my inclusion in the Jewish community, even when I stumble. At times when I feel sheepish if

I forget to ask a guest if they keep kosher, or when I don't know the words to a certain prayer, this memory reminds me that blunders don't mean banishment; they show us a way we can be better without showing us the door. And in a way this is even more reassuring than if we had never made a mistake at all.

I recently left the professional world of interfaith work to join a non-profit that works to improve the educational experience for immigrant, asylee, and refugee youth. My experience as an outsider there—an American-born White woman with privilege both seen and unseen—is not unlike my experiences entering interfaith spaces. I have stumbled plenty. For example, a (non-Hispanic) colleague had informed me that we should stop using "Latinx" and instead start using "Latine." I did so in front of a Hispanic board member, who gently informed us that "Latine," while used by some people, is considered problematic by others (herself included), and she suggested we not use it. Was it embarrassing? Sure. But, it highlighted for me, as did my interfaith work, the importance of owning your mistake, considering its implications, and taking time to learn more about how it came to happen and what you might do differently in the future.

Piglets and *Iftars* on Zoom, Oh My!
Kathryn's "Overthinking" Mistake

Lexi's story brings back fond memories; but it also reminds me of my own mistakes during those years. At that time, I was freshly out of graduate school. Although I had gone from student researcher to assistant director of The Pluralism Project, the kind of nerves Lexi describes were still very present in my work. Despite my best intentions, I screwed up many times. There was the time my outfit was not appropriate for the occasion, or the time I mixed up the halal and kosher catering orders. The most egregious was when I scheduled a major conference that conflicted with a holy day I hadn't thought to include in our consultations. But, as Lexi noted, recalling cringe-worthy missteps can be a good thing: the learning continues.

Religious diversity became an interest to me when I was a child. I was the daughter of a Lutheran pastor; my closest friend was a rabbi's daughter. As children of religious leaders, we shared a lot in common. We would commiserate about living in the "fishbowl" of our faith communities, and having to accompany our fathers on countless visits to members of their respective congregations. Other forms of religious, cultural, and ethnic diversity—such as our faith community's participation in welcoming of new immigrants and refugees—shaped my childhood as well.

Unlike Lexi, my own upbringing was within a single tradition: Christianity. I grew up in a household where my father was a pastor, and my mother worked for the denominational publishing house. My extended family included several other pastors and church workers, and our activities were always planned around the holy days and ordinary rhythms of church life. I came of age in the Evangelical Lutheran Church in America (ELCA), a denomination formed in 1988 by the merger of three Lutheran churches in the United States. One of the more progressive "mainline" Christian churches in the United States, it is part of the five-hundred-year-old Lutheran movement launched during the so-called "Protestant Reformation." When I went to divinity school as a young adult, I could have pursued ordination; but I felt called instead to lay leadership at the intersection of ecumenical (or intra-Christian) and interreligious work. I wanted to help the church claim its responsibility to be in unity with other Christians, and to seek justice and peace for all of creation in partnership with people of other religions and worldviews.

Today, I am responsible for the ecumenical and interreligious relations of my denomination, both nationally and globally. The formative experiences of my childhood, coupled with what I learned during my years as a student researcher and staff person at The Pluralism Project, have given me a firm foundation for what I do. I've discovered that advancing professionally has not exempted me from making mistakes altogether; I've simply gotten smarter about how I learn from them.

A key part of this shift is not letting my shame and embarrassment keep me from reflecting differently on various types of mistakes. Are they mistakes that impact how we are perceived by our partners, such as my inappropriate outfit? Are they mistakes of exclusion, such as the mis-scheduled conference? The most challenging for me are missteps I make in overthinking. This happens when I give deference to what I think I "know" about interfaith relations instead of following my heart or trusting other people—a kind of opposite to the mistake Lexi shared above. The result may be that my words and actions stifle the potential for authentic engagement. These missteps occur most often when I am trying something new, such as parenting in an interfaith space.

During my tenure as my denomination's executive for ecumenical and interreligious relations, I have had the privilege of serving as cochair of the "Shoulder to Shoulder Campaign: Standing with American Muslims, Advancing American Ideals." Now over a decade old, this campaign was formed by Jews and Christians who wanted to stand in solidarity with their Muslim neighbors in the context of rising anti-Muslim bigotry and violence in the United States. In addition to outstanding staff leadership, this coalition has a remarkable executive committee. My colleagues are deeply committed and never hesitate to roll up their sleeves to serve. During the pandemic, Shoulder to Shoulder quickly pivoted to move its inter-religious programming online. Doing so allowed for greater participation of people across the country, and it also supported creative approaches to diversifying programming. In the spring of 2022, one such program was a multifaith children's *iftar* to explore themes of sharing and belonging, featuring two Muslim women authors of children's books. This event provided an opportunity for the wider community to join Muslims in breaking the daily fast during the holy month of Ramadan.

As the mother of four young children, I was excited to participate with my family—to share with them the meaningful mission of this organization I am so proud to be part of in my daily work. We rushed home after school pick-ups to log on to the program. As we enjoyed the authors reading from their picture books, one of my twins ran off to grab a stuffed animal—a six-foot-long, green-and-yellow snake. He wrapped it around his neck and carefully settled back in to listen. In no time, his twin sister had to join the fun. Off she went, returning with a stuffed animal she had received from the tooth fairy that same morning: a plump, plush, pink piglet. Oh, my!

I could feel my anxiety growing. What on earth would my colleagues—not to mention strangers—on the call think if a Christian child showed up to an interfaith *iftar* boasting about her pig? All I could think of was pork. It seemed *haram*, or forbidden, rather than the harmless gesture it was. With a quick eye to the mute button, I quietly suggested to my daughter that perhaps she could hold her piggy out of view, and added that I would follow up to explain why later. I didn't quite know what was wrong, or even *if* it was wrong; I simply knew I wanted to be sensitive to my partners' religious restrictions and sensibilities. Perhaps even more so, I wanted to affirm to myself that I was raising a child who shares those sensitivities. But it all happened so fast.

Before I knew it, we were called upon to share. The other participants immediately drew the children into the conversation. Of course, the stuffed snake provided an easy entry point. But then, my daughter unmuted our computer and chimed in with her brother, saying, "Well, I have my pig, but my mom told me I shouldn't share it with you." Oh, dear God, was I embarrassed. The misstep was not, as I feared, my daughter bringing her piggy, but me trying to prevent her from being herself in this precious, interreligious space—a space intended to cultivate sharing and belonging, of all things! As I explained my intentions and apologized to my daughter, it was a meaningful time of growth for me. She was quick to extend grace, offering the consolation that "we all make mistakes."

In hindsight, and in sharing this story with my Muslim and Jewish colleagues, they could appreciate what I was trying to do. They also assured me that they were not offended; in fact, a few of them added that their kids have stuffed pigs, too. They could appreciate that my intention, though misguided, was for our neighbors of diverse religious identities to experience a sense of belonging in our presence. I have learned a lot from this one small mess-up, about myself as a parent and, also, as an inter-religious practitioner. There is room for everyone to show up—piglets and all—fully as who we are. My daughter was teaching me this lesson all over again.

Upon Reflection

As people who work professionally in interfaith spaces, we get plenty of opportunities for missteps. We have come to see this as less of a curse than a blessing. Over the years, some of our mistakes have been major, causing ripple effects of harm and hurt feelings, challenges and obstacles in our interreligious work. These big gaffes have been key moments for learning. But more often than not, the small mistakes have been what has changed us most. Why is this? We believe it is because they can show us our deeper aspirations for interreligious understanding. The dissonance we feel is less overwhelming than those major mistakes, and those feelings can help us to explore the distance between our actions and our intentions, and gives us a chance to make meaningful changes. Think of it this way: when we trip, we have the opportunity to catch ourselves before we fall.

In this way, our missteps can increase our capacity to cultivate interreligious spaces of grace where mistakes are expected—and even affirmed—as evidence of our commitment to engage. When we share openly with others what we have learned from our missteps we can contribute to creating a culture of learning for all. As interreligious spaces are, by nature, spaces where differences can be defining, we can expect that missteps will be made, and often! When we are at peace knowing that our differences can and very likely will trip us up, our "should have known better" and "overthinking" moments are a particularly meaningful source of reflection: they build trust, help us practice authenticity, and—eventually—allow for taking greater risks together. In this way, our missteps can, over time, lead us to discover our deepest interreligious intentions. When we intentionally stop ruminating and start reflecting, we begin to see our truest intentions behind our awkward actions. We can see in ourselves the desire to relate with sensitivity and care for our interreligious partners and to build connection across difference.

While we shouldn't lose ourselves in self-criticism over those small moments, perhaps we can re-frame that continual replay in a positive way: it encourages us to think about how we can be better partners in this interreligious work. Those uncomfortable feelings signal to us that we now have an opportunity to reflect on where we fell short while reminding us of the differences we are hoping to both honor and bridge. Our minor missteps have major impact when we allow them to serve as a mirror, showing us our bigger intentions and hopes for interreligious understanding. The shame of feeling like we should have known better, while a difficult emotion to experience, is an indication that we want to keep striving. We know we *can* do better. That knowledge can be hard to face in moments when we falter, but it is an important reminder of all the work there is to do—with ourselves and in our world.

Perhaps most importantly, when our interreligious partners show us kindness and grace in those mortifying moments, it can transform shame into humility. By practicing authenticity, we build trust, which is the foundation for all of the most meaningful and impactful interreligious relations. Those moments of grace remind us that we are welcome in that space, blunders and all. They help us cultivate interreligious spaces where mistakes are not only expected, but welcome, serving to affirm our mutual intentions to learn, grow, and transform the world together.

Chapter 2

WHAT'S IN A NAME?

On Acknowledging the Individual before Us

DAVID D. GRAFTON

To the nursing staff, this woman had appeared quite disturbed and anxious. I was at the hospital by chance, as I had been visiting members of my congregation that day. I was wearing my clerical collar, so I was publicly identifiable as some kind of religious figure. As I walked past the nurses' station, one of the nurses intercepted me and asked, "Would you mind stopping in to see the patient in room 102? Her name is Mary. She asked for a minister."

"Certainly," I replied. When I arrived at room 102, I found two patient names written on the white board next to the door: "Mary" and "Sophie." There was only one patient in the room. The bay closest to the door was empty. Perhaps she was out for tests or had been discharged? In the bed farthest from the door, near the window, was an elderly and frail woman with a full head of gray hair. She had an oxygen mask on her face, covering her nose and mouth. She had been suffering from emphysema and was now on full oxygen. The machine was making a constant gurgling noise in the background.

"Hello, Mary," I said. "I'm Pastor Grafton. The nurses said that you were asking for a minister to come and speak with you. I'm a Lutheran pastor. I hope that's okay; would you mind if I spoke with you?"

The woman looked up, surprised. She seemed to gather herself and then nodded, yes. I sat down in the chair next to her; and she said, "Thank you for coming." She looked at me for a moment and then began to talk about her life.

"I'm a Baptist, you know," she said.

"Wonderful," I responded. "It sounds as if your faith has been important to you."

"Oh, yes," she said; "and I am ready to meet my Lord."

She went on to talk about her life, family, and husband. How she worried about her husband as he did not have God in his life. She was fine with her soul, but worried about his, and what would happen when she was gone. I listened for some time, and when she seemed to be done, I asked if I could pray with her. She nodded yes.

I prayed for Mary by name, thanking God for Mary and God's presence in her life, and asked God to let Mary feel God's presence and comfort during these final days. I acknowledged Mary's love for her husband and that God would hear Mary's concern for him. When I finished, I looked up. With labored breathing, she nodded from underneath her mask.

"Thank you," she said in a muffled tone. "Now, what's your name again?"

"I'm Pastor Grafton."

"It's good to meet you, Pastor Grafton. I'm Sophie. Thank you for visiting."

Stunned, I smiled wryly and slunk out of the room. The bed #1 patient who was out for tests: she was "Mary"!

An Exchange of Names

I had been leading an adult education series for a congregation during the season of Lent to learn about their Muslim neighbors. This White, middle-class, progressive congregation had decided to learn about Islam, and they reached out to me. I agreed, under the condition that we would invite several Muslim colleagues and friends to come in and speak to them as well. They seemed enthusiastic about this proposal.

The series was, by and large, a huge success. After the introductory session, I encouraged the members to write down all the questions that they had about Islam and submit them anonymously. I would then work them into the coming sessions without ascribing the questions to particular people. I find this to be a helpful method, as often well-meaning individuals with very good questions feel embarrassed to ask. So, they don't, which stifles the learning process. This method frees them to let me know what is on their minds. It also allows me to rephrase questions and put a positive spin on the topic. After the first two weeks of general material, I then asked Muslim colleagues to come and speak about various topics and their own views of Islam.

Apparently, the series was publicized in the local community. By the third week, attendees included a number of Muslim visitors. Perhaps they were intrigued. Perhaps they were worried about what these Christians were saying about Islam. Probably, both. In any case, their presence turned out to be a bonus. They treated us to a wonderful variety of Muslim perspectives.

One week, a young *Muslima* college student came. The topic that day was "Jesus in Islam." This is always an interesting topic for Christians, who usually are surprised to discover the importance of Jesus ('Isa) in the Qur'an and the depth of resources about him as an important prophet in Islam. After I gave a brief overview of some of the passages related to Jesus ('Isa), the young woman raised her hand. I was delighted. She began to ask me questions about the divinity of Jesus and how we could call him "God's son." She posed the most excellent questions! However, our exchange was provoking nervous laughter and shifting of bottoms in the audience. So, I opened the discussion to the group by asking them to share their own views on what this title meant to them. After a wonderful conversation that barely scratched the surface of the topic and our understandings, the session ended. I approached the young woman: "Can I ask your name?"

"Yes," she said, "I'm Refia."

"Thank you for your questions and for being here today, Refia," I said.

I could see that a woman from the host congregation was waiting to speak with Refia. I moved away to give her space. "Thank you for coming," the woman said, and quickly extended her hand to shake Refia's. Refia shyly extended hers and smiled. "Now, what is your name?" the woman asked. "My name is Refia," said the guest. "RE-FI-YA?" responded the congregant; "I have never heard of that name before. Can I call you Rebekah? That I can remember."

Introductions involve an exchange of names. In them, we offer up whatever part of ourselves we are willing to share. That is no small matter of importance. Names can reveal much about the history and meaning of a person, their important relationships and family. Having someone else provide one's name is also a matter of trust. In offering up our name to another, we open ourselves up to them. Introductions require the skill of listening well; they also require attentiveness to the person in front of us. What's in a name? Quite a lot.

Relationality

Without delving headlong into the Aristotelian discussion of whether or not a word is tied essentially to a "thing" or whether it is only representative of that "thing," it is important for us to recognize the significance of names as an opportunity for relationality.

Relationality, of course, is a two-way street. So, taking care to hear the name and all that this name entails—its past, its current identity, and its potential future—can open us up to reflect on our own past, current identity, and potential future. Recalling Martin Buber, we might "experience" people in that we might meet them, speak to them, and see them. We might hear a name and the accompanying brief introduction. That is good and important and necessary. But, Buber invites us to something deeper than experiencing other people. He invites us into relationality with them. For this, says Buber, is what human beings are created for— seeking relationships. As we are introduced and hear that name and as we listen to the story, the person before us is no longer an "It" but has become a "Thou" in relation to "Me"—to use Buber's terminology. When we begin the journey of a relationality, we are able to have what he calls the "You moments," in which we are opened up to the identity of the person in front of us.[1] This does not happen easily or quickly. But the first step is being open to hearing someone's name.

So then, taking the time to invite someone to introduce themselves, to actively listen to the response and the words that are shared, and then taking the effort to correctly pronounce that name is the first step before all else. In these introductions, we learn something important about our partner. Carelessly not listening, mispronouncing, or worst of all, making light of the name because it may be unique or different or because we are not able to pronounce it derails the whole opportunity of interreligious engagement.

What's in a Name?

> What's Montague? It is nor hand, nor foot,
> Nor arm, nor face, nor any other part
> Belonging to a man. O! be some other name:
> What's in a name? That which we call a rose
> By any other name would smell as sweet. . . .[2]

"What's in a name?" opines Juliet. Caught up in the past and the present over which she did not originally create, she laments that her love for Romeo could take place in any other time or place regardless of his name. She was in love with him, but he was a Montague. For her, that did not matter. Oh, but in the end, the names do matter. Shakespeare's Juliet falls victim to the reality that the names they bore have meaning beyond their mere letters. They carry a history and associations and identity. It is through the name that the relations are originally created.

More often than not, names are given—by parents, grandparents, family members, communities, or even a religious ceremony. In some cultures, an individual's name is given in memory or in honor of a parent, grandparent, or other ancestor. It is also not uncommon that people take on new names at significant moments in their lives. This is especially true in religious communities, where at a conversion, baptism, naming ceremony, ordination, or wedding, a person will take on a new identity to mark the transition. On other occasions, a parent might be renamed after the birth of a child.

People are often also named for their place of origin. During the years I taught at a seminary in Egypt, I learned a great deal about the cultural and religious traditions about names. In Arabic, the "*nisbah*" is an adjective that denotes a relationship of a person to a place. These names are recognized in American society as one's last name or surname. For example, al-Dimashqi denotes someone from Damascus. However, the regional or local associations may be even more interesting. For example, Shenouda al-Suriani is a prominent Egyptian Christian monk. His *nisbah* places him not from Syria but from the monastery of the Syrians in the Wadi Natrun desert in Egypt, an important monastery in the history of Coptic Christianity. The *nisbah* reveals an important religious history of the Copts, and Shenouda's association with it, and by extension the importance of that name in Coptic history.

A name may record a connection to family. While Americans often do not think about the origins of our own surnames, they too have a history. Among Scandinavian Americans, the suffix "son" denotes a lineage: John-son or Carl-son. Among Americans of British descent, the common surnames of Smith or Baker can possibly be traced back to an ancestor's profession: the smithy, the baker, etc.

For people of faith, it is important to reflect on how the divine is expressed through names, as those names figure so powerfully in the ongoing spiritual lives of Jews and Muslims, for example.[3] In the Islamic tradition, the 99 Beautiful Names for God (al-Asma al-Husna) represent various attributes of God, "the Just," "the Forgiving," "the Merciful." However, they do not capture the totality of the essence of God. In other words, while God can be represented by these attributes, they do not contain God completely, and God is beyond the human definitions of such words. Likewise, in the Hebrew scriptures the prophet Moses wishes to know "who" is the one to whom he is speaking at the burning bush, and by what name shall God be known.

> God said to Moses, "I am who I am." He said further, "Thus you shall say to the Israelites, 'I am has sent me to you.'" God also said to Moses, "Thus you shall say to the Israelites, 'The Lord, the God of your ancestors, the God of Abraham, the God of Isaac, and the God of Jacob, has sent me to you.'" (Exod 3:13–15, NRSV)

The tetragrammaton—four letters that describe "I am who I am" or "I will be who I will be"—is not able to capture God's name completely, and for many Jews is unutterable. Nevertheless, as Hillel Ben-Sasson notes, the 99 Names and the tetragrammaton both represent "the possibility of God's original redemptive presence" and affirm "the existence of a relational attitude to God, a human accessibility to divine presence."[4] These letters and words go beyond the descriptors to something sublime and "wholly other" that cannot be contained. And yet, these human definitions or descriptors are how believers can find solace in some kind of relational aspect with God.

Likewise, in our relationality with our fellow human beings, names mark the individual before us but represent so much more. Deep and committed interfaith or multifaith dialogue requires that we be honest with ourselves and our interlocutors. This requires time, patience, and trust. It does not happen quickly or easily. The first step, however, is to offer up our name and to invite the other to introduce themselves by their name(s). If we do not take the care to listen first to each other's names (and pronoun preferences), how will we explore together our views of the divine or that which is the ground of our being—our ultimate concern?

Perhaps, my encounter with Sophie could have started like this: "Hello, I'm Pastor Grafton; the nurse mentioned to me that you wanted to see a minister. What is your name?"

Notes

1. Martin Buber, *I and Thou,* trans. Walter Kauffmann (New York: Charles Scribner's Sons, 1970), 84.

2. William Shakespeare, *Romeo and Juliet*, act 2, scene 2.

3. Hillel Ben-Sasson, "Representation and Presence: Divine Names in Judaism and Islam," *Harvard Theological Review* 114, no. 2 (2021): 219–40.

4. Ben-Sasson, "Representation and Presence," 224.

Chapter 3

DEFLECTING MYSELF
A Failure of Leadership

HANS GUSTAFSON

"My name is Hannah and I was raised in the Jewish tradition," remarked an undergraduate student at a multifaith meeting of university stakeholders comprising students, staff, and faculty. We were introducing ourselves and our religious identities. *Wow,* I thought to myself, *what a clever way to [not] answer the question of stating your current religious identity. I'll have to remember that and use it myself in the future.* However, for the moment, when it was my turn to self-identify, I would deflect the question and fail to demonstrate authentic leadership.

"What is your religious identity?" I hated that question. I am not always comfortable stating my religious orientation, especially to people I'm meeting for the first time. Nor is it always appropriate to ask those from marginalized (sometimes stigmatized) groups to openly declare their religious identities. I still wince reflexively when the question comes up in group settings.

What are you? What is your religious tradition? "I'm just a guy," or, as Billy Joe Shaver sings, "I'm just an old chunk of coal." Such was the response that played out in my head. My preference would be to shrink from this question altogether and minimize any uniqueness or significance of my religious orientation. In reality, a canned preemptive introduction came out of my mouth: "I'm a non-Catholic who teaches at a Catholic university." Most of the time, this would satisfy the inquirer. They probably concluded that I was either a non-Catholic Christian (that is, Protestant Christian) or more precisely, given my Scandinavian name (Hans Gustafson) and place of birth and residence (Minnesota), that I was just another Lutheran Christian. This wouldn't be too far off the mark, as I was indeed *raised in the Protestant tradition* with Lutheran parents and grandparents. Furthermore, and after all, the well-known Minnesota mythmaker Garrison Keillor once half-jokingly quipped that Minnesotans are "Lutheran people. Even the Catholics up here are Lutheran."[1] Perhaps my inclination to deflect or downplay any significance of my religious identity stems from my implicit ancestral inheritance of the societal norms lurking among Scandinavian immigrants to the United States, articulated in Aksel Sandemose's Laws of Jante, such as, "Thou shalt not believe thou art something [special]," and "Thou shalt not believe anyone is concerned with thee."[2] At a Catholic university, stating that I'm non-Catholic can sound appropriate within the institutional context. If pushed further, I state that I was raised in the Protestant Christian traditions. Rarely does the conversation go further, and I walk away relieved to have once again avoided having to fully reveal my present religious orientation, which, like an increasing number of Gen-Xers such as myself (and younger), is sympathetically agnostic and most accurately and awkwardly described as nonreligious, nonbeliever, and nonaffiliated (in the traditional sense of these words).

Religious labels are often imperfect, and many people do not like to be labeled and put in a box. I am not an antireligious person. My professional life is dedicated to understanding, learning from, and building relationships between and among religiously diverse individuals and communities in service of common public goods. Although I may be nonpracticing or nonreligious, I am also a champion of religion, civic religious pluralism, and freedom both *of* and *from* religion. While I may be nonreligious today, I might become religious tomorrow. I often reflect on Wilfred Cantwell Smith's thoughtful response to a student who asked, "Professor Smith, are you Christian?" To be sure, Smith was indeed *a* Christian (an ordained Christian minister in the Presbyterian Church in Canada to boot), but to the question "are you Christian," Smith replied "Am I Christian? Maybe, I was, last week. On a Tuesday. At lunch. For about an hour. But if you really want to know, ask my neighbor."[3] Such is the understanding, in part, of my own religiosity as one who values striving to live in (and always falling short of) the way of Jesus and other exemplars of practical ultimate wisdom. Perhaps I will again one day be a religious person, a believer (with faith), or religiously affiliated with a community of practitioners.

In short, I have "holy envy" of the faith, community belonging, and belief that many religious people have. However, in the spirit of Krister Stendahl, who made popular the concept of holy envy, as much as I might be open to those beliefs myself and to socially sharing in religious community, I am honest enough to admit that I presently do not explicitly share the religious beliefs, nor engage in the rituals, of many religious people. Although I may implicitly or *anonymously* practice values held by religious traditions, they are not religious practices for me.[4] I have no desire to disingenuously convince myself of an underlying divine metaphysic to my life's experiences. However, I do strive to remain open to the spiritual wisdom of my peers and any genuine religious faith it may inspire in me down the road. As Stendahl taught, I am comfortable in the present with rejoicing in the religious beliefs and practices of others without "grabbing" or "claiming" them for myself (for they are not mine to take). I enviously (but not jealously) celebrate the beauty of their religious beliefs, behaviors, and belonging without appropriating them for, or forcing them on, myself.[5]

A Failure of Leadership

This is a story of my failure: a failure of trust, a failure of vulnerability, a failure of authenticity, a failure of leadership. Trust, vulnerability, and authenticity are foundational for successful leadership, especially in interfaith spaces. Karen Kimsey-House, cofounder of the Coaches Training Institute (CTI) and coauthor of the Co-Active Coaching and Co-Active Leadership model, observes, "When leaders are human, vulnerable, and real, people feel connected personally and trust blossoms."[6] Every time I deflect a question about my religious identity with a canned, noncommitted, hedged response, I fail to meet the moment; I fail to seize the opportunity to be *authentic, vulnerable, truthful*; to build *trust* and to demonstrate *leadership*.

Deflecting the question can be a failure to be *authentic* by owning my religious identity as one among an increasing many who check the box "nothing in particular."[7] Deflecting the question can be a failure to be *vulnerable* by being fully honest about my messy and humanly imperfect (non)religious orientation as someone who currently has few, if any, traditional religious beliefs but cares deeply about and envies the religious wisdom of others (and is open to the possibility of sharing some of those beliefs in the future). Deflecting the question can be a failure to *trust* my colleagues, friends, and family to understand my religious orientation and accept me nonetheless as an equal partner and colleague in interfaith bridge building. Deflecting the question can even be a failure to tell the *truth* (or, more accurately, to tell a *fuller truth*) by navigating the interaction from a purely transactional perspective that favors avoidance of outing myself as "nonreligious," lest it affect my professional standing among my colleagues, students, and peers. Being existentially truthful—that is, being outwardly truthful about core aspects of myself and others—can seemingly clash with the utilitarian value of telling half-truths (for example, "I'm a non-Catholic raised in the Christian tradition"). Choosing the latter (utilitarian value) over the former (existential truth) can result in a failure to choose dignified existential truth for its own sake alone and not for some secondary utilitarian end.[8]

Ultimately, deflecting the question is a failure of *leadership* at a most fundamental level: failure to be real, to be human, and to be myself. Warren Bennis, pioneer of leadership studies, famously preached that "to become a leader, you must become yourself; become the maker of your own life."[9] The Co-Active Leadership model maintains that "leadership begins as an inside job."[10] That is, an individual must first discern their purpose to lead from personal values, convictions, and experiences that come from deep within. According to leadership scholars James M. Kouzes and Barry Z. Posner, leadership "is first an inner quest to discover who you are and what you care about, and it's through this process of self-examination that you find the awareness needed to lead. . . . The mastery of the art of leadership comes with the mastery of the self, and so developing leadership is a process of developing the self."[11] Failure to be open, honest, vulnerable, and authentic can inhibit your ability to be the maker of your own life. Allowing the fear of others' perceptions to dictate who you are and what you become may ultimately cause you to feign a false self, donning a mask for the sake of others.

Although leadership may begin with the self, it includes and ends with others; and the process of knowing and developing one's self often requires others to help an individual discover their deepest values, convictions, and experiences. Kimsey-House recognizes, "People know when the truth is being spoken. They do not have to be told. When those in charge tell the truth and speak openly, trust naturally occurs."[12] Conversely, people can sense vague inauthenticity, which causes them to second-guess and possibly mistrust. Abbey Lewis of Harvard Business Publishing, a leading producer of transformative leadership development programs, similarly observes, "Most people can spot an inauthentic person a mile away, and they'll instinctively distrust that person. Authentic leaders must be willing and able to talk about their values, about what makes them tick."[13] In spaces of intentional collaborative interfaith encounter striving to form relationships across difference in service of common aims and goods, effective and authentic leaders emerge by taking risks, being vulnerable with their (non)religious values, visions, and practices, and by trusting others to accept them for who they are today.

If the aspiration of symmetry, while acknowledging obvious asymmetries, is a foundational principle of interfaith engagement, and if I expect others to be vulnerable and authentic in trusting me with, and being honest about, their complicated religious orientations, then I have the mutual responsibility to trust others with, and be fully authentic about, my messy dynamic religious orientation as well. They can handle it. Like me, they are complicated humans making their way through a sophisticated suffering world. And if they can't handle it, and it appears my risking vulnerability and authenticity has failed, then I can rest assured that, at the very least, I've *failed forward* by learning something about them and myself in the process, which is an essential value for leadership in religiously diverse spaces.

Failing Forward

Billy Joe Shaver sings, "I'm just an old chunk of coal." However, the following lyric preaches, "but I'm gonna be a diamond some day." Leaders welcome failure as an invitation for growth. It was a watershed moment for me when I understood that "there is no leadership without risk, and there is no risk without failure."[14] When I accepted the image of "failing forward . . . the only way a baby learns to walk or a leader learns to lead,"[15] I gave myself the permission, freedom, and motivation to accept risks and failures as necessary for growth—not only in interfaith leadership or leadership in general, but in the greater scope of a flourishing life. Risk, failure, transparency, authenticity, vulnerability, and building trust all contribute to self-actualization, or the journey of becoming more fully human. They hold the potential to fuel the process of knowing more intimately who you already are, which is an inner journey all leaders must take. Vinita Bali, an Indian business leader with experience leading and serving several multinational corporations, suggests that "leadership is less about what we do and more about what we become—and in the process how we influence and learn from those around us."[16] In addition to considering the necessary values of authenticity, vulnerability, and trust for effective interfaith leadership in multifaith settings, this reflection is also an attempt to own the mistakes and failures of my past, to trust others to understand them, to commit to failing forward for growth, and to take that uneasy and unstable baby step with nervous excitement while falling forward with outstretched arms toward those around me for support.[17]

Notes

1. Garrison Keillor, *Life among the Lutherans*, ed. Holly Harden (Minneapolis, MN: Augsburg Books, 2010), 148.

2. Aksel Sandemose, *A Fugitive Crosses His Tracks*, trans. Eugene Gay-Tifft (New York: Knopf, 1936), 77–78.

3. Recounted by Amir Hussain in "Building Faith Neighbors: Church Colleges and Muslim Communities," *The Cresset: A Review of Literature, the Arts, and Public Affairs* 73, no. 4 (2010): 31–38.

4. *Anonymously* here refers to practicing something without knowing it.

5. For more on Holy Envy, see Hans Gustafson, "Suppressing the Mosquitoes' Coughs: An Introduction to Holy Envy," in *Learning from Other Religious Traditions: Leaving Room for Holy Envy,* ed. Hans Gustafson (Cham, Switzerland: Palgrave MacMillan, 2018), 1–12.

6. Karen Kimsey-House, "How to Build Trust as a Leader," *LinkedIn* (July 6, 2017), www.linkedin.com.

7. Pew Research Center, "Nothing in Particulars," *Religious Landscape Study,* 2014, www.pewresearch.org.

8. Inspired by Hannah Arendt, psychologist Svend Brinkmann differentiates between existential dignified truth and the utilitarian value of truth. The former, which is more human and dignified, chooses truth for its own sake while the latter chooses truth for the sake of something else, such as health, security, happiness, success, and so on. See Svend Brinkman, *Standpoints: 10 Old Ideas in a New World* (Cambridge, MA: Polity Press, 2018), 71–77.

9. Warren G. Bennis and Patricia Ward Biederman, *The Essential Bennis* (Hoboken, NJ: John Wiley and Sons, 2015), 214; cited in James M. Kouzes and Barry Z. Posner, "Leadership Begins with an Inner Journey," in *Contemporary Issues in Leadership*, ed. William E. Rosenbach, Robert L. Taylor, and Mark A. Youndt (2nd ed.; London: Taylor & Francis Group, 2014), 119.

10. Henry Kimsey-House and David Skibbins, *The Stake: The Making of Leaders* (San Rafael, CA: Co-Active Press, 2013), 26.

11. Kouzes and Posner, "Leadership Begins with an Inner Journey," 117.

12. Kimsey-House, "How to Build Trust as a Leader."

13. Abbey Lewis, "Good Leadership? It All Starts with Trust," Harvard Business Publishing Blog, March 4, 2021, www.harvardbusiness.org.

14. Kimsey-House and Skibbins, *The Stake*, 35.

15. Kimsey-House and Skibbins, *The Stake*, 35.

16. Vinita Bali, "Leadership Lessons from Everyday Life," in *Contemporary Issues in Leadership*, 235.

17. Kimsey-House contends, "when the courage to risk failure and the transparency of owning mistakes is balanced with a clear commitment to learning, trust grows quickly." See Kimsey-House, "How to Build Trust as a Leader."

Chapter 4

ALWAYS ASK

Reflections on the Boundaries Religions Set

AIDA MANSOOR

A religion may provide guidelines regarding what foods its followers may consume. It may set limits on casual physical contact between women and men. It may encourage the offering and receiving of hospitality. Sometimes, the intersection of limits with hospitality and graciousness is complicated. Here are some illustrations.

Hand-to-Hand Contact

In the United States, in many situations, handshaking is strongly encouraged. Similarly, during an interfaith gathering, attendees may be instructed to hold hands with whoever is next to them—for a prayer or to convey friendship and fellowship. These scenarios present a dilemma for Muslims. Some will shake or hold hands, out of a sense that this is the hospitable, gracious, and polite thing to do. Others will not, due to their own notions of modesty and conveyance of respect. They believe that even casual physical contact between a woman and a man who are not spouses or siblings is un-Islamic.

Like many Muslim women, I feel reluctant to shake a man's hand. I am also reluctant to offend. What to do? When one of my Muslim friends attends an interfaith service at which she anticipates handholding, she strives to position herself between two women. If the congregation is asked to hold hands, she is well situated! Others I know avoid shaking hands by making sure their arms are full!

Those are strategies of people who prefer not to shake or hold hands. But, what if you are the person reaching out? If someone declines to shake your hand, what should you do? Ten years ago, I attended the wedding of a good friend of mine. The groom was not Muslim. However, he had

24

worked in Egypt, so was familiar with Islamic etiquette. After the ceremony, as the couple walked down the line of well-wishers, the groom hugged and kissed each person. However, when he came to me, he paused; he sensed that I was not going to extend my hand. So, he placed his right hand over his heart, smiled, and bowed his head. I was happy to do the same. This is truly the best way, I think, to greet people if they feel uncomfortable shaking hands. If someone does not reach out to shake your hand, simply take your right hand and place it on your heart while smiling and bowing your head.

In February 2020, I was invited to give a talk during the Sunday Vespers service at a private boarding school for boys. I had done this previously, so I knew what the procedure would be. The whole student body would proceed into the chapel. They would sing a hymn. This would be followed by several readings and my five-minute sermon. Then, during another hymn, the school principal and masters and I would proceed to the main door where each student would shake my hand in thanks. The previous year, I had shaken the hands of five hundred young men.

I asked myself how I could make this year's visit a different experience. Rather than ask the school principal to intervene, I made my sermon all about the ways we show gratitude, love, and respect to one another. I talked about how our U.S. culture encourages a firm handshake, but that there are cultures where this is not the right way. I spoke about eye contact—about how, in some cultures, looking someone in the eye can be disrespectful, but in other cultures, the opposite is true. I told them of my reluctance to shake hands—so, how respected I felt at the wedding when the bridegroom paused, simply placed his right hand on his heart, and smiled while bowing his head.

When I had finished, we sang a hymn. I proceeded to the door with the principal, and I waited to greet the five hundred young men. Each one of them greeted me in the way I had described: right hand on heart. I was so surprised!

A month later, when we all were in lockdown due to the COVID-19 pandemic, I received a note from the school thanking me, saying, "Especially at this time when we have been told not to shake hands due to Covid, we know what to do: place our right hands on our hearts, smile, and bow our heads in greeting."

Ask Why

A few years ago, while serving as a hospital chaplain, I visited a patient who had lost so much weight after surgery that his nurses were worried. "Mr. Khan refuses to eat," one nurse told me. "He has not eaten for days.

Every time I try to encourage him to eat, he shakes his head and says, 'No.' What can we do? All he eats is ice chips." The situation was so dire that they were considering the possibility of tube feeding.

As they told me this, Mr. Khan's adult daughter walked in with a bowl of homemade soup. The nurses immediately told her that her father refused to eat and hoped she could change his mind. To their astonishment, Mr. Khan took the bowl of soup in his hands and smiled. He finished the whole serving and asked his daughter in Urdu for some more. The nurses were stunned. They asked his daughter what was the secret in the soup. When they were told that it was very basic chicken noodle soup they were shocked. "We brought him chicken noodle soup, and he refused it. We even brought him fruit-flavored gelatin, but he refused that too."

What the daughter helped the nurses understand was that the hospital-made chicken noodle soup was not *halal* (prepared according to Islamic rules). As for the gelatin, it is served in many hospitals to patients after surgery because it comes under the category of a "clear fluid" and is light on the stomach. However, in the United States, gelatin often contains porcine ingredients. Mr. Khan was well aware of this; and, like most Muslims, he wanted to avoid it on religious grounds. Once the nurses and staff also were aware, they read the menus with Mr. Khan and his daughter, taking note of which meals he could order and which he would avoid on religious grounds. They also agreed that, if any of Mr. Khan's medications contained gelatin or alcohol, they would advocate for a suitable replacement. With this change in his care, Mr. Khan improved quickly and soon returned home.

Nowadays, most hospitals and medical staff are well aware of the religious dietary requirements of their patients, which makes life much easier for everyone.

The Gift One Can't Receive

Mention of the surgery patient's reluctance to receive medications containing alcohol reminds us that alcohol is an issue for many Muslims, due to verses in the Qur'an that instruct us to avoid it. There are even some Islamic traditions that advise not to deal with alcohol in any way. Buying, selling, even carrying alcohol is discouraged. Some Muslims may avoid going to any gatherings that serve alcohol. My husband and I sometimes receive gifts of alcohol, especially at Christmas and New Year. We used to pass them on to people who were not Muslim; but we still felt guilty, because another Islamic tradition advises us that when we give gifts to others, we should only give of what we love.

So Muslims are left with three options: accept the gift but pour the liquid down the drain to avoid drinking it; accept it but pass it along to others; or explain, as politely as we can, that we cannot accept the gift—and we give it back. It is such a dilemma. A few years ago, it took me a few hours to dispose of a bottle of wine because I had great difficulty opening it. I did not have a corkscrew; so, I made a makeshift one with a screwdriver and a large nail.

I do not want to offend. I feel people would feel offended if they knew I was pouring away their gift. I am sure they would be offended if I refused to accept it. My suggestion is that, if you are considering giving a gift to a Muslim, fresh fruit or chocolates may be the way to go. Better yet, ask. Have a conversation and discuss gift options. Demonstrating that you are aware of possible sensitivities can greatly strengthen a relationship.

Clarifying Conversations

Yet, even when we think we have had a clarifying conversation, things can go awry. A few years ago, I was invited by my good friend, Sally, for dinner at her home. She knew that, as a Muslim, I try my very best to keep to the dietary rules and regulations prescribed by my faith. In the Qur'an, we are advised not to eat foods that originate from a pig, because it is considered unclean. She told me that she had a new salmon recipe that looked scrumptious. I was all in favor of this—I love salmon. When I arrived, Sally mentioned that the salmon took a considerable time to wrap. I had no idea what she meant. Maybe, I thought, it was a kind of Salmon Wellington dish where the salmon fillets are wrapped in puff pastry. My anticipation was rising. We all sat around the table waiting for the star dish to arrive.

The dish was placed in the middle of the table and uncovered with a fanfare—and there, to my dismay were those same salmon fillets that I had imagined, wrapped in bacon! Initially, I was speechless—mainly because I knew how much time and energy Sally had put into all the preparation and cooking. She had taken the trouble to ask me about my dietary requirements, and I had told her that I did not eat pork. I had failed to mention that I did not eat bacon, lard, ham, gelatin, or any porcine product. I apologized. She was so gracious in her disappointment—and she whipped up an omelet just for me.

Even though I have lectured about Islam and dietary rules for many years, and think that I am aware of and sensitive to the dietary needs of others, I still have moments where I fail dismally. Only last March, I made a mistake when trying to offer hospitality to a colleague at work. She was new to our institution, so I wanted to welcome her specially. I decided I would make a pot of hot tea, which I would serve with my favorite chocolate muffins from a local store. As she walked into my office, I felt her discomfort. She was Christian. It was Lent. She had given up chocolate for that time. Not only that, but my new colleague was also on a gluten-free diet, and the muffins were certainly not gluten-free. I, who thought I was aware of most food-related missteps, was now caught in one.

My new colleague had gone out of her way to ask me about my dietary requirements, but I had neglected to ask about hers. I had told her all about my new tree-nut allergy and the sensitivities for a *halal* diet; but I had neglected my responsibility to ask what her food sensitivities were. Thankfully, she had brought a lemon cake that was not only free of chocolate and lard but was also gluten-free and made from a flour that was not nut-based. Thanks to her thoughtfulness, our teatime together was a great experience.

Reflection

Conversations about food rules and other sensitivities are important. They help us all feel valued and understood. As we saw in the case of the surgery patient, they can even be life-saving. Where intentionality is demonstrated, missteps can be overcome, and a good relationship will continue.

Chapter 5

A Sikh and a Jew at the Airport
Lessons on Handling Misinterpretations

Or N. Rose

A shiny red, mid-sized rental car pulled up to the curb and from it emerged a very tall, dark-skinned man with an off-white turban, long graying beard, and boyish smile. "Come, my friend, let me help you with your bags. On a hot day like this, we can all use some help." With that, he whisked me off to the Kansas City airport. I had come to the Midwest from my home in Boston to attend the annual conference of a major interfaith organization. One of its officers, a Sikh scholar whom I'll call Amardeep, had graciously volunteered to give me a ride to the airport.[1]

A wise and warm person, Amardeep engaged me in meaningful conversation as soon as I settled into the car. We had a wonderful time together, discussing the similarities and differences between our faith traditions and the issues facing each of our minority communities in the United States. Although we had just met at the conference, we went deep quickly. Before I knew it, we had arrived at our destination.

Amardeep kindly stepped out of the car into the humid summer air to help me with my bags and to say goodbye. Before parting company, I thanked him for the ride and for the conversation, then gave my new friend a big hug. (I come from a family of huggers!) With that, I headed for the check-in counter. I didn't communicate with my Sikh friend again for several months.

In December 2009, I traveled to Melbourne, Australia, to speak at the Parliament of the World's Religions. One morning, as I walked through the crowded hallways of the conference center, I heard someone call my name. To my pleasant surprise, it was Amardeep. After briefly catching up, he invited me to attend a session he would be speaking at the following day. "I will be sharing the end of our Kansas City story," he said with a mischievous grin. "You don't know it yet, but I promise it is interesting."

Intrigued by Amardeep's enigmatic description of the conclusion of "our" story, I arrived early for his session the next day. When it was his turn to present, he spoke passionately about his involvement as a Sikh in interfaith projects. He ended by telling our airport tale.

"As Or gave me a hug, I noticed that two baggage handlers standing nearby were looking curiously at our embrace. After returning my car to the rental facility, I walked past the airport doors where I had left Or and saw the two men still standing there. They smiled at me and said hello; I reciprocated. Then one of the men commented on how moving it was to see a Jew and a *Muslim* hug in public. (They correctly identified Or's *yarmulke* as a Jewish head covering but were clearly confused by my turban). At that moment, I did not feel it was important to correct the mix-up between a Muslim and a Sikh, so I let it slide. And then, the other baggage handler remarked, 'You are living the future today!' I smiled and walked away; they had gotten it right after all."

As my friend finished his story the audience applauded. I, of course, rose quickly from my seat, jogged to the front of the room, and gave him a big hug!

I have thought about this story many times since first hearing it from Amardeep at the public session in Melbourne more than a decade ago. On the one hand, we have made significant strides in the North American interreligious movement in recent decades. On the other hand, we obviously have much more work to do. How many people in Boston, Kansas City, or elsewhere in the United States could accurately differentiate between a Muslim and a Sikh on the street, let alone know anything substantive about their religious lives? Further, both communities continue to suffer from bigotry, including violent attacks. Adding to the pain of this ignorance and hatred, there have been incidents in which Sikhs have been harassed or abused by bigoted assailants who misidentified them as Muslims.[2]

I have also thought about my Sikh friend's response to the baggage handlers. When is it best to let things slide? When should one correct such a mistake? It is equally important to consider *how* to make this correction. These questions need to be considered contextually. In making a correction, what do we hope to achieve? What is the best way to accomplish our goals?

In this case, I can certainly understand why Amardeep chose not to upend the narrative of the airport workers: it was a brief and passing interaction with well-intentioned strangers. They should have been commended for their encouragement of warm Jewish–Muslim interactions. May we be blessed to live in a world in which seeing a Jewish man hugging a Muslim is considered unexceptional.

And yet, the ignorance of the baggage handlers—and of countless other Americans—is real and requires redress. As the scholar of religion

Stephen Prothero and others have observed, we suffer from religious illiteracy in this country and throughout the world, contributing daily to division and strife.[3]

In fact, in discussing this experience with me, Amardeep said that he now could imagine rewinding this scene. In his new version, he would thank the two men for their good wishes. Then he would, calmly and kindly, explain to them that he was, in fact, a Sikh, and would share with them why he wears a turban. If they demonstrated interest, he might even say something about the importance of head covering in different religious traditions. This led me to reflect on various situations in which I have had to make similar decisions as a Jew, attempting to embody my values with integrity, compassion, and wisdom. When have I spoken up and how did I choose to do so? Were my words or actions effective? Why or why not?

This episode also led me to think again about my own ignorance and biases, the ongoing need for discernment and learning, and the ways people have chosen to call me "in" or "out." In sharing our Kansas City airport story, my Sikh friend offered his listeners an opportunity to consider anew the complexities we all face in trying to engage thoughtfully across lines of difference.

Notes

1. A version of this essay was published as Rabbi Or Rose, "Interpreting an Embrace: A Jew and a Sikh in Kansas," in HuffPost (May 24, 2010), www.huffpost.com.

2. See, e.g., Kat Chow, "Long Before They Were 'Apparent Muslims,' Sikhs Were Targeted in US," National Public Radio (January 2, 2016), www.npr.org.

3. See, most recently, Stephen Prothero, *Religion Matters: An Introduction to the World's Religions* (New York: W. W. Norton, 2020). See, too, his earlier volume, *Religious Literacy: What Every American Needs to Know—And Doesn't* (New York: HarperCollins, 2007).

Chapter 6

The Tour

Lessons from an Interfaith Itinerary

Marcia Moret Sietstra

Without a doubt, the most exciting youth trip of my career as a pastor was the trip to Chicago. The trip provided our youth with new cultural and interfaith experiences that were unavailable in our hometown in South Dakota. Our visits included an art museum, aquarium, ethnic restaurants, and three faith communities: a huge Black church, a Korean Buddhist temple, and a multi-ethnic mosque. Our popular youth group leader, Traci, had prepared an excellent folder of material about each faith community, plus space for daily journaling and questions to guide evening discussions.

By Sunday morning, we had visited the cultural sites on our itinerary. It was now time to visit three faith communities that were different from our own. We attended early worship at Trinity United Church of Christ, on the south side of Chicago, where we were a row of White faces in a sea of Black and Brown worshipers—many of them dressed beautifully in bright, bold, colorful clothing that would have been called "Sunday best" when I was a child. We admired the gorgeous variety of hats worn by many grandmothers and some younger women as people streamed into the sanctuary. Imagine our surprise at the beginning of the service when Rev. Jeremiah Wright invited us to stand so he could introduce us. And then, as we sat down, the entire congregation stood up and applauded us! It was a hearty welcome that set the tone for the lively service, with two choirs leading rousing gospel music, and preaching interspersed with the call-and-response style of congregational participation.

Next, we traveled to a Korean Buddhist temple. We were graciously welcomed to participate in a guided meditation and then a worship service—which ironically, reminded all of us of our own congregation's worship style much more than the service at Trinity UCC. The kids were politely interested, but had found Trinity UCC more exciting. That evening the kids shared their reflections about the similarities and differences in ways in which people worship. We adults were feeling very good about the experiences we had arranged for them.

Monday morning was to have begun with a tour of an Islamic high school, followed by an afternoon of volunteering at a clothing distribution project on the South Side. But, the clothing distribution site was unexpectedly closed for the day, so we decided to check out of our hotel and leave for home immediately after the morning tour of the Islamic school, instead of spending another night in Chicago.

When we reached the school that morning, our kids piled out of the vans and were met on the sidewalk by Maryam, the representative from a local Muslim outreach organization that had set up the tour. She greeted Traci and me, then turned to the male host and students and introduced me as "the pastor." As she did so, I stepped forward and eagerly reached forward to shake the hand of the young man standing nearest to me. Three of the young men and the adult male host stared at me without moving a muscle, and the fourth young man standing closest to me actually took a step back. In that moment, I realized my mistake. While Traci and our own youth group kids stared silently, I dropped my hand, smiled broadly and continued my friendly greetings.

I had hesitated for only a second, but Traci said later that the moment seemed to last much longer. My youth group members were accustomed to seeing their pastor treated with respect, deference even, and the Muslim young men's refusal to shake my hand made some of them uncomfortable. My own fifteen-year-old son was in the group, and as we entered the school, I glanced in his direction. His mouth was set in a tight line, and I could see he was upset.

We were warmly ushered into the school and entered a long hallway to begin our tour. Out of earshot of our hosts, the kids near me were quietly asking what had just happened. Why were the young men so rude to Pastor Marcia? I quickly explained that some Muslim men shake hands with women, but many Muslim men believe it is wrong to touch a woman who is not a family member. It was all I had a chance to whisper quickly, and not all the kids heard it.

As we walked down the hall, we could see into the classrooms of elementary-age students, which looked familiar. Once the bell rang, older students spilled out into the hallways. The familiarity ended. All the older girls wore head coverings. We had prepared our youth to expect this, but they were still wide-eyed. The Muslim students looked equally solemn as they observed us.

We were led through an impressive science lab and several other areas of the school before finally entering the mosque area. When we entered the prayer space, our male guide explained the importance of prayers in Islam and gestured across the room indicating that the men and boys gathered in this space. He explained that women usually prayed at home. On occasions when women did attend the mosque, they sat in a balcony area located above the back of the main room.

Our group was invited to ask questions. While there were many thoughtful questions, there was particular interest in the role of women in Islam. Someone asked why the elementary-age girls didn't wear head coverings like the older girls. Maryam carefully explained that the hijab is optional for younger girls, but that at puberty most girls start wearing head coverings because they believe that more modest dress is necessary after a girl's cycles begin. Someone else asked if a woman could choose to sit on the main floor where the men sat, if she preferred that to the balcony. Maryam explained that all women were expected to be seated in the separate area during prayer time so they would not be a distraction to the men. After a lively question-and-answer period, the tour ended.

Unfortunately, we left for the ten-hour drive home right after the tour, so I didn't have an opportunity to debrief the entire youth group that day. In fact, because the youth group didn't meet in the summer, I never found an occasion for the entire group to reflect on our Muslim tour. It was only much later that I discovered what a mistake that was, when—months later—Traci happened to mention to me how shocked she was by the refusal of the Muslim young men to shake my hand. She shared her feelings with me:

> When the young men refused to shake your hand, I thought, Oh boy! We've offended them in the first minute of our visit! I became uncomfortable in my female skin and that stayed with me the whole time we were there. I couldn't shake the feeling.
>
> I worried that you and I, and maybe our girls, were dressed inappropriately and would cause offense, even though we'd all taken care to dress in long sleeves and pants. I was so aware that my pants were a little tight from eating so much fabulous food on our trip and I wished I had a sweater to wear!
>
> I remember wondering if our girls were uncomfortable when they heard explanations for the dress-code change when a girl started her cycles—and the reason women had to sit apart from men so they wouldn't be a diversion to the men. I still remember looking up when they pointed out the women's seating, and thinking, *Really? Women have to sit in that dark balcony way back*

there? Honestly, the gender divisions made it difficult for me to believe Islamic women were thought of as equal, or that their strength was really recognized.

It had been my idea to give our youth some exposure to other religions in hopes that we could reduce fear and distrust of Americans who practice minority religions. Had my plan backfired? Had I caused the youth group leader and the students—including my son—to be more resistant to Muslims?

From my vantage point today, I think our Muslim visit was a mixed success. I clearly made more than one mistake that day; in fact, I can easily spot three. My offer of a handshake was the first. I did it out of habit and, probably, a lack of awareness. As I recall, I was surprised to find that *American* Muslim men would avoid shaking hands, even though I was aware that some Muslims elsewhere in the world did so. I naïvely assumed that Muslims in the United States would have embraced American cultural practices.

The second mistake I made was not allowing time for debriefing after the tour. I was a novice at doing interfaith work, and I had not yet learned how important it is to take the time to let students discuss their shared experience and unpack all the questions, perceptions and misperceptions generated by it. If we had made time for discussion after the tour ended, I could have corrected the misperception of male rudeness in the refusal to shake my hand. I could have provided a broader view of women in Islam by explaining that the social customs of a country also influence religious customs, and that many Muslim women are highly educated, hold positions of authority, and live egalitarian lifestyles that they believe are based on Islamic teachings of equality.

My third mistake had to do with the format of our visit. It would have been a much richer learning experience if our youth group and a similar group of Muslim high schoolers had participated in conversation with each other or worked on a charitable project together. Instead, we took a tour that was bound to illustrate differences—in particular, the hijab and segregated seating—two customs that are not easily understood across lines of cultural and religious difference. Conversation and relationship-building could have focused on shared values, instead.

Imagine if the youth had met in pairs or groups of four to talk about things they have in common, choosing from a list of sample questions to get started, for example:

- What are your favorite extracurricular activities?
- What holidays does your school dismiss for?

- What stereotypes do you wish people did not have about your religion?
- One thing that I like about my religion is . . .
- Have you ever been to South Dakota, and would you like to visit us there?

Or imagine if our youth group and a group of the Muslim students had participated together in a service project. Working side by side, each would have discovered that they share, in common, the value of caring for one's neighbors. Learning by doing is one of the most powerful teaching methods we have.

Over the years I've been able to help facilitate some unique interfaith youth projects. One of my favorites involved the creation of an interfaith youth Lego robotics team. The city newspaper had featured a front-page story about a local Muslim Youth Lego Robotics Team that won a regional competition. So, we asked clergy in our interfaith group whether youth in their church would want to learn how to compete in Lego robotics if the Muslim team would teach them how. We would fund all the necessary Lego supplies. A small Presbyterian church was excited to accept the offer! So over the course of many months, the Muslim kids taught the Presbyterian kids what they knew, which led to the two Lego teams, along with two sets of parent advisors, collaborating on a big robotics project involving the wider Presbyterian congregation.

Relationship-building experiences like these encourage reciprocal learning, rather than one-way learning. When we planned our visit to the Islamic high school, we did it so our youth group could learn about their Muslim peers. The Muslim youth had just as great a need to learn about their Christian peers. If we had created opportunities for them to actually talk or work together, the learning would have been in both directions, and would have been a much richer experience for everyone involved. Nevertheless, I believe our tour of the Islamic high school and mosque actually *was* a success in several ways.

- We demonstrated that it's okay to make a mistake, to admit it, and to move on.
- We demonstrated a willingness to enter unfamiliar spaces and maybe even experience some discomfort as we seek to understand the religious practices of our fellow Americans.
- We reduced fear of the religious other when the kids saw how much they had in common with members of an inner city Black church, with practitioners of Korean Buddhism, and with Muslim teenagers—who, like them, are learning how to become faithful adults in their particular religious tradition.

It's not surprising that we made these mistakes. We were novices in interfaith dialogue. At one time, we are all beginners in this work; so we do well to extend grace to our counterparts as we cross lines of religious difference on the road to understanding one another. Grace allows us to enter unfamiliar space with curiosity instead of fear. Over the years that I've been involved in interreligious work, I've become increasingly comfortable, even when mistakes are made. Curiosity, humility, and grace became my most valuable companions in unfamiliar spaces.

Chapter 7

DISCERNING A DUAL IDENTITY
A Case of Tightrope-Walking

JON M. SWEENEY

> The honest religious thinker is like a tightrope walker. It almost looks as though he were walking on nothing but air. His support is the slenderest imaginable. And yet it really is possible to walk on it.
> —Ludwig Wittgenstein[1]

When Michal and I married in early 2010, we were often with friends who would ask about my religious identity. She is a congregational rabbi, and I've been a Christian all my life. She liked to answer their questions with a short quip: "When we were first engaged, Jon converted . . . [pausing, for effect] . . . to Catholicism." Everyone who was Jewish would laugh. It took me a while to catch on. Why was this funny?

I had thought there might have been an unease with Catholicism on Michal's part; and why not feel uneasy, since I entered the Roman Catholic Church in 2009, when abuse scandals were all people heard of Catholicism? Even a Jesuit priest friend, when I said, "I'm finally becoming a Catholic," responded, "Why?!" Not to mention the Catholic Church's history of anti-Judaism and antisemitism. I was uneasy myself. But that's not why it was funny. I soon realized the joke was: he converted, but not to Judaism, as might seem likely. Because when does a Christian marry a rabbi (who wants to remain a rabbi) and not convert to Judaism? It was almost unheard of at the time.

From the start, Michal and I felt we had more in common with each other religiously and spiritually than we often had with some of our coreligionists. We were well matched, even if our religions often were not.

Each religious tradition has tools for living, meant to help carry and sustain us, make us wiser about the world and ourselves, and turn us into better human beings. Religious people are like tightrope walkers, to

38

use Wittgenstein's metaphor quoted above, outfitted to make it across that slender line; and somehow it usually works.

They are distinctive—that walking, those tools—from tradition to tradition. And the tightrope walker doesn't usually incorporate other circus performance techniques into walking the line. They focus on doing one thing well. This is how I've usually felt about my religious life, even though I've also been curious about the lives and practices of others. I have learned much and often from Muslims, Buddhists, Hindus, Jews, and Indigenous people. This curiosity rose to a new level when I began to study and pray with frequency in synagogue and at home. My religious life became abundantly Jewish. Since 2010, I have been in synagogue far more often than I've been in church.

To be a decent rabbi spouse, I need to be involved in the congregation; but I also want to be involved. I love Jews and Judaism, and I love religion. Yet I remain a Catholic. I go to Mass and love that too. I spend time each year at a Trappist monastery. I often pray the canonical hours, especially the "night watch" in the early hours before dawn. I'm a Catholic writer and editor who spends all day most days immersed in the subjects of my first love.

So I am a frequent participant in Jewish services and practices, but I am not Jewish. There are boundaries that I observe. For example, I would not wear a tallit, and it would not be appropriate for me to say Kaddish— or even to recite the *Shema* with the feeling that I've observed in others when they recite it.[2] Each Shabbat, when I am with others saying Kaddish, I stand in support of the mourners, as do the others not in a year of mourning or not observing a *yahrzeit* (anniversary of the death of a close relative), and I say the repeated "Amen" and other communal responses as members of the community do. However, I do not pray the Kaddish as a Jewish mourner.

I wear a *kippah* if I am a guest in a synagogue or home where wearing one is expected. I will join a group *aliyah* ("going up" to the Torah scroll when it is open and read in synagogue, considered an honor for Jews) as a member of the community, but I would be uncomfortable if someone suggested I should be given an *aliyah* by myself, or with just one or two other people. The exception to this will take place soon, at our daughter's bat mitzvah; I will stand there with my wife and beam.

I am an active participant in our weekly Torah study group. I contribute ideas and questions in the way that others do, but sometimes I deliberately mention that I'm not Jewish; I'm most likely to do this when saying something that is at all critical. For a Catholic to say, *I don't like that in Torah*, is very different than for a Jew to say the same. I'm not a little bit Jewish. I'm not half-Jewish. But this is my unique situation.

There are other people—particularly those born with one Jewish and one Christian parent, raised in both traditions—who have good reasons for being half-Jewish and half-Christian. They might say, *How could I be anything other?* I cannot know their experience. I can only know my own.

Similarly different from me is the person who converts from one tradition into another and then may find affinities between the two, overlappings, or convergences. I recently wrote a biography of just such a person—the Lakota medicine man Nicholas Black Elk—who made a sincere conversion to Roman Catholicism in mid-life, is likely to become a Catholic saint, but who also never saw it necessary to put away his Lakota pipe, his great visions, or his traditional dance.

I am in a religious position that some would consider messy, but where I feel fortunate, as both synagogue member and permanent guest. I learn much, am blessed often, by my participation in Jewish services, prayer, and study. But the lines I don't cross are important for me—and, I think, for my Jewish friends. Similarly respecting religious lines, I would happily join a Lakota friend in his sweat lodge and fast and chant and pray, but I wouldn't ever build one in my backyard. And after participating in a sweat lodge ceremony, I would never imagine calling myself a little bit Lakota. I might feel differently if I looked upon the formalities of religion as limitations, but I don't see or experience religion that way. I am willingly Roman Catholic, fully aware that any person may also be. If I want to wear a tallit in synagogue, I should ask to be recognized as Jewish. Otherwise, I'm pretending, or playing, with serious and important things.

Borrowing from another's religious tradition is a kind of stealing often called "religious appropriation," and it has been usefully defined by Liz Bucar in a recent book: "when individuals adopt religious practices without committing to religious doctrines, ethical values, systems of authority, or institutions within the context of existing injustice."[3]

A Catholic friend once described to me her own deep attraction to Judaism, and how a Jewish friend successfully dissuaded her from converting. Her friend said: "I know you, and I know that your imagination is filled with Jesus. You can't cease being a Catholic, or a Christian, simply because you're unhappy with your church. You're filled with Jesus. It's inside you." This is as it should be. I mean, this is how religion is supposed to work in us. It shouldn't be easy to leave, or join, and we shouldn't be casual with another's. My friend, somewhat reluctantly, agreed with her friend's advice. She's still a Catholic many decades later, and will remain so, though she loves Jews and Judaism as I do.

I have another friend, a rabbi, not my wife, who a quarter century ago encouraged me not to be casual with the religious practices of another tradition by pointedly saying, "How would you feel if I took a little nibble of the Eucharist?" He was metaphorically and literally right on. That would be offensive to the emotion I place in this essential practice of my tradition. Similarly, I feel it would be inappropriate for me to place my feelings too deep within Jewish religious practices.

If you are Christian, imagine that a snack food company began to market Holy Communion chips and that the appeal of receiving the body of Christ easily and flavorfully took hold with millions of people who never saw a priest or the inside of a church. And if this seems farfetched, let me suggest it's not inconceivable that Beijing might seek to unhinge the power and authority of the Roman Catholic Church in China using such a scheme. And who could accomplish this better than marketers of snack food?

To use someone else's religious symbols, liturgies, or practices as an outsider who doesn't share in that religious tradition's commitments is to cause offense. And to claim a religious identity without sharing in that religion's commitments is even more fraught. The first is incidental; the second is fundamental. There is a head and a heart to religious living. Like the person who learns to speak another language, but will always dream only in their first language, the words of my head and heart turn and return on and to my Christianity. No matter how much I learn about that other language. No matter how affectionate I am for the people who speak the other language.

There is also a citizenship to religious life. Even if you didn't choose your citizenship, because you were born with it, you choose whether or not to remain where you are or to change countries.

If there's a continuum of fluid religious identities, at one extreme end would be the nineteenth century Bengali holy man, Ramakrishna, who claimed to experience the Divine in a variety of religious-specific manifestations. In addition to his Advaita Vedanta and Vaishnav Bhakti devotions, he was also at times, he said, Christian and then Muslim, and so on. I haven't known many people who would claim something similar. At the other end of this fictional spectrum of pluralists might be me, since I pray and worship and study with Jews more often than with Catholics, and yet I never describe myself as a little bit Jewish. I am no longer a stranger in a Jewish congregational setting (spiritually speaking or literally), but I remain a frequent and knowledgeable guest.

Here's where it becomes most tricky: religions are mediated ways that we experience or express the Divine. For some of us, there are also unmediated experiences or expressions, and it is when these take place in less familiar religious places or congregations that we begin to move outside a singular religious identity. One of my favorite spiritual writers, Thomas Merton—who remained a faithful Catholic but curious about nearly every religious tradition he encountered—understood this well. In his *Asian Journal* Merton wrote, "The contemplative life must provide an area, a space for liberty, of silence, in which possibilities are allowed to surface and new choices—beyond routine choice—become manifest." For him, this included contemplating a series of stone standing, sitting, and reclining Buddhas in India. "[L]ooking at these figures I was suddenly, almost forcibly jerked clean out of the habitual, half tied vision of things, and an inner clearness, clarity, as if exploding from the rocks themselves, became evident and obvious," he wrote in his journal.[4]

It makes perfect sense that these experiences might happen while praying or studying or praising in a religious setting that is unfamiliar. Sparks fly when we encounter Spirit outside the confines of where we usually contain it. This is why I wish unfamiliar religious confines on every person living. They lead to epiphanies and to moments of profound connection. My unscientific study tells me that people clearly rooted in one religious tradition, open to experiencing another, are more likely to find affinities for the other than are those people who simply stay home. But be careful, then, not to offend anyone, not to overstep the lines, that are there for everyone's good.

There is also an alliance to be made with religious people. I threw in my lot with the Jewish people many years ago, and that means something. I have a Jewish wife, with whom I am raising a Jewish daughter. Their future is also my future. As a very real example, I sometimes sit in shul with one eye on the front door, imagining how quickly I would throw a chair at a dangerous intruder, or how I might jump in front of someone charging the rabbi.

In summary, let me put it this way: Who would I offend if I were too Jewish in my practice, or in my claims of religious identity, due to my other religious commitments? After the Shoah, I imagine the answer to be, any Jew who rightfully thinks: *These ways of being who I am put me in danger in the world. What risk are they to you?*

Notes

1. Ludwig Wittgenstein, *Culture and Value, Revised Edition*, ed. G. H. von Wright (New York: Blackwell, 1998), 84e.

2. The *Shema* is to Judaism as the Lord's Prayer (the "Our Father") is to Christianity. "*Shema yisra'el adonay eloheynu adonay ehad*," "Listen, Israel, the Lord is our God, the Lord alone" (Deut 6:4).

3. Liz Bucar, *Stealing My Religion: Not Just Any Cultural Appropriation* (Cambridge, MA: Harvard University Press, 2022), 2.

4. Thomas Merton, *The Asian Journal of Thomas Merton*, ed. Naomi Burton, Brother Patrick Hart, James Laughlin (New York: New Directions, 1975), 117, 233–35.

Part II

Presumptions

Chapter 8

THE POWER OF PRAYER
(TO MAKE THINGS AWKWARD)
On Learning Interreligious Leadership

JACK GORDON

There's a photo, somewhere, of about one hundred young adults standing around a series of circular tables, filling the breadth of the gym / social hall of a Latter-day Saints chapel in Washington, DC. Everyone is holding hands, their eyes closed, many with heads bowed. A moment of silent meditation and contemplation at the end of a momentously successful day-long interfaith summit, attended by dozens of aspiring young leaders eager to overcome differences and find solidarity together. As the principal organizer of the event, I'd called on a friend who was a terrific orator in the Black Christian tradition to close us out with some inspiring words, a nondenominational prayer to connect the spirit of faith and community that had brought us together.

"Was anyone else weirded out by the prayer at the end of the summit?" read one tweet afterwards. "Totally," responded another. "First time I've ever been to an interfaith event where we were all made to pray together. What was *that* about?" The negative response to what I'd intended to be a sincere moment of reflection caught me off guard. What's more, it pointed to a group of attendees who had shown up ready to fully participate and yet felt disappointed, if not mildly offended: atheists and secular humanists. The irony was not lost on me: I myself have never been wholly convinced there is a God.

As a child of a mixed marriage—Conservative Jewish on my dad's side and culturally Christian on my mom's—I'd grown up going to synagogue weekly, became a bar mitzvah, and had a decent education in Torah. I took the stories more as fables and subjects for debate, not a literal truth. God was a character in the narrative with at times questionable motives and a skewed sense of justice. In my day-to-day life, I didn't turn to God for

45

assistance. Moreover, I tended to consider people who lived by faith with a heavy dose of skepticism.

In college, I began to study the Bahá'í faith, and was enamored of its message of unity for humankind and revolutionary teaching of Oneness. The Writings of Bahá'u'lláh helped me open up to a more expansive view of the universe that embraced the Divine and saw the beauty in the interconnection and interdependency of all things. I began to pray in a way I had rarely experienced before and was buoyed by the experience. All the same, I never left behind a certain feeling of skepticism. Although I gained a greater appreciation of the role faith had in the lives of many people I knew, there were still times I felt it was a bunch of fairy tales.

One thing I prided myself on, however, was an openness to learn from people whose experiences were difference from mine. I knew from my own upbringing that traditions didn't always fit neatly into a box. I had a strong Jewish identity and yet I had a nominally Christian mother. To top it off, we'd celebrate Christmas at—plot twist!—our Bahá'í grandmother's house. In college, I still identified as culturally Jewish, even though I had a Bahá'í religious practice. I claimed both while still not being sure there was a God—and felt no conflict within me all the same. So, far be it from me to judge someone who said they were this type of Christian or that one, this type of Muslim or another—especially if they shared my interest in exploring interfaith collaboration.

Millennials, and even more so Gen Z, are not only increasingly diverse in terms of our families and social groups, but multidimensional in terms of our own identities, especially when it comes to religion and belief. When we bring young people together to talk about the role of religion in society and how we use our beliefs to inspire action, how can we *not* make space for those who don't neatly line up with a traditional affiliation?

I was already in my late twenties by the time I got started in interfaith organizing in DC. Looking around me, I saw that many local institutions were led by folks who were one or two generations ahead of me. As a member of the board of the largest regional interfaith organization in the DC area, I was often the youngest person in the room—by at least a decade. So, I started seeking out peers: assistant ministers, program associates, children's class teachers, events coordinators, and social entrepreneurs working at faith-based institutions and nonprofits or volunteering their time with their communities. I made friends quickly. Together, a handful of us started planning an annual summit for young faith leaders in the DC area.

I knew our success lay in casting a wide net, being bold in our outreach and extending warm invitations to as many people as we could find, regardless of their affiliation. Year after year, I made it a goal to push beyond the people we'd convinced to participate in the previous summit: to make the pitch to more groups; to encourage the sole contact to invite their friends the next year; to find out, if someone had moved, who'd taken over a role. We grew our event year after year, at least doubling its size by the end of my tenure as lead organizer. More importantly, we launched dozens of friendships along the way. But, that first year, I didn't know what I was doing.

To be honest, I didn't really have a lot of experience with interfaith events up to that point. It made sense to me that there'd be some sort of closing that would help us process the joy and exhaustion from the day. Closing with everyone holding hands and having time for a communal prayer and meditation—the people we'd have in the room would be used to doing that. Sure, we were in a church, but we understood that not everyone was Christian. We weren't going to pray "in Jesus's name." If there was mention of God and being united as people of faith, I figured that folks would come to it with their own understanding and, y'know, get it.

Upon reflection, I see how that assumption must have been weird for the atheists in the room. Some had trained with the Interfaith Youth Core, where folks are called to speak from their own experience, but there's never a group ritual like a prayer. They were staunch religious freedom advocates, knowledgeable in religious history and traditions, and had shown up eager to participate. I later learned how unwelcome atheists and secular humanists are often made to feel at interfaith gatherings, when organizers and participants too easily emphasize the "faith" part of the equation, more than the interconnection—the opportunity to learn from others with a different set of beliefs, albeit similar values.

After the event, I called up a couple of the more vocal dissenters to discuss what they'd felt and how we could have made them feel more welcomed and included in that moment. There was no ill will—just a desire to improve on a promising start. I made sure that from the next year on, we had at least one atheist on the planning team. When we met a year later, we had a humanist invocation to kick off our event. Secular humanist groups contributed financially to support the growth of the event. They were as integrated as any religious organization.

It was certainly not the only mistake I made in those early years: I couldn't understand why planning the event for a Saturday was a big deal if we weren't getting interest from that many observant Jews anyway. ("It just comes down to numbers!") I falsely categorized Unitarians as a denomination of Protestant Christianity. ("You're basically the same thing, right?") And, once, at a planning meeting, in a moment of exasperation, I reflexively cursed "Jesus Christ!"—much to the visible shock and discomfort of LDS and Catholic committee members. I'm sure there were many other faux pas along the way, but none that overshadowed the immense bond of friendship that was created through this series of highly successful gatherings year after year, particularly between those who were part of the various generations of planning teams.

As the COVID pandemic restrictions relaxed, just about ten years after the first DC Young Adult Faith Leaders Summit, a number of us agreed it was time for an informal reunion. We had been in our twenties and early thirties then. Now folks were married, had babies (if not two or three), had graduated from seminary and PhD programs, had become executives, had run for office, were leading their congregations. In short, we'd gotten old! We joked we needed a "DC Middle Aged Interfaith Leaders Summit" now.

I looked around the gathering—Jews and Catholics, Latter-day Saints and Bahá'ís, Muslims and Protestants, humanists and folks with multiple identities—and felt pride for the friendships we'd grown and sustained over the past decade. But, ironically, I've also come to a place where I'm not in touch much with the next generation. As the father of an emerging adolescent, I know many more ten-year-olds than I do twenty-year-olds or even twenty-five-year-olds. As I watched our children play together, I wondered how growing up in this milieu would affect their outlook on the world. In fact, this is intergenerational work as much as it is interreligious. The joy and challenge of each generation is that we must open the door further, draw the circle wider, to help more see they have a place and feel welcome.

Chapter 9

Relics in the Chapel

On Dangers Inherent in Experiential Learning

Soren M. Hessler

Unwittingly, and with the best of intentions, I very nearly imperiled an entire family line of potential priests. Permit me to explain.

In 2018, Hebrew College instituted a requirement that all new rabbinical and cantorial students take a three-course sequence engaging other religious traditions: a foundational seminar in Jewish and religious pluralism, followed by an immersive introduction to Christianity and a vibrant study of Islam.[1] At the time, I was the associate director of the college's Betty Ann Greenbaum Miller Center for Interreligious Learning and Leadership while also serving part-time on the ministry staff of Boston University's Marsh Chapel. I had been ordained by the West Ohio Conference of the United Methodist Church a few years before and was working on a PhD in practical theology—also at BU. I was eager to be in the classroom more; so I was thrilled when the dean of the rabbinical school and my boss approached me to consider developing the curriculum for the Christianity course. Together, we envisioned a course focused on the histories, beliefs, and practices of contemporary Christian communities with a primary objective of equipping future Jewish institutional leaders to better navigate relationships with Christians for the sake of cooperative justice work in the world.

These courses, taken in successive years, would meet on the Tuesday through Friday following the Martin Luther King holiday in January. While instructors for the other courses decided to meet at Hebrew College, I wanted to immerse students in a variety of manifestations of Christianity in Boston by holding class in churches and other Christian organizations.

I was moved by Zalman Schachter-Shalomi's remembrances of encounters with Howard Thurman while a student at Boston University.[2] As he told the story, he found himself on campus very early one morning nearly seventy years ago, looking for a place to *daven*. He entered the chapel and happened upon a man whom he assumed to be the janitor. The man suggested he come back the next day and see if he found the lower chapel more suitable for prayer. Schachter-Shalomi did that. To his surprise, the brass cross had been removed, candlesticks had been lit, and the Bible had been opened to a Psalm.

The young rabbi was thinking of enrolling in a course taught by Thurman, the first African American dean at a predominately White higher education institution in the United States, so he asked to meet with him. When he arrived for that appointment, he realized that Dean Thurman himself was the man who had made the chapel more hospitable. As Schachter-Shalomi wondered aloud to Thurman whether his "anchor chains" were long enough to entrust his education to a Christian, Thurman responded, "Don't you trust the *ru'ah hakodesh*?" Stunned again by Thurman's insightfulness, he resolved to study with the Baptist mystic.

I was aware of the import of Reb Zalman and Dean Thurman to the Hebrew College and Boston University communities respectively. Therefore, I sought to begin the course in a place formative in the relationship between these two significant religious figures: Boston University's Marsh Chapel, and more specifically, the lower-level, more intimate Robinson Chapel. As Thurman had done, I removed the brass cross from the lower chapel for the first day of class. I began the day with introductions and a review of the syllabus. Students then read Schachter-Shalomi's remembrance of his encounter with Thurman. They met with the current dean of Marsh Chapel for a candid conversation about people's "anchor chains"—those things that keep us anchored in our own traditions and the import of hospitality in interreligious encounter. The opening morning session went off without a hitch in Robinson Chapel. We took a break, after which a colleague was to provide an art and architecture tour of the main nave as a way of helping orient students to how one Christian community understands and relates to its liturgical space.

As we arrived in the chapel narthex, my colleague mentioned that the ashes of Boston University president Daniel L. Marsh (the visionary and namesake of Marsh Chapel) and his wife, Arline Woodford Marsh, were interred in the nave.[3] One of the students quickly spoke up. He explained that he could not be in the presence of human remains, so he asked me to excuse him from the remainder of the tour. I quickly consented. He left; the tour proceeded. During the question-and-answer session that followed, a student asked whether it was common for churches to contain remains of dead people. My colleague and I explained that the practice of housing relics of significant Christians in churches is incredibly common in Roman Catholicism. Contemporary Protestants are less likely to revere the relics of saints. However, some continue the practice of burying significant people in church crypts or otherwise interring them in churches. We both also noted that many university churches were the final resting places of significant university figures.

I then learned from one of the students that the student who had asked to be excused was a *Kohen*, a descendant of the Jewish priestly class, who took very seriously the prohibition found in Lev 21:1 for sons of Aaron not to be defiled by a dead person. I had not even thought about Daniel Marsh's ashes being a problem for anyone setting foot in the chapel, let alone creating a potential ontological crisis for a student. As we moved to the lunch break, I frantically called colleagues at Hebrew College. Had I inadvertently ruined this young man's entire life? Was I causing all of my other students to become ritually unclean? Did we need to not meet in any other churches? And why did my Jewish colleague, who approved of my course plan and who had been to Marsh Chapel many times and knew of the Marshes' ashes, not warn me that utilizing Marsh Chapel for the course could be a problem?

My Hebrew College colleague got a good chuckle out of my predicament. He then explained that Hebrew College is home to a wide range of personal opinions about the appropriate conduct of *Kohanim*. Among this institution's candidates for ordination, very few are *Kohanim*. This particular student had a very traditional view of observance of ordinances related to the priestly class. Thankfully, while on our tour of BU's chapel, we had always been at least four cubits from the Marshes' ashes, and the student had never entered the nave itself. The dean and I agreed that, in the future, students could petition to be exempted from the site visit portions of my course. We both felt that for the vast majority of Hebrew College's students the site visits were a valuable educational experience; but if they would present an ontological dilemma, they should not be required. From then on, when future iterations of the course involved travel to a site that contained human remains, I would take care to notify participants well in advance of the first day of class. Over the years, such disclosures have sparked interesting conversations—often marked by students wondering what would prompt me to make such a disclaimer!

The entire incident helped me to refine and focus the pedagogical style of the course, which I have described as "nothing off limits."[4] I am transparent about the good, the bad, and the complicated when it comes to Christianity and equally transparent about the limits of my own knowledge about Christianity and Judaism. I also encourage students to ask all their questions about Christianity. In the midst of talking about why "sometimes the minister is a girl" or how Unitarian Universalists fit into intra-Christian politics,[5] students often ask me if it was important to remain celibate while single in order to be ordained. It makes for quite the teaching adventure. I learn so much about both Christianity and Judaism from their questions. Ultimately, I think this mutual humility and vulnerability between teacher and students does help prepare students to engage thoughtfully with Christians as they seek to make meaningful difference in the world.

My chapel misstep has made me much more cognizant of what spaces are, and should be, used for intentional interreligious engagement and how relics both literal and figurative powerfully shape a space. Daniel Marsh designed Boston University's chapel to have no fixed cross in order to make the space more hospitable for all people—a revolutionary move in the early twentieth century. However, his interment there has actually made the space less hospitable—at least for some. I continue to ponder whether the benefits of utilizing a historic Christian chapel for expressly interreligious programming can outweigh the barriers to hospitality created by the relics it houses.

Notes

1. Soren M. Hessler, "The Association of Theological Schools, Accreditation, and Graduate Education for Non-Christian Religious Professionals," *Journal of Interreligious Studies* 35 (March 2022): 70.

2. Renditions of Schachter-Shalomi's encounter with Thurman are found in Zalman Schachter-Shalomi, "What I Found in the Chapel," in *My Neighbor's Faith: Stories of Interreligious Encounter, Growth, and Transformation*, ed. Jennifer Howe Peace, Or N. Rose, and Gregory Mobley (Maryknoll, NY: Orbis Books, 2012), 207–10, and Zalman Schachter-Shalomi and Edward Hoffman, "Widening Horizons: From New Bedford to Boston University," in *My Life in Jewish Renewal: A Memoir* (Lanham, MD: Rowman & Littlefield, 2012), 87–94.

3. The marker of Daniel Marsh's ashes is also featured in the university's virtual tour of Marsh Chapel. See "Discovering Marsh Chapel," *BU Today*, https://www.bu.edu/today/projects/marshchapel/.

4. Soren M. Hessler, "'Nothing Off Limits': Pedagogical Reflections by a Christian Teaching Christianity at Rabbinical School," in *Deep Understanding for Divisive Times: Essays Marking a Decade of the* Journal of Interreligious Studies, ed. Lucinda Allen Mosher, Axel Marc Oaks Takacs, Or N. Rose, and Mary Elizabeth Moore (Newton Centre, MA: Interreligious Studies Press, 2020), 109–13.

5. Foundational readings for the class include Kathryn House, "Sometimes the Minister Is a Girl," in *Faithfully Feminist: Jewish, Christian, and Muslim Feminists on Why We Stay*, ed. Gina Messina-Dysert, Jennifer Zobair, and Amy Levin (Ashland, OR: White Cloud Press, 2015), 188–93, and Abigail Clauhs, "'The Cathedral of the World': Interconnection in Difference," in *Words to Live By: Sacred Sources for Interreligious Engagement*, ed. Or N. Rose, Homayra Ziad, and Soren M. Hessler (Maryknoll, NY: Orbis Books, 2018), 31–41.

Chapter 10

Rude Awakenings

A White Buddhist Reflects on Religious and Racial Equity

Wakoh Shannon Hickey

A small circle of meditators gathered in a side chapel off the main chapel of our seminary campus. We lit a candle on the altar table and sat silently for half an hour. On every entrance to the space a sign was posted, saying, "Meditation in progress, please help to maintain the silence." Every week, people walked through the side chapel, talking and going about their business as if we weren't there. When I asked classmates not to do this, several responded, "Well, this *is* a Christian school"—as if that provided a license to be rude. Almost all of the weekly meditators happened to be Christian. None of the intruders would have dreamed of traipsing blithely through the sanctuary during the weekly Protestant service in the main chapel. It was as if sitting quietly simply did not register as a religious practice deserving comparable respect.

For six years, I was the only Buddhist student at that seminary; I led the meditation group for two years. As a rare Buddhist graduate, I earned both an MA and MDiv there. The school belongs to an interfaith consortium near a major research university, and I gained a solid background in both Buddhist and Christian studies. I was well prepared to earn a PhD in religious studies elsewhere. To my surprise years later, I even found myself teaching introductory biblical studies, among other things, to many undergraduates at two liberal-arts universities. My seminary education has been indispensable to my work as a Buddhist chaplain in academic settings and as an interfaith chaplain in medical contexts. I am deeply grateful for the excellent education I received, the lasting relationships I made with seminary classmates, the healing I did from youthful experiences of toxic Christianity, and the deeper faith and clarity of purpose I developed during those years. I am most grateful, however, for the painful lessons my experience as a religious minority in a Christian environment taught me about the experiences of racialized minorities in majority-White environments.

I came to see my own White privilege and White liberal racism more clearly. Although it was often frustrating and lonely, it was also salutary. I don't think there is any better way for a member of a dominant group to develop empathy for minority groups than to experience minority status directly, at length.

A large proportion of my seminary classmates were LGBTQIA+ people, so I felt quite comfortable as an out lesbian. As a Buddhist, however, I experienced countless microaggressions—a term that hadn't been coined yet. I was tokenized repeatedly by well-meaning, liberal Christians who knew nothing about Buddhism or its diversity, yet who expected me to represent and speak for all of it. What a stark look in the mirror it was for me, a White convert who had lived and worked in majority-White environments most of my life and had little understanding of my own White, liberal racism.

Fortunately for me, Buddhism had a certain cachet as "cool," particularly the Zen Buddhism I practice—unlike Islam, which was vilified after the 9/11 attacks on the World Trade Center and Pentagon. The 9/11 attacks occurred during my fourth year of seminary, as I began a residency as a hospital chaplain. While the U.S. president and his cabinet beat the drums for war in Iraq and Afghanistan, violent attacks increased dramatically on Muslim Americans and Sikh Americans (who were mistakenly perceived as Muslim). Zen Buddhism, however, was a relatively blank canvas on which people projected images of serenity and spontaneity.

My experience of monastic Zen training bore little resemblance to those stereotypes: it is extremely demanding, physically and emotionally; tightly scheduled from well before dawn to well after dark; chock-full of ritual formalities and chanted liturgies. Having to deal with my classmates' and professors' misconceptions, assumptions, and downright ignorance was exhausting.

On one occasion I read a poem at the ordination of a Christian classmate. I wore meditation robes and a Zen-style stole, because I thought it would make visual sense to the people assembled. The poem I read was neither Buddhist nor Christian, but spoke of prayer as opening one's whole self to the vast circles and cycles of being. My friend and I had chosen it jointly because we both found it meaningful, and because it spoke to the themes and images of the rest of the service. Afterward, a Christian pastor commented that my participation made the service interfaith.

It was *not at all* an interfaith service: it was a United Church of Christ ordination, conducted according to the UCC Book of Worship. I was participating as a friend of the new minister, whose ministry and theology I supported, even though I did not share it. The pastor's comment reflected the assumption I have encountered so often: that a Buddhist body at the front of the sanctuary automatically makes a service "interfaith." This is tokenism: including a member of a minority in a group to create an appearance of diversity, but not addressing the person's actual differences or needs.

I have been invited countless times to participate in so-called interfaith services. I appreciate these invitations, but in almost every case, the service is designed according to a Protestant format and held in a church full of pews, and I am asked, usually at the last minute, to plug in by reading a Buddhist text, leading a couple of minutes of meditation, and/or ringing a bell. This gives people an opportunity to feel good about being "interfaith" without having really to take seriously the fact that I am coming from a completely different religious perspective, and my religious experiences and practices are radically different from theirs.

Buddhism is nontheistic, for example: it does not refer to God. The notion is considered irrelevant to the spiritual path leading to liberation from suffering. I can and do use "God-language" regularly in my work as a hospice chaplain, because my role there is to serve people of any faith (or none), to meet them where they are, and to speak in religious or spiritual terms that are meaningful for them. I certainly believe in powers greater than the "self" enclosed within my skin, yet my faith is not oriented around a transcendent deity imagined as a "being," or as having a personality, or as directing human affairs, as is presumed in many mainstream Jewish, Christian, and Islamic theologies. As Lucinda Mosher says, "God is the answer to a question Buddhists don't ask."

The best description of God I've found thus far comes from the late Episcopal bishop John Shelby Spong, who articulated a nontheistic Christian theology of God as the power of "life-affirming love." It is found in the ways animals tend their young, plants turn toward sunlight, and we care for those dear to us. It is always accessible, but neither omniscient, nor omnipotent, nor "personal."

I suspect that consciousness is more than a mere product of brain activity, but I don't believe in a "soul" or "essential self" that transmigrates or that exists as an independent, enduring entity apart from the body. I find the idea that everything is impermanent, and therefore interrelated and always transforming, to be deeply comforting, because nothing is ever lost, only changed. I also practice repentance regularly, but not to a god; I don't believe in "sin." I take my ethical vows seriously and believe in karma and rebirth, but like most modern Buddhists I regard heaven and hell as states of mind—both deluded, both temporary.

When I convened a chapel service during seminary, I adapted several Buddhist practices to a Protestant format, because it seemed impractical to have people meditate for thirty or forty minutes, then join in another thirty or forty minutes of full prostrations, incense offerings, and chanting, partly or entirely in Japanese. That is the daily religious practice of Sōtō Zen temples. The "sermon" is a separate event, often lasting about an hour. I did ask participants to remove their shoes before entering the chapel and to remain silent before the service, which created a sense of sacred space novel to many.

An interfaith group to which I belonged later, on the East Coast, hosted an annual Thanksgiving service, and wanted to include a Buddhist element, though no Buddhist was available to participate. The Christian and Jewish organizers wanted to recite part of a traditional Zen chant before meals:

> Innumerable labors brought us this food; may we know how it comes to us. Receiving this offering, let us consider whether our virtue and practice deserve it. Desiring the natural order of mind, let us be free of greed, hate, and delusion. We eat to support life and to practice the way of Buddha. This food is for the Three Treasures, for our teachers, family, and all people, and for all beings in the Six Worlds. The first portion is for the precepts; the second is for the practice of samadhi; the third is to save all beings. Thus we eat this food and awaken with everyone.

Asked about this, I said they were welcome to include it, but the point of the Zen meal ritual is to take just enough food to sustain one's health so that one can continue practicing for the benefit of all beings. It's the opposite of the American custom of feasting at Thanksgiving. They wisely left the chant out.

In Zen tradition, we enter meditation and ceremony halls silently, barefoot and bowing. We don't walk down the center aisle or pass in front of the altar. I still wince when people have ordinary conversations in church before a service, or walk through the space as if it were a theater, or place sacred texts on the floor.

One year, during my tradition's major annual religious observance, a seven-day meditation retreat, I tried to maintain silence on campus for a few days. I found it nearly impossible, because other people seemed to feel so awkward or insulted when I responded to their greetings by handing out slips of paper explaining what I was doing. When I lived in a campus dormitory, I was amazed that a paid manager was expected to do all the cleaning; in a Zen community, everyone participates in a few minutes of general cleaning every day, which is why Zen temples are typically immaculate.

What would interfaith education or services look like that truly took account of participants' religious differences? In twenty-five years of involvement in interfaith organizations, I have rarely had occasion to find out. It takes a lot more time, conversation, and planning than most conveners want to spend. In a climate of increasing religious polarization, however, it might be a useful exercise for prospective clergy, especially those from mainline Christian denominations.

The best interfaith service I have experienced was a winter solstice gathering in which a series of different religious practices and readings on the theme of light were offered side by side, with little effort to integrate or comment on them. It felt more meaningful and instructive than what usually passes for "interfaith" services, in which a collage of elements from different traditions is assembled in a superficial way that does not truly honor any of them.

Another tiresome experience is being expected to speak for all members of one's minority group. A classmate once stopped me on campus and asked me to describe "the Buddhist perspective on physician-assisted suicide," a topic he was exploring for an ethics class. I asked, "What sort of Buddhist do you mean?" He looked blank. I said, "A Theravadin perspective would be different from a Māhāyana one." He looked more blank. He clearly was unfamiliar with even the major categories of Buddhism (Theravāda, Māhāyana, and Vajrayana), much less the multiple variations within those categories. Buddhism is as diverse as Christianity; I certainly cannot speak for all of it.

I am a Western convert to one specific Japanese form of Zen. Several other forms of Zen—as well as many other Buddhist denominations—developed in Japan and elsewhere across Asia. My perspective is completely shaped by my social location, as I learned in seminary. Because of that education, I also see Zen rather differently from some of my Zen teachers, who had not engaged in much historical-critical study of the tradition. I'm usually willing to discuss issues from my own perspective; I have recommended and loaned many books; I can identify resources. However, I appreciate a question that shows the questioner has done a little "homework" and has at least some background.

Like members of any minority group, I speak the religious language of my own community *and* the language of the dominant religious culture, in Christian dialects ranging from fundamentalist Pentecostalism to liberal Protestantism to Catholicism. But very few Christians speak the languages of Buddhism or Zen. So although I found most of my seminary faculty supportive and open, I spent countless hours and pages of text explaining the basic assumptions and vocabulary of my tradition before I could even begin to grapple with the theological questions I was asked to consider in classroom assignments.

When absorbing lectures, textbooks, sermons, and the like, I expended enormous energy translating Christian concepts and assumptions into terms I could understand and use. I didn't even realize how *much* energy, until I took a class in religious education with a group of Unitarian Universalists, many of whom are not Christian, and who don't normally use theistic language. I am stunned by how effortless our theological conversations felt by comparison.

I certainly don't expect Christians to censor themselves about their love of God or their faith in Jesus. I am grateful, however, for the Christians I have met who recognize that not everyone shares their assumptions and language about the sacred, and who find ways of expressing broad religious themes in more inclusive terms.

I am grateful to have spent six years (and tens of thousands of dollars) wrestling seriously with Christian scriptures, history, theology, and ethics. It certainly helped me to function better as an educator and as a professional chaplain, and it broadened and deepened my understanding of Christianity enormously. It also helped me to understand, in a much more visceral way, why majority-White graduate schools and employers often have trouble retaining the talented people of color they recruit. I had heard from Black, Asian, and Latina friends in majority-White schools and workplaces how exhausted they felt by the additional emotional and intellectual demands of functioning in those cultures, but I didn't have any visceral sense of what they meant. Now I have an inkling.

How might seminary education create Christian ministers who are well rooted in their own traditions, but do not fall into triumphalism? How can committed people of any faith work in genuine *partnership* for justice, compassion, and peace, with people who don't share their religious assumptions? First, it requires leaving one's comfort zone and immersing oneself in other communities and worldviews. Mere *proximity* to religious differences is not *engagement* with them. For meaningful interfaith relationships to develop, all parties must come to the encounter informed, willing to let go of fixed positions, and open to being shaken and changed by the process.

Chapter 11

AN ACORN IS NOT A TREE
Avoiding Assumptions in Faith-based Coalitions

RACHEL S. MIKVA

Long before reproductive rights were under assault to the degree they are today, I invited a friend to attend a rally planned by the Religious Coalition for Reproductive Choice (RCRC). The organization describes itself as "a broad-based, national, interfaith movement that brings the moral force of religion to protect and advance reproductive health, choice, rights and justice through education, prophetic witness, pastoral presence and advocacy." The RCRC website gathers Buddhist, Catholic, Hindu, Jewish, Muslim, Protestant, and Universalist Unitarian perspectives supporting reproductive justice. Since individuals and organizations on the other side of the debate often try to assert an exclusive claim on religious values, I believe that RCRC's affirmation of reproductive rights as a matter of religious freedom is essential.

The rally unfolded as you might expect. Speakers from different spiritual lifestances emphasized the importance of women and families making reproductive health decisions without shame, stigma, or legal coercion. They shared their traditions' teachings about abortion—a varied and nuanced chorus of religious insight. They spoke about all the issues that are part of reproductive justice—sexual education, food security, paid leave, affordable childcare, health care—not simply keeping abortion safe and legal. Then someone introduced a song composed for the occasion, "An Acorn Is Not a Tree," and my friend began to fume.

He had come to support women's bodily autonomy and religious freedom, including the right to choose what they believe about the beginnings of life. But, he did not personally distinguish between a fetus and a human. In the analogy of the song, he believed an acorn is morally equivalent to a tree—even though he refused to impose his religious convictions on others. He saw himself as both pro-choice and pro-life. How could

59

the organizers, committed to a big tent on reproductive justice, erase him from the coalition?

As we reflected together on this experience, we recognized the risks in making assumptions about what brings people to a cause. Interreligious collaboration to advance the common good is crucial, but we cannot presume that allies share our religious or ethical perspectives just because they are on our side.

The most obvious strategy to avoid this error is to ask questions. Invite people's stories. Model how to speak *within* rather than *for* a coalition, just as we learn to speak from rather than for a religious tradition. This practice applies across a range of issues. In combatting the climate crisis, there must be room for those who engage the work through the ethic of "creation care" and those who deny the existence of a creator. In fighting for criminal justice reform, there must be room for those who believe in rehabilitation and those who assert the fundamental corruption of the human soul, for those who are there to resist human rights violations and systemic racism, and those who are moved more by the waste of state resources.

Interreligious leaders have long been aware of some ways we stumble across internal differences amidst prayers, songs, statements, speeches—even with the food we serve and the time we schedule. How often have I been in a prayer circle of activists with my Christian brother who tries to speak for all of us "in the name of Jesus Christ our Lord"? How often have I been invited to events on Shabbat? We have learned to identify our particularity, so that my Protestant clergy partner may say instead, "I offer this prayer to you, O God, in the name of Jesus Christ my Lord, even as each of us approaches the Divine or transcendent in our own way." And the invitation for an event that cannot avoid Shabbat adds, "Rabbi, I know that this is scheduled during your Sabbath. If you are not able to join us, we can explore other ways for you to participate in our efforts."

We do not have as much experience, however, thinking through issue-specific coalition theologies. So we must make it a habit to inquire: What brings you to the table, and how is it informed by your spiritual lifestance?

Since I advocate understanding something of our stories, let me share one small piece of a long and complex narrative regarding abortion. A greater percentage of American Jews than Christians support a woman's right to choose whether or not to carry a pregnancy to term. Recent Pew research reports that 83% of Jews are pro-choice. Christian opinion is recorded within subcategories: 66% of Black Protestants, 60% of White, nonevangelical Protestants, 56% of Catholics, and 24% of White evangeli-

cal Protestants believe that abortion should be legal in most or all circumstances.[1]

If you trace this difference back through layers of history, religious
texts, and public policy—sometimes having more to do with gender
politics than religion—you may find translation of a single word in the
Hebrew Bible at the root. In the only explicit reference to legal consequences when a pregnancy is disrupted—in this case a miscarriage—the
text makes a distinction between the status of the fetus and the mother:
"When men fight, and one of them pushes a pregnant woman and a miscarriage results, but no other damage (*ason*) ensues, the one responsible
shall be punished when the woman's husband exacts it, paying a fine
based on reckoning. But if other damage ensues, the penalty shall be life
for life, eye for eye, tooth for tooth . . ." (Exod 21:22–25).

Death of the fetus is not considered murder, or it could not be reconciled with a fine. Even manslaughter would require that the assailant
flee to a city of refuge. The familiar trope of life for life applies only if the
woman is otherwise harmed. Targum Onkolos, an early Aramaic translation, makes it more explicit—rendering "no other damage ensues" as "the
woman does not die."

The Vulgate matches the Targum here, but the Septuagint (the Greek
translation that became influential in early Christianity) translates the
Hebrew word *ason* (damage) as "form" (*exeikonismenon*, literally "made
from the image"). The change yields a very different understanding: if
the fetus is unformed when the woman miscarries, the penalty is only a
fine; if it is formed, the law of *talion* applies. The central question becomes
the nature of the fetus, not the welfare of the woman. Although both
the Hebrew and Greek texts were "Jewish" in origin, these Judean versus Alexandrian perspectives came to shape Jewish versus Christian
approaches to questions of abortion—distinctions that impact us to this
day.[2]

Judaism is undeniably life-pursuing—"*Choose life*," Torah teaches
(Deut. 30:19)—but it does not mean anti-abortion. Jewish tradition teaches
that abortion is a religious imperative if the woman's life is in danger. It
teaches that her life continues to take precedence over that of the fetus
until the majority of the body has emerged from the womb; only then is
it a *nefesh*, a living human being. Within the Reform movement, where
I belong, there is overwhelming consensus that abortion should remain
legal in most or all circumstances. There are contemporary Orthodox
legal scholars who maintain that endangering the woman's life is the only
instance that justifies terminating a pregnancy, but many others interpret
the woman's well-being more broadly—each selecting a range of rabbinic

texts to support their perspective. We recognize and even celebrate the multivocality within our tradition, and the vast majority of Jews do not want the state deciding the question for us.

If the interfaith world could surface more such stories that shape our diverse attitudes toward reproductive choices, perhaps it would be more broadly understood how these are questions of religious freedom. (The history of Christian teaching and practice is far more diverse than most people know as well.) As one interreligious group argued in a brief submitted in *Dobbs v. Jackson Women's Health* (2021), "Abandoning the viability standard would erase the only credibly coherent line anyone has yet identified that preserves even a modicum of respect for the many different faith perspectives that the people of this nation hold dear."[3]

There are other lessons we may learn from the acorn. In building interreligious coalitions, we must forgo litmus tests whenever possible, and let alliances focus on single issues when necessary. Political and religious progressives can make common cause with conservative Catholics in the fight against capital punishment, for example, without expectations of partnership on reproductive justice or LGBTQIA+ equality.

It is sometimes difficult to bracket a matter that feels urgent, or to sit down with folks who do not stand with us on other issues. Organizers of the Women's March and the Movement for Black Lives felt this tension around the Palestinian–Israeli conflict; the resulting public statements ended up marginalizing Jews of all races who support women's rights and BLM if they also support the right of Israel to exist (even if they are critical of Israeli policies).

Religious and secular LGBTQIA+ efforts sometimes exclude Jewish Israeli groups with charges of pinkwashing—covering up the sins of the Occupation with progressive policies on gender and sexual orientation. Ostracizing these groups, many of which actually challenge Israeli policies regarding the Occupation, is a kind of essentialization we have long resisted in interreligious work. A whole group cannot be made to stand for the actions of some. The "-washing" epithet also ignores the interreligious principle of pragmatism over purity; an imperfect ally is still an ally. The boundary marker I use for how big the tent can stretch in coalition work is whether someone present will be directly harmed by the participation of others who have been invited in.

Mostly I am interested in finding ways to expand the tent. Some potential allies are invisible to us because they do not identify with familiar -isms, or they do not belong to congregations, or they are marginalized within their own religious communities. We need to learn their stories.

In addition, many people who have been involved in interreligious engagement identify as theological and political progressives. The values often naturally align. In the work of social transformation, however, it is far too narrow a coalition. To build broader and stronger bridges, we need to think outside the box. There are countless allies with a more conservative orientation who recognize the dangers of Islamophobia and antisemitism, the urgency of environmentally sustainable policies, the tragic absurdity of easy access to assault weapons, the threat of Christian nationalism, and other issues that challenge us today.

Even for those of us who have been doing interreligious work for a long time, a bigger tent can create uncomfortable spaces. I have thought about this challenge a lot in terms of evangelizing groups having to set that work aside in order to join with people of diverse faiths, or queer allies trying to partner on poverty issues with groups who restrict LGBTQIA+ rights.

Recently, I was drawn to consider a surprising linkage that ties back to the question of reproductive rights. At an April 2022 panel discussion sponsored by the Aspen Institute's Religion and Society Program, Rev. Mitch Hescox spoke about needing to have the right messenger with the right message to move people toward social action. His example? He spoke to evangelical Christian groups about the climate crisis in the language of right-to-life. It was utterly compelling if I put myself in their shoes, and simultaneously unnerving. Am I co-opted in partnering with them? Do I lend legitimacy to their voice on abortion and accidentally abet the stripping of women's rights and religious freedom? Or can I take comfort that their passion inspires work we can agree on as well?

If we can navigate these concerns and be present in uncomfortable spaces, if we are careful about presumptions and expectations that restrict room at the table, interreligious coalitions will grow stronger in their justice-seeking efforts.

Notes

1. "Fact Sheet: Public Opinion on Abortion," May 17, 2022, www.pewresearch.org.

2. Portions are adapted from Rachel S. Mikva, "Abortion," in *The Encyclopedia of Jewish-Christian Relations* (Berlin: Walter de Gruyter, 2019, and ongoing).

3. *Dobbs v. Jackson Women's Health*, "Brief of Americans United for Separation of Church and State, American Humanist Association, Bend the Arc: A Jewish Partnership for Justice, and Interfaith Alliance Foundation as *Amici Curiae* in Support of Respondents" (2021), 22, www.supremecourt.gov.

Chapter 12

NOT IN THE NAME OF JESUS

On Being True to Ourselves

HUSSEIN RASHID

In *Bobby*, a Bollywood movie, there's a song called *"mujhe kuchh kehnaa hai"* (I have something to say). It is a "call and response." The male lead says, "I have something to say"; the romantic interest responds, "I have something to say too." They constantly interrupt each other in politeness, interfering with what we presume is their mutual declaration of love. At one point, the male lead makes reference to a story about the dangers of politeness: people standing in front of a train keep saying, "After you," back-and-forth, until the train leaves without them. I think about this song a lot when I'm entering a new interfaith relationship. Sometimes, it is possible to be too polite, to the extent that we miss getting anything from the other person, or to even really hear what the other person is trying to say.

In 2011 I had a wonderful opportunity to be a Muslim scholar-in-residence at Virginia Theological Seminary (VTS). The goal was to help prepare the seminarians for work in multireligious environments, both through formal education in a class on the Qur'an I offered, and by interacting with me. We shared meals, watched TV, and socialized together.

One of the highlights during my time at VTS was attending weekly morning prayer meetings—times of reflection together for a group of students and a faculty member. I was invited to various prayer groups. During the early part of my stay, as we were learning how to engage with each other in meaningful ways, I had two very different experiences of them.

In one meeting, the students spoke to one another of their learnings as religious community leaders, and then they turned to prayer and song. In that part of the meeting, they sang and praised God profusely. I was invited to join, and I gladly did so. It was lovely experience in an absolute sense, and one that made me feel welcomed in community.

In the other meeting, the students also spoke to one another of their learnings, and then they turned to prayer and song. In that part of the meeting, they sang and praised Jesus profusely. I was invited to join, but could not always do so. As a Muslim, I love and revere Jesus. I spent a week of my course at VTS on Muslim devotionals to Jesus. However, I do not recognize Jesus as God or the son of God. Yet, even with this group, where I could not fully participate, I felt welcomed; and it was a lovely experience.

I was struck by the differences between the practices of the two groups. I went back to the first group and asked why they did not include references to Jesus in their worship. In order to make me feel welcome, which they thought would come from full participation, they chose to consider what might be theological red lines for me, and to structure their worship around those considerations.

The second group did also consider my theological limits. They let me know before they started their meeting that their worship would explicitly call on Jesus as God, and I was welcome to participate as I felt comfortable. They shared with me everything they were going to do, so nothing came as a surprise; and I could make informed decisions about what I was doing.

These different approaches were a learning moment for all of us, as I spoke to both groups about my experiences and how we could improve our interfaith interactions. With the first group, they wanted me to be welcomed and present and participate. I was able to do that based on how they set up their space. However, my presence and participation were not informed. More importantly, my hosts were not fully present. They limited themselves in trying to give me space. In hindsight, we agreed that this was not actually productive to building open and transparent relationships.

Their intentions were good. They were not only being good hosts, but also recognizing the large power imbalance that resides in interfaith activities. Organized Christian and Jewish communities bring resources, training, and experience to interfaith events that Muslims cannot yet match. They also knew that interfaith work in the United States was defined by Christian experience of intrafaith difference, and the hegemony of Christian language and thinking that permeates the country. The way they structured the morning was an attempt to offer a more equitable space. In discussion though, we agreed that it was still an exercise in power, because I was not consulted and was unaware of the limits they had put on themselves. They still had control of the situation, and were having me expose myself, while they concealed part of who they were. It was considerate, but not equitable.

The second group was much more transparent about their positionality. They were honest about who they were and what their commitments were in ways that were articulated to me prior to our worship. I was not only able to make informed decisions, but more importantly they demonstrated how to distribute power without compromising who they were. Just as they were going to be true to who they were, I was invited to be true to who I was. I could participate, I could be silent, I could leave. My agency was not impinged; it was accentuated.

Focusing on etiquette and protocol, just like focusing on the product, keeps us from the hard work—the work that actually produces results. The end goal of our activities, not in the grand "create a better world" sense but in the more immediate "do a joint event way," is not actually the goal in my opinion. It is the way we engage with one another that gets us to build trust, to build community, and to cause offense.

When I speak of offense, I do not mean the idea of causing intentional harm. We learn of difference when it emerges, and sometimes that learning comes from unexpected experiences. Because they are unexpected, these events are violations of manners and etiquette. In certain contexts, they can be read as provocations. If someone offers me a drink of alcohol, they are either unaware of or are dismissive of my beliefs as a Muslim. Both instances cause offense. The second situation requires a different essay. The first situation is an invitation to talk and learn from each other, if the goal is to understand we are different, and difference is a blessing from God, as the Qur'an teaches me (49:13), and an opportunity to deepen my understanding of myself and another person.

Turning back to my prayer groups, the second group told me who they were, lived who they were, and created an environment for me to do the same. As a result, I could come to them and ask, how do I present Muslim understandings of Jesus, which are often at odds with broad Christian theologies, without causing offense? They encouraged me to make their peers uncomfortable and have them question their assumptions, to encourage them to think about how to minister in a multireligious context. I would offend, they assured me, but I would not be offensive.

With that knowledge, I could talk about the relationship between Christianity and colonialism, and how some Muslims saw the ways in which those speaking loudly for Christ were the ones happiest to kill in his name, as this poem by Kaifi Azmi conveys:

> Go to those jungles of Vietnam
> Its crucified cities and desolate villages
> That have been crushed and burnt by Bible-readers
> They have been calling out to you for a while.[1]

I could share how deep the love of Jesus is in Muslim traditions, as ascetic, as healer, and as revolutionary. For example, in an epistle from the Ikhwan al-Safa (the Brethren of Purity, who wrote in Iraq across the ninth and tenth centuries) it states,

> Christ is said to have known that he could not manifest himself openly to people, given their state of ignorance, imprisoned as they are in Nature and the Material. Hence, he took the disguise of a physician and healer and wandered from town to town, preaching, mingling with the residents, and piquing their curiosity with parables. He would then initiate select listeners and offer them a Gnostic vision in which the soul is called to awaken from the sleep of ignorance and escape from the prison of the body, to ascend finally into the celestial spheres and the realms of divine majesty.[2]

I could not have these conversations without transparency, respect, and trust. My contrasting experiences offered me significant material to consider when entering into an interfaith relationship. In addition to the often-unacknowledged questions of power, there are also limits to politeness. Attempts to be overly cautious for fear of offense, without consultation with our partners, keeps us in the same place. We do not get to know one another, discover one another, and engage with difference. The train to interfaith community left the station, and, offering the other to get on it, we were not on it.

Notes

1. Quoted in Raza and Ali Hussain Mir, *Anthems of Resistance: A Celebration of Progressive Urdu Poetry* (New Delhi: India Ink, 2006), 79.

2. Quoted in Oddbjørn Leirvik, *Images of Jesus Christ in Islam* (New York: Continuum, 2010), 79.

Chapter 13

INTERRELIGIOUS ORIGIN STORIES
To Begin, and to Begin Again

HEATHER MILLER RUBENS

In 1986, the ninth National Workshop on Christian–Jewish Relations was held in Baltimore, Maryland. Local clergy, lay congregants, and Baltimore business leaders attended the conference together and were transformed. In their social and personal lives, they had experienced the divisiveness and harms of antisemitism in Baltimore, and they understood that interreligious learning and dialogue were necessary to undo this structural and societal problem. And so, these Jewish and Christian friends began to meet regularly. They decided together that sustained, interreligious theological education would help dismantle antisemitism and strengthen the Baltimore community, and perhaps even change the wider world. Thus, the ICJS was born—with its first name—the Institute for Christian and Jewish Studies. ICJS came into existence within the context of historic changes in Christian–Jewish relations. Indeed, White Christians sitting down with Ashkenazi Jews in Baltimore to learn about each other's religious practices and beliefs and dreaming together how they could cobuild a better city was previously unthinkable. It was slow work—developing interreligious friendships and trust in the shadow of the Holocaust's horrors—but it was necessary work. This is the origin story of ICJS.

What tales do we tell of our interreligious beginnings? And how do interreligious origin stories (both metanarratives and narratives) shape the quality of our interreligious encounters? Origin stories have enduring value. They are foundational for meaning-making. However—particularly in moments of growth, expansion, and transition—origin stories should be revisited. They should be reclaimed when they are helpful; they should be rewritten or revised when they hinder the work at hand.

In 2013, after twenty-five years as a Jewish–Christian dialogue organization, the Institute for Christian and Jewish Studies (ICJS) expanded its mission to include Muslims and the study of Islam; in 2016 ICJS changed its name to the Institute for Islamic, Christian, and Jewish Studies.[1] In the midst of re-visioning and rebranding ICJS during the 2010s, we should have revisited our origin story. Failing to do so proved to be a misstep with consequences—from which much was learned. ICJS needed to be able to honor our beginnings, and at the same time we needed the courage to begin again.

Our origin story had served us well for decades, but was not up to meeting this moment of expansion. Our mistake was in canonizing our origin story without recognizing that the metanarrative of Christian–Jewish relations was not able to, nor meant to, hold Muslims and Islam. We tried simply to incorporate Muslims into a largely White Christian–Jewish dialogue that had been going on for nearly three decades. To use an analogy, we asked our Muslim partners to pull up a folding chair to the Christian–Jewish dialogue table. This was inconsistent with our methodology, our origin story, and indeed our mission—which is the urgent and essential work of dismantling religious bias and bigotry by building learning communities where religious difference becomes a powerful force for good.

For several years, ICJS has been looking for new metanarratives that can hold the complex interconnected hatreds of antisemitism, Islamophobia, anti-Black, anti-Brown, anti-Asian racism that challenge our communities today. We are doing a lot of listening to local narratives that are unfamiliar to us; we are seeking a broader coalition of Baltimore cobuilders for the interreligious society. To extend the analogy, we are trying to put away the folding chairs and build new interreligious dialogue tables together with new partners so that we have four: a Jewish–Muslim table, a Christian–Muslim table, a Jewish–Christian table, and a Jewish–Christian–Muslim table.

The Importance of Origin Stories, Metanarratives, and Narratives

Longstanding interreligious and interfaith organizations must grapple with *local* origin stories specific to their particular efforts and institutions, as well as the more *global* metanarratives that shape the stories of interfaith relationships. The *local* origin story of the Institute for Islamic, Christian, and Jewish Studies (ICJS) began in 1987 when ICJS was founded in Baltimore, Maryland. The more *global metanarrative* around the founding of ICJS was grounded in the framework of Jewish–Christian relations, developed in a post–World War II, post-Shoah, North Atlantic context. In 2013, a quarter century later, ICJS sought to expand its mission to include

Muslim communities and the study of Islam. In many ways, we were beginning again as an organization and needed to sit with our own origin stories, exploring how both metanarratives and local origin stories were in relationship with the mission expansion.

ICJS was founded in the context of historic changes in Jewish–Christian relations that began in a post-Holocaust, post–World War II environment. A critical moment in beginning this metanarrative of transforming and restructuring Jewish–Christian relations starts with the Roman Catholic Church's Second Vatican Council and its 1965 document *Nostra Aetate: The Declaration on the Relation of the Church to Non-Christian Religions*.[2] The theological work begun by the Roman Catholic Church was part of larger developments in the field of Jewish–Christian relations after the Holocaust that prioritized a need for Christians to reckon with anti-Judaism and antisemitism within Christian tradition.

This broader metanarrative deeply shaped the founding of ICJS: Jews and Christians had a chance to begin again; to reset and reframe; to create a new Jewish–Christian relationship. The power dynamics between the two communities and problems in their past relationship were self-evident to the founders: (White) Christians and (European) Christian culture had engaged in the *teachings of contempt* vis-à-vis Jews and Judaism for centuries, which created the theological and political environment that made the horrors of the Holocaust possible.[3]

Particular social contexts and local histories also must be attended to when thinking about interreligious origin stories. Baltimore has a long and shameful history of racial and religious discrimination toward its Black and Jewish residents. Baltimore earned the disgraceful distinction of being the first city in the United States to enact a municipal segregation law, in 1910.[4] The U.S. Supreme Court invalidated segregation laws in 1917. From this point, segregation of both the Black and Jewish communities in Baltimore moved from government policy to more informal and insidious forms of segregation practice by property developers and real estate agents. As Baltimore expanded in the early to mid-twentieth century, the Roland Park Company played a major role in creating the neighborhoods it developed in the northern part of the city as exclusively White, Christian enclaves. Through explicit neighborhood covenants, as well as unwritten mandates enforced by real estate agents, the Roland Park Company excluded both Blacks and Jews for more than half a century from upscale neighborhoods in north Baltimore.

When the ICJS was created in 1987 by Christian and Jewish leaders from Baltimore's business and congregational communities, an important first step needed was for (White) Christians to do the vital work of self-reflection and self-criticism. What was the Christian role in perpetuating and continuing anti-Jewish prejudices in Baltimore and in the greater world? What role did Christian theologies, Christian scriptural interpretations, and Christian traditions play in the lead up to the Shoah, and in dividing Baltimore?

To reckon with both the local narratives of prejudice and discrimination, as well as the metanarratives of post-Holocaust Jewish–Christian relations, ICJS launched the Maryland Interfaith Project. Through this initiative, 1988–1991, nearly two hundred clergy and lay people from eleven Christian denominations conducted a sustained theological inquiry into the ways their Christian beliefs, teachings, and practices perpetuated anti-Jewish prejudice and fostered antisemitic animosity. This self-critical work by Christians was crucial preparation for a Christian–Jewish interreligious encounter. Indeed, for many Jewish partners it was a precondition to build the trust necessary to enter into an honest dialogue with Christians. It was a strong foundation upon which Jews and Christians in Baltimore constructed a dialogue table.

Beginning Again: Engaging Muslims and the Study of Islam

The September 11 attacks and the protracted U.S. wars in Iraq and Afghanistan made expansion of ICJS's mission to include Muslims and the study of Islam seem imperative to our leadership. However, the metanarrative behind this expansion was fundamentally Islamophobic. Muslims were being caricatured in the popular media as members of a violent religion. In the North Atlantic context, a culture of suspicion and surveillance of Muslim individuals and institutions were being fed by accusations that Muslims represent an internal threat to Western democracies. Consequently, in many interreligious and interfaith events, when the audience question-and-answer session occurs, there is a tendency to demand that Muslims answer for acts of terrorism committed by members of their faith around the globe, and to explain how passages in the Qur'an appear, to some readers, to justify violence. Regrettably, ICJS was not fully immune to the story of Islam in the United States that was shaped by this security-lens metanarrative.

A few mistakes are clear in hindsight. We did not give ourselves enough time and moved too quickly. Creating friendships, building trust, and gaining new literacy (both learning and unlearning) are slow work. They require patience and careful, attentive pacing. ICJS hired a Muslim scholar and began offering courses and programs without doing the foundational community work of developing trusting relationships of mutual learning with a robust number of local Muslim partners. As a successful

Jewish–Christian dialogue organization, with over twenty-five years of experience, we figured our existing methodologies and good intentions would carry us forward during this transition. We failed to reinstate the successful model of the ICJS Maryland Interfaith Project. (That is, we did not engage in a sustained theological inquiry into ways in which Christian and Jewish beliefs, teachings, and practices were participating in anti-Muslim prejudice in our community.) We did not recognize that, as an organization, we were not merely expanding our mission; rather, we truly were beginning again.

For instance, an important aspect of expanding the mission of ICJS to include Muslims is that it forced us to explore issues of race and religion in our interreligious efforts. With the inclusion of Muslims in our mission and our interreligious work, ICJS not only increased its religious diversity, but also its racial diversity. Muslim Americans are the most racially diverse religious community in the United States, where Islamophobia is deeply tied to anti-Black and anti-Brown racism.[5] In Maryland, Muslim Americans come primarily from the Black, South Asian, and Middle Eastern communities. In welcoming Muslims into ICJS, we incorporated people of color into our programs, staff, and leadership. The expansion of mission in 2013 forced us to begin to wrestle with our institutional whiteness. (The founders and most participants in our programs over the years had been White or European-heritage Christians and White Ashkenazi Jews within the majority Black city of Baltimore.) As an institution built and devoted to promoting understanding across religious difference, ICJS needed to explore the complex ways religion and race intersect in our religious communities, in our city, and in our country.

Correcting Mistakes and Beginning Again, Again

At the critical juncture of expanding our mission, we made a mistake: we omitted a vital step of reinterpreting and reimagining our origin stories, narratives, and metanarratives. Thankfully, in the ten years since then, we have had a chance to begin again the effort to develop resilient relationships with Muslim partners and communities. ICJS is now working to cobuild a better Baltimore, and a better world. That includes the crafting of new stories to tell together.

I hope that the ICJS experience may be instructive for others. I encourage everyone committed to interfaith and interreligious encounters to pay careful attention to the ways in which origin stories, narratives, and metanarratives shape the possibilities of such work. The stories we tell about ourselves and our origins matter deeply. To ignore or forget their power is a mistake. Interreligious partners should cultivate a regular practice of attending to questions such as: What are the interreligious origin stories operative in your interreligious work? How do metanarratives and local narratives shape your interreligious encounters? What are the possibilities and limitations of your origin stories? If you need to begin again, what story would you tell?

Notes

1. In July 2016 I became the executive director of ICJS after Chris Leighton, its founding executive director, retired. I had joined ICJS as the Roman Catholic scholar in 2011 and took on the role of executive director amidst this organizational expansion of mission, audiences, and work.

2. For the complete text of *Nostra Aetate,* see https://www.vatican.va/archive/hist_councils/ii_vatican_council/documents/vat-ii_decl_19651028_nostra-aetate_en.html.

3. I put the terms *White* and *European* in parentheses because ICJS at the time of its founding in 1987 would not have used those adjectives to describe itself or the project of Jewish-Christian relations. But I think they are important adjectives added to augment the retelling of our organizational origin story in the 2010s as we embarked on mission expansion to include Islam, and in light of more recent scholarship interrogating the whiteness of interfaith and interreligious projects in the North Atlantic context.

4. Antero Pietila. *Not in My Neighborhood: How Bigotry Shaped a Great American City* (Chicago: Ivan R. Dee, 2010).

5. Institute for Social Policy and Understanding, "American Muslim Poll 2017," www.ispu.org. Muslims were the only religious group surveyed with no majority race, as compared with Jewish, Catholic, Protestant, and nonaffiliated respondents. According to the survey, American Muslims are 24% White, 25% Black, 18% Arab, 18% Asian, 5% Hispanic, and 7% mixed.

Part III

CONVERSATIONS

Chapter 14

How Did You Wake Up?

*Missteps on the Journey toward an Ethos
of Honesty, Curiosity, and Sensitivity*

Daniel Berman

"How did you wake up?" My college suitemate asked me this question during one of those late-night, everything-is-on-the-table, no-holding-back, jarringly honest conversations you have at 3:00 a.m. when you're exhausted and your heart just feels open—an African American young man who grew up in the Bronx on one bed; a Jewish kid from a small town on the coast of Maine on the other.

He asked me this question because I had just published an article in *The Columbia Daily Spectator*, the Columbia University student newspaper. The article was making some waves on campus. An unrestricted $30 million gift had been made to the college, and the administration announced its plans to renovate our student center. I wrote an article of protest, asking how we could possibly justify that decision when the current student center—which seemed perfectly fine to me—was surrounded by poorer, predominantly African American neighborhoods. I was confused and angry by the living contrasts of deep poverty and great wealth. I viewed the college's decision as a choice to perpetuate that contrast, not repair it.

When my friend asked me, in response to this article, "How did you wake up?" I told him a story. A few months earlier, after a night out with my friends, we took the subway back uptown to 116th Street, got off the train, and started walking toward the wrought-iron gates on campus. Those gates seemingly reached to the sky, distinguishing the campus from the surrounding neighborhoods.

There were many homeless people living on the streets on those blocks, and late at night they were often asleep on the sidewalks; and it's New York City, so everyone was out late at night, and there wasn't much room on the sidewalk to maneuver in a group. Just before entering campus, maybe thirty steps before the gates, a man lying down on the street was in my path. I jumped over him, and continued through the gates.

"That was the night," I told my friend. I was shocked by what I did, the brutal casualness of looking the other way. Skipping over that man, I understood: certain lives are valued and certain lives are not.

I grew up in a home where the trauma of the loss of much of my mother's family in the Holocaust was present. We felt it mostly in its silence, but it was there. I understood the implications for my mother, and more distantly, for us. I saw the pain in my grandparents' eyes. I understood the history of dehumanizing others.

But that personal experience of looking away, realizing *you are participating* in a system of saying, "these lives matter, these do not"—that's how I woke up. That's when I fully noticed the brokenness, and felt responsible to call it out. Just a few blocks up the street, years earlier, Rabbi Abraham Joshua Heschel had written:

> There is immense silent agony in the world, and the task of man is to be a voice for the plundered poor, to prevent the desecration of the soul and the violation of our dream of honesty . . . morally speaking, there is no limit to the concern one must feel for the suffering of human beings, that indifference to evil is worse than evil itself, that in a free society, some are guilty, but all are responsible.[1]

Over the last thirty years, I have felt close to and distant from that call to conscience and consciousness at different moments in my life. Like so many others, I felt it strongly after the killing of George Floyd, a forty-six-year-old Black man who was handcuffed and pinned to the ground by a police officer's knee on a Minneapolis street corner. I was angry and sad. I was taken back to my studies during college of the Harlem Renaissance, and the eerily prescient image painted by the author and activist James Baldwin. "It demands great spiritual resilience," he wrote, "not to hate the hater *whose foot is on your neck*, and an even greater miracle of perception and charity not to teach your child to hate."

I attended protest rallies and gave sermons to my congregation encouraging people to stand up, not idly by. It felt somewhat empty, though. More than anything, we felt the conflict inherent in a sense of moral clarity and political powerlessness. One of my community members had previously worked for a Black Christian pastor, and after hearing one of my sermons, reached out to me to connect with the pastor. I was not totally sure yet of my long-term goals, but I was clear that I wanted—needed—a human connection, a relationship of support and solidarity. I called the pastor, and we spoke for an hour about our paths to ministry and that tension of hopefulness and helplessness weighing on us and our communities.

We decided to expand our conversion to include other Black Christian pastors and rabbis. We called and invited dear friends whom we both knew and trusted to be part of our ongoing discussions. In the first few months, the group was fluid—people attended for a week and left, or came only occasionally. Sensing the difficulty of this disruption, we asked for a commitment to be together for an hour a week. We knew this would be a bold ask; we were pastors and rabbis after all! But we knew it would take both courage and discipline to show up, and that was the tone we wanted to create in this group. "If we are going to do it, let's do it," we said to one another. A group of seven emerged, three Black pastors, one White reverend, and three rabbis.

We discussed potential structures for our weekly conversation. We could take turns sharing a teaching and facilitating the discussion. We could agree to read a text ahead of time and come prepared to discuss and respond to it. Ultimately, we decided to prioritize building personal friendships, and that our discussions would be more free-flowing, with one guiding question: "what's on your heart right now?"

We met every week online. That guiding question was both liberating and unnerving. There was a lot of space to share and listen—too much space, at times. We fell into some common traps of early group dynamics: difficulty managing the delicate balancing act of when to step in and step back, different skills in facilitating the group, and varying comfort levels in sharing personally. We experienced early dissonance in our shared goals and understanding of the purpose of our commitment to one another. In hindsight, having a clearer structure and something specific to respond to may have offered some protection from these common group missteps.

This became particularly clear to me one afternoon. We had been discussing the complex, painful, and sometimes violent history of Christian missionary work, so we were a bit on edge already when one of the pastors asked to learn more about Jewish approaches to conversion into Judaism. We discussed the ancient, classical Jewish sources, which express a serious note of concern and caution to anyone considering conversion to Judaism. Before accepting a potential convert into a process of learning and discernment, the rabbis were required to turn away a potential convert three times, a test of resiliency and determination. We discussed our more modern, progressive approaches to conversion and what it means to openly and lovingly welcome a person into Jewish faith and life into the Jewish community.

It was at that point I decided to improvise. I remembered a TV episode that had seemed so poignant and moving when I saw it years earlier. In it, a Black Christian woman wants to convert to Judaism, a path that begins because kosher meals tasted better than common prison food. She decides to learn about Judaism as a way to gain access to kosher meals and along the way discovers a genuine love for the faith. The scene I decided to show to the group through our screen-share function portrayed this woman at a table with two Jewish women prisoners and a rabbi who had been brought in to listen to her, and—as suggested by tradition—to turn her away three times before agreeing to guide her through a full process of conversion.

I remembered the scene as depicting a Black woman prisoner yearning for authentic connection to Jewish religious faith and spiritual practice. I remembered her claiming through tears that she had finally found her people. Only a few minutes into sharing the clip, however, I realized I had made a terrible mistake. I looked at the posture and eyes of everyone else in the group. They all seemed surprised, if not stunned, by both the clip and my choice.

The scene did portray a woman who had undergone a spiritual awakening inspired by deeply held Jewish values such as theological questioning and inclusion. It also portrayed a painful, angry rejection of Christianity, culminating in a heart-stopping line, uttered by the woman's Jewish friend, that when she goes to the *mikveh* (Jewish ritual bath), she can then wash off her "Christian filth."

I had no memory of that aspect of the scene; I simply had not seen or heard it. Now, suddenly, surrounded by my new friends in an intentional multiracial, multifaith group dedicated to honest discussion of race, faith, and social justice, I introduced a painful and strange clip that offered almost nothing of substance. Rather, I feared, it eroded trust or even others' desire to be part of this group.

How would the group react? They were, as I imagined, surprised, and discouraged. One of the pastors asked me why I felt moved by the scene, and I did my best to share that I connected to the sense of spiritual seeking, an experience that just feels so rare sometimes. I then began to apologize, asking a few times for the group's forgiveness—for my oversight and insensitivity, and for my poor choice in not respecting the group enough to put more thought into what I would be sharing.

Each member of the group graciously accepted my apology. But I could also feel a breakdown in trust that would have to be built back up. I wondered: Were we ready to deepen our discussions and take on difficult kinds of questions? Might the group's discussions be expanded to examine not only our communities' shared history and moral sensibilities but also the blind spots we carry?

I carry the misstep with me constantly. Earning trust in a group that asks you to share what your heart is carrying is not easy. Developing an ethos of honesty, curiosity, and sensitivity is not easy. Most importantly, however, forgiveness, in this group at least, was, quite simply, full of grace. Three years later, we still meet every week, and constantly make mistakes. We are dear, trusted, and close friends. We know one another well enough to notice what we're all carrying in that day—personal experiences with racism and antisemitism, the exhaustion of ministry during the isolation of a pandemic, the anger and distress we feel after horrifying mass shootings—and encourage one another to lay it out there, with all its pain, which we will hold together.

Notes

1. Abraham Joshua Heschel, "The Reasons for My Involvement in the Peace Movement," in Susannah Heschel, ed., *Moral Grandeur and Spiritual Audacity: Essays* (New York: Farrar, Straus & Giroux, 1996), 224–26.

Chapter 15

THE PROBLEM WITH WHAT I SAID NEXT
A Question of Intrafaith Solidarity

NANCY FUCHS KREIMER

Me: Sarah, I need your help.

Sarah: Always happy to help you. What do you need?

Me: I have been asked to write a chapter for a book about mistakes
        made in interfaith work. Can you help me think about that theme?
        As a rabbi, have you had an experience of a mistake being made?

Sarah: I have! Remember the wonderful winter solstice parties we used
        to give ourselves every year in our monthly Jewish–Christian
        clergy group? How we looked forward to all the latkes and advent
        customs and poetry?

Me: Indeed! Those were precious times.

Sarah: Well, I recall a mistake that happened about a decade ago at our
        meeting in January, after one of those lovely evenings. Mary had
        sung a carol. I shared that there was a line in it that did not land
        well for me as a Jew. I don't remember why now, something prob-
        ably on the triumphalist side. It's not important what it was. Mary
        had offered it as a song she loved; she did not ask us to sing along.
        But the song had been hard for me to hear, and I wanted to tell the
        group how it made me feel. Perhaps to open a conversation. We
        were all good friends. Then, a mistake was made.

Me: Who made it?

Sarah: You.

Me: Oh, my! I don't remember this at all! What did I do?

Sarah: You jumped in right after I spoke. You said, "That line was no
        big deal." I don't remember what you said next. Something about
        why it did not matter; that it did not really mean what I thought
        it meant; and that the song was just fine with you. I do remember
        how I felt. Unsupported. What happened to the virtue of solidar-

ity? Of Jews sticking together, especially when the non-Jews are listening. After you spoke, everyone seemed happy to let it drop. I have not thought about that evening in years. But, you are looking for a misstep. There you have it!"

Me: Hmm . . . I need to think about this.

***

So think about it, I did! First, I wondered what was going on for me. Perhaps, the line had not struck me as problematic, so I opened my mouth to "speak my truth" without stopping to consider my friend Sarah and how she might hear my words. Or maybe I *had* seen what Sarah saw, but my attention and compassion were trained on Mary, who had shared her beloved carol with "the best of intentions." Perhaps I was trying to take care of Mary's feelings. I am typically conflict adverse. It is not surprising that I took on the role of the great "smoother-outer." (Old habits die hard.) Or maybe, as a long-time veteran of the interfaith world, I was simply showing my less experienced Jewish friends how to handle little things like this. I can imagine I was eager to display my credentials as an evolved interfaith interlocutor. Maybe I even thought that I was doing Sarah and the other Jews a favor.

While I'm always interested in knowing what goes on in my own "endlessly fascinating" head, the questions I really needed to ask were different. Was this a misstep at all? And if so, what kind of misstep was it? Thinking about the goals and norms of multifaith conversation, what was my mistake and how could that evening have unfolded differently? First, I concluded that my mistake, while not a grievous one, was indeed a mistake. My friend felt I had let her down. As she saw it, a "member of the tribe" had failed to show up in solidarity with her sister Jew. If I had said anything at all to non-Jews in the room, I should have taken her "side." As a matter of Jewish solidarity, it occurred to me that my choice was unaligned with other choices I made on a regular basis. As a participant in interfaith encounters, I would always request the most compatible to kosher options (though it was not my personal practice). I wanted to make sure that my fellow Jews who had the most significant needs would get them met. Similarly, as a matter of solidarity, I would not attend certain interfaith events on Shabbat, even though the attendance would have fit with my own Shabbat observance. When I move from the realm of ritual to that of substantive issues, things get more nuanced. In conversations in multifaith settings about contested issues within our own community, solidarity is more complicated.

Diversity within our Jewish communities is a given. The old joke "two Jews, three opinions" continues to resonate as truth. A truth in which we take pride. Except when we do not. When a topic becomes an issue between the Jews and non-Jews in the room, I can recall many interfaith moments when the Jews in the group presented a united front even when I knew that their views are actually quite diverse. We love to reference the Talmud—where the rabbis disagree about everything—although we rarely point out that these are not disputes intended for non-Jews' ears. I imagine that some Jews would praise our keeping our most divisive conversations to ourselves as solidarity and condemn the breach of a presumed consensus as disloyalty.

Solidarity is a capacious concept. It could mean solidarity with the Jews in the room, or at least the Jew who has just spoken up. But it also might mean solidarity with other Jews who are not present and whose positions are minority ones. Or non-Jews whose interests have not been served well by the comment a Jew just made. I recall times when I have let a minority Jewish position go unspoken, or not spoken up for those others who have no voice. In those moments, I feel a twinge of survivor guilt, knowing that I am included here because I can clam up about some of these other solidarities that I hold dear. Hannah Arendt, in 1942, wrote from a different perspective on solidarity than the ethnic/national one arising at that time. While not advocating "collective suicide" for the Jewish people, she wrote about restoring "the solidarity of the human race."[1] Seeing one's responsibility as greater than group solidarity puts the conversation in a different light. In places where I do not know or trust the "good intentions" of others, solidarity with a majority Jewish opinion can be a good choice. In other cases, it may be a narrow and particularistic understanding of what loyalty entails.

Is solidarity really the correct frame? Viewing that miniature story through the lens of Mussar (a Jewish spiritual discipline of character cultivation), I saw my misstep from many angles. First, a bit of textual excavation. In the Torah, we read:

Ki tir'eh chamor son'acha rovetz tachat masa'o, v'chadalta me'azov lo, azov ta'azov imo. (Ex. 23:5)

If you see an ass, i.e., a donkey, that belongs to someone who hates you, collapsed under the weight of its load, and you are inclined not to help, you must nonetheless help your enemy get his sorry ass off the floor.[2]

The Mishnah picks up on this and in a long list of virtuous acts includes, "Who shares in the bearing of a burden with his colleague" (Avot 6:6).

The idea enters the Mussar classic *Mesillat Yesharim* this way: "A man should strive to be of as much help as possible to those who are weighted down with some burden." And in the next generation, Rabbi Simcha Zissel of Ziv wrote about "bearing a burden with one's neighbor" as the equivalent of loving one's neighbor as one's self. [3] Which brings us to my Mussar teacher, Rabbi Ira Stone, who centered his Mussar method, designed to help contemporary Jews grow their souls to live responsible lives, on the idea of "bearing the burden of the other."

So how did I do that evening? First, I had failed to "bear the burden of the other"—my closest other in the room, my friend Sarah. She had taken a risk, and I left her hanging. I did not notice her burden; or, noticing it, did not find a way to carry it with her. As for Mary, one might say I viewed her burden superficially. Perhaps better than my protecting her from a rueful moment, Mary would have rather learned what Sarah (and perhaps others in our group) heard in that song. By shutting down that conversation, I had failed to bear Mary's burden as well. Failing two others in one hasty utterance, I had certainly failed my own Mussar's aspirations of careful speech with attention to the other. Finally, perhaps the "other" in the room with a burden was the group itself. The need of the group is to have the richest and best conversation possible. Because I spoke up the way I did, the group missed out on a conversation we might have had. Perhaps, too, things would have gone better if a different container had been created in which this diversity could be aired. Perhaps the question could be phrased as one of character: what is "right speech" regarding intrafaith diversity in multifaith conversation? We were a self-led group, and no one stepped up. Which brings us to consider the role of a leader as creator of contexts for such encounters.

When I cotaught religious leadership for a multifaith world with Reverend Katie Day at Reconstructionist Rabbinical College and Lutheran Theological Seminary (now United Lutheran Seminary), we noticed that our students did not hesitate to let each other know that there existed a spectrum of positions among us on fraught topics such as officiating at interfaith weddings or Israel/Palestine. Yet, speaking up in disagreement with another Jew, let alone all the other Jews in a room, did not come easily to the Jewish students in multifaith settings. As in my case, when they did, it sometimes happened clumsily; a painful moment ensued, and we hastily moved on.

In this course, we utilized the pedagogical tool of the Fishbowl, set-ting up a "safe space"—or better, issuing an invitation to be brave. Chris-tians sat in the outer circle to listen as Jews, sitting in the inner circle, conversed among themselves. Then we switched positions and roles. This allowed us to normalize a spectrum of views, indeed, to *request* an airing of that diversity rather than to wait for one student to decide to take on a colleague. Structural interventions like the Fishbowl make it easier for us to argue among ourselves like Talmudic rabbis, framing differences within a subgroup as something expected and welcomed. We allow space for those disagreements in solidarity with the whole group's goal of learn-ing more about one another.

Here is my takeaway from my friend Sarah's honesty. Even in a long-standing group like ours, where good will abounds, solidarity more widely conceived is not easy. Managing intrafaith diversity well, as indi-viduals and as leaders, is one way of bearing the burden of the group itself. One needs to deeply trust a group to want to make it a priority. If I had it to do over again, I would have said, "That carol landed differently for me, and I would love to tell you all about it, but first let's hear more from Sarah. Maybe the rest of you might also want to share." Do I do that regularly? No. But I can try. And if I were the facilitator, I would have pointed out what a lovely moment this was. "Nancy just said something that was different than what Sarah said. Thank you, Sarah. Thank you, Nancy. What a beautiful opportunity for us all to learn. Let us begin. . . ." Sometimes, these would be the right moves; other times not at all. In the end, the Mishnah gives us an oft-quoted but hazy piece of guidance. "An argument for the sake of heaven will endure; but a debate not for the sake of heaven will not endure" (*Pirke Avot* 5:17). So, our ultimate "other" to whom we owe our solidarity is none other than "heaven," or the Divine. What that means in any given situation is a matter of discernment. That is why multifaith work, when done with care, is so challenging.

***

Me: I thought about what you said. I want to say, quite simply: I was wrong. No excuses, no explanations, no long stories. I made a mistake.

Sarah: It really was not a huge deal at all. If I had wanted to pursue things, I could have.

Me: I know. That is why I am grateful to you for remembering and giving me this opportunity to think about it. I am sure I have made other, bigger errors. Some I remember. Some I do not even know—especially if they were made across differences of race, gender, age. It is so hard to admonish each other, even when there are no power differentials!

Sarah: I know. That is why I am grateful for our tradition of *teshuvah*—of turning, repentance, forgiveness. They say that before God created the world, God first created seven things: The Torah, Gehinnom, the Garden of Eden, the Throne of Glory, the Temple, Teshuvah, and the Name of the Messiah (*Pirkei de Eliezer* 3). It seems to me that when we meet one another in relationship, we meet across worlds, even if just the separate worlds of two close friends. Yet, before there was even any world at all, God saw fit to create the possibility of repentance. God knew we were going to make mistakes. It's built into the structure of the world. Breaking and repairing.

Me: I like that idea. I think we need to hold on to it when we do the work of multifaith encounter. Set that idea right at the start of our encounters, like God placed it at the beginning of the world. We are going to make mistakes with one another, and we will forgive each other. That is how we will all grow.

Notes

1. Geoffrey D. Claussen, *Modern Musar: Contested Virtues in Jewish Thought* (Philadelphia: Jewish Publication Society, 2022), 293.

2. Translation by Irwin Keller, https://www.irwinkeller.com/itzikswell/2009/02/parashat-mishpatim-saving-your-enemys.html.

3. Moses Hayyim Luzzato, *Mesillat Yesharim: The Path of the Upright*, trans. Mordecai M. Kaplan, introduction and commentary by Ira F. Stone (Philadelphia: Jewish Publication Society, 2010), 197.

Chapter 16

When the Head Gets in the Way of the Heart

An Interreligious Conversation that Went Wrong

Jeffery D. Long

It is not at all uncommon for me to receive letters and email messages from former students. I have kept in touch with many of them through the years, often through social media. I am pleased to say that some of them have become my dear friends. I have been invited to their weddings—and have officiated at two. They may tell me about a major life event or achievement: a new job, a promotion, an award, acceptance into a prestigious academic institution, a new home, the birth of a child, and so on. Some have also turned to me for career advice, relationship advice, or spiritual advice. And, of course, there are always the requests for letters of recommendation.

I was not surprised at all, then, to see an email one morning from someone who had graduated more than a decade previously. I'll call him Michael. I remembered him as a thoughtful and sensitive young man whose interest in the subject matter I taught clearly extended beyond the intellectual. Michael was a spiritual seeker. A devout Protestant Christian, he had a very open mind and was keen to learn all he could about the beliefs and practices of other people. The one course that he took with me was on Buddhism. I know there was a period in which he took a deep interest in Islam as well, and pursued study abroad in order to further this interest.

We stayed in touch for a couple of years after his graduation, but at the time I received this particular email, it had been about ten years since our last contact. This was also not at all unusual. I have had former students who have stayed consistently in touch with me through years, others who have been in contact intermittently, and others who have simply gone their own way. I had assumed Michael was in the last group.

But, given our earlier relationship—one that I always found pleasant and mutually respectful—I was pleased to see an email from him in my inbox. What I could not see in that moment was that this message would begin an interreligious conversation with a former student that was destined to go terribly wrong!

I opened Michael's message. It was short. He greeted me, told me he had converted to Roman Catholicism, and then informed me that *he forgave me* for "teaching Buddhist meditation at a Christian college."

This message was odd in several ways. First, it did not sound like the Michael I had known. I even wondered if someone else had hacked his email account. Perhaps someone pretending to be Michael was sending this message to me.

The content was also strange. I do not teach specifically Buddhist meditation at the college where I work. For students who are interested, I teach a very basic meditation practice that is the foundation of forms of meditation taught in many traditions: a simple stilling of thoughts through a focus on the breath. Given the multireligious character of our student body, I think it is important that I not be seen as proselytizing or promoting any specific form of spiritual practice. Moreover, my Hindu religious commitments compel me to avoid proselytizing at all. I frequently begin my courses by reassuring my students that, "It's against my religion to try to convert you to my religion." I want my students to understand and appreciate the traditions I am explaining to them—including, but not limited to, the one I practice. I want them to cultivate empathy across religious boundaries. If I am trying to "convert" them to anything, it is to an open-minded appreciation, even for views that they themselves do not hold.

I should also note, because I think it is relevant to the larger issues with which this essay is engaged, that I do not teach meditation in the classroom. To be sure, there are professors in my field who offer meditation practice as part of their curriculum.[1] I certainly respect the pedagogical choices they have made; but I personally do not find inclusion of meditation in the classroom environment to be productive—at least for achieving the objectives I have for my teaching. At the same time, given the fact that many of my students do want to learn this practice, I make it available outside of class by leading a monthly meditation session in our college library. The aim of these sessions, again, is not to proselytize, but to make available to students an experience that they might not otherwise have and to enable them to share in some of its benefits.

Michael may have thought I was teaching "Buddhist meditation" because, if I recall correctly, he took my Buddhism course during a brief period—fairly early in my teaching career—when, bowing to pressure from both students and colleagues, I did include meditation practice in my courses. This would typically occur once a semester, and I clearly indicated that it was optional and that the practice we would pursue would be nonsectarian in nature. One of the many reasons that I no longer include meditation in the classroom is that the classroom is full of subtle, unspoken expectations and pressures. I suspect there were students who meditated, not because they had any interest in the practice but because they felt it was expected by me or by their fellow students—despite my reassurances that it was optional. I am also quite confident that there were students who simply closed their eyes and sat there without really making any effort to meditate. As any experienced meditator can tell you, it is very easy to get a sense of the people in a room with you when you engage in this practice. At the risk of sounding "New Age-y," there is a definite change in the energy of a room when everyone in it is meditating, and a quite different energy when some people are meditating and others are not. As I often explain to students and colleagues, I do not promote meditation in the classroom because it is bad for both the meditation and the classroom. The meditation is disrupted if there are people in the room who do not really want to do it, and the classroom dynamic is disrupted if students feel that something is being imposed on them—even if efforts are made to reassure them that this is not the case.

As for Michael's concern about my teaching Buddhist meditation at a Christian college: Elizabethtown College, where I teach, does have a historical relationship with the Church of the Brethren. This is an Anabaptist denomination with historical connections to the Mennonites and the Amish. Indeed, our college houses one of the world's leading centers for the study of Anabaptist and Pietist traditions.

The Brethren heritage of the college, however, while certainly shaping our identity and our curriculum, does not dictate it. The Brethren are themselves a noncreedal tradition, so there is no such thing as Brethren heresy, for example. In fact, I have found the local members of the church to be quite open to learning about various religious traditions. I have been invited to speak at the church, on multiple occasions, on Hinduism, Buddhism, and Jainism. The church has also hosted interfaith events in which I have participated as a Hindu representative. It is also the case that very few of our students or faculty are actually members of the church. It is thus more accurate to call Elizabethtown College a college with a Christian heritage than a "Christian college"—if, by this term, one is referring to a college where Christianity overtly shapes everyone's daily life. Faculty are not required to sign a statement of faith or to belong to a church. We have professors and students of many religions and of no religion.

I felt, therefore, when I received Michael's email, that he was factually mistaken—both about my teaching Buddhist meditation and in his characterization of the identity of our college. More disturbing than that, though, was his statement that he "forgave me," as if I had been doing a bad thing by teaching meditation to students.

I was not at all disturbed by the fact that Michael had converted to Roman Catholicism. I come from a Roman Catholic background myself. Although I have since found a home more suited to me in the Hindu community, my feelings toward the Catholic Church are largely positive, even if I disagree deeply with some of its doctrinal claims. I have many Catholic friends, including a number of theologians whom I know as colleagues, and we have very warm and close relations.

Probably, the first misstep I made regarding Michael's email was to respond at all. I had thought of simply not replying. But his message was so odd and so different in tone from all of our previous communications that I felt concerned for his well-being. In that spirit, I wrote back.

In my response, I told Michael that I thought it was wonderful that he had found a home in the Catholic Church—that it was a great tradition and that I was grateful for my upbringing in it. I also told him that there really was nothing for him to forgive: that I was not trying to proselytize or to promote Buddhism through teaching meditation, and that I am Hindu in any case. (I have often, as a non-Indian Hindu, encountered people who found my religious identity confusing, and who then described me to others as a Buddhist.) I did not engage with him about the "Christian college" part of his message, although he would repeat this claim a number of times in our subsequent exchanges—all of which occurred via email.

Michael's response to this was quick. He had known already about my Catholic upbringing. He told me that it was time for me to "come home," to renounce Hinduism and return to the Roman Catholic Church.

I wrote back about my great respect for the Catholic Church and the fact that Hinduism, as I understand it, is a tradition that encompasses the core teachings and practices of many religions. Sri Ramakrishna, the founder of the tradition to which I adhere, found God-realization through the practice of many traditions, including Christianity, and concluded that all of these paths lead to the same Infinite Reality. I told him I was not trying to proselytize, and that he should stick to his faith. But, I wanted him to understand and respect why I made the choices I had made and that it was not his place to compel me to make different ones.

Michael's next move was to send links to websites promoting Catholicism, including a video of a talk by a former Hindu who had become Catholic. I responded in kind, sending a video of a talk I had given about how I came to Vedanta.

Michael's tone then became more aggressive. He began to make, frankly, ridiculous claims about Hinduism, based on stereotypes and misconceptions about the tradition. I responded to each of these with facts and argumentation. For example. Michael asked, "Why do Hindu monks spend all of their time meditating, instead of helping people like Mother Teresa did?" I responded that the monks of the Ramakrishna Order run the largest relief organization in India. He responded that he "seriously doubted" whether monks could run such a relief organization and asked for me to give evidence for this claim. I responded by sending him a PDF of the Ramakrishna Mission's annual report, which is publicly available online.

This was when things went seriously downhill in our conversation. I lost my patience. In my next reply to Michael, I wrote: "I am a professional scholar as well as a practitioner of this tradition. I have been studying it longer than you have even been alive. Do you really think these one-liners from you are going to make me question all of my life's choices and change my faith?" This made him very angry. He replied that America was a "Christian nation" and that I should go to India if I really wanted to be Hindu. He concluded his last email to me by writing, "I think what you do is evil."

This disturbed me. I have studied religious extremism enough to know that the belief that "the other" is evil is often a condition for committing violence. Although Michael never threatened me, it was clear that he really believed that I was doing something evil in teaching students about traditions other than Christianity at a "Christian college" in a "Christian nation." Wanting to get a more objective pair of eyes on the situation, I informed my dean about my correspondence with Michael. He informed our campus security about the situation and recommended that I stop replying—which I did. I never responded to the email in which Michael told me that he thought what I was doing was evil. I never heard from him again. So, the end of the matter seems to have been reached.

What Could I Have Done Differently?

Readers will no doubt have many ideas about the mistakes I made in my interaction with Michael. Although responsibility for the end result—namely, what appears, at the moment, to be an irreparably broken relationship—ultimately lies with both of us, writing this essay has given me an occasion to reflect on what I could and should have done differently to have helped bring about a different, more positive conclusion to our interaction.

My self-assessment is that I erred in responding in kind: forwarding Michael links when he forwarded me links, offering counterarguments when he made his criticisms, and believing that he would, at some point, simply acknowledge that he was out of his depth and give up on his efforts to convert me. This was the outcome for which I was aiming.

I erred, I believe, in failing to heed an inner voice that I have generally learned to trust through the years. That inner voice was prompting me to take the conversation to a different level: to ask Michael, "Why did you convert to Catholicism? Tell me your story." I never did this, and I wish I had. I think our conversation might have gone very differently had it not been about doctrine and who was "right" about Hinduism. Michael would likely still have been very dissatisfied with any outcome other than my "coming home" to the Catholic Church, but he might have felt that he had been truly heard. I doubt he got that sense at all from the conversation we had.

One important lesson from this conversation-gone-wrong is this. While doctrinal differences and differences of interpretation are truly fascinating, and exploring them can lead to deepened mutual understanding, there are occasions in which pursuing them interreligiously can be counterproductive. Developing the skill of discerning when to lead with the "head" and when to lead with the "heart" is, I have found, essential to successful, productive interreligious interaction. If there is already a foundation of trust and mutual respect, serious conversations about differing perspectives can be illuminating, perhaps even leading to a deepening of the relationship itself. If, however, such a foundation is either absent or questionable, one must tread with care. It will be wiser to follow the heart rather than the head—leading with empathy and compassion rather than with the intellect alone.

Notes

1. See, e.g., Judith Simmer-Brown and Fran Grace, *Meditation and the Classroom: Contemplative Pedagogy for Religious Studies* (Albany: State University of New York Press, 2011).

Chapter 17

WHAT DID HE JUST SAY?
The Importance of Knowing Why We're Here

NISA MUHAMMAD

I had been the assistant dean of religious life at Howard University only a few weeks when a student (I'll call him Bilal) contacted me for help. We exchanged the requisite greetings of *"as-salaam alaykum"* and *"wa alaykum as-salaam."* This meeting took place late in the spring term. So, to get the conversation started, I asked him what his plans were for the summer. "I'll probably be renewing my marriage," was Bilal's casual reply. What did he just say?

For a moment, I was speechless. While the student also said he planned to work at a summer job, I was laser-focused on his statement that he planned to renew his marriage. I asked him to tell me more about renewing his marriage. He said his marriage expired in August. However, he was considering renewing it for another six months. My brain was swirling, trying to remember whether this topic had been covered in some course I had taken. Had I ever learned anything about renewable marriages? Are they similar to renewable energy? I drew a blank. Was his wife Muslim? He said no.

Trying not to sound alarmed or baffled, I dug deeper. How long had he been married? "Almost a year," Bilal told me. "It's a temporary marriage. I've already renewed it once." My eyebrows raised. "How many times do you plan on renewing it?" I wanted to know. "I'm not sure," he said; "I was thinking about letting it expire next year."

What? I was keenly aware there was a young woman involved in this. What does she think about this arrangement? I wanted to know that, too. "She loves me," Bilal explained. "She wants to be together. She was in an abusive relationship before me." I thought the abuse was continuing, but I kept that to myself. Then, aloud, I asked, "Does she know that at any point in time, you can decide not to renew this marriage and go about your business?" He replied, "She's not Muslim, so she doesn't understand everything." I'm now shaking my head. Finally, I blurted out: "Do her parents know she's in a temporary marriage?" He said he was not sure what she had told them.

My mind was now racing with questions and emotions. In my head, I could hear the voice of Malcolm X, speaking in Los Angeles in 1962: "The most disrespected person in America is the Black woman. The most unprotected person in America is the Black woman. The most neglected person in America is the Black woman." I'm a Black woman with a Black daughter. This young man's situation had started to feel personal.

I pressed: had he met this woman's parents? "Briefly," Bilal replied. I kept asking; he kept answering without hesitation. In my mind, each answer he gave me made the situation sound even worse; and, with each question, my voice got more strident. Imagine how it sounded when I asked: "Has this marriage been consummated?" This time, Bilal did not come right back with an answer. He just sat there, looking at me. I knew I had crossed a line. But, hell! Without apology, I stared right back at Bilal, waiting for him to answer. Eventually, he said: "Yes. The marriage has been consummated. She's my wife. Of course, we've consummated the marriage." For some reason, that answer made me angrier.

My phone rang. This conversation was over. To my surprise, Bilal promised to visit my office the next time he was on campus.

That was the first of a few conversations I had with Bilal about his marriage. Honestly, I don't even remember whether Bilal had told me his reason for contacting me in the first place. I'm sure it wasn't to discuss his marriage, but that's where it started and ended. From our conversations, I learned that this "temporary wife" lived with her parents; this "temporary husband" lived with his parents. They got together whenever possible, spent time together, studied, and had date nights. I, a chaplain, felt unprepared for what I was hearing.

Howard, like many universities, has a multifaith team of chaplains. I considered asking one of these colleagues how they would handle something like this. A non-Muslim perspective might be helpful. I imagined myself sitting with one of the Christian chaplains. I imagined myself saying, "Rev. So-and-So, what do you know about temporary marriages? I have a student who wants to renew his marriage in a few months. How would you handle this?" I imagined that, looking aghast, Rev. So-and-So would ask, "Is his wife a Howard student?" And I'd reply, "No, she's not a Howard student. She's not even Muslim." In my imagination, my colleague now gave me a bewildered look.

This imaginary one-on-one helped me grasp that I was concerned that the young woman was more "girlfriend" than "actual wife." I took a deep breath and made a quick *dua* (prayer). This allowed me to put my concerns aside. I could now remember I was a chaplain. I would be ready for the next talk with Bilal.

In preparation, I created for myself a crash course on temporary marriages.[1] The books and articles I read reminded me of what I already knew: *zawāj* (marriage) is essential to a Muslim's life. It is a sacred union between a man and a woman. In Islamic Law, *zawāj* is defined as a legal contract that gives to each party the right to enjoy the other. It is the foundation for families, a significant part of society. The Qu'ran says: "And among His Signs (is) that He created for you from yourselves mates that you may find tranquility in them; and He placed between you love and mercy. Indeed, in that surely (are) Signs for a people who reflect" (Surat al-Rūm [30]: 21). Was that what my student had with his temporary marriage?

My research reminded me that, for Muslims, marriage means following the path of Prophet Muhammad (peace and blessings be upon him). He married and encouraged Muslims to marry. In Islam, according to Muslim scholars, two types of marriages are seen in Muslim societies. For many couples, marriage is a permanent contract ended by divorce or death. For some couples, marriage is contracted temporarily. *Mut'a* is a marital contract that is limited in time from the outset and expires when the time limit has been reached. It was seen in Arabia before the revelation of the Qur'an. It was also seen in various other parts of the world. For example, temporary marriages were practiced for centuries among Peruvian Indians in the Andes, in fifteenth-century Indonesia, ancient Japan, and elsewhere.

While this temporary marriage has been practiced for centuries, it is controversial in Islam. It has become a feature that distinguishes Sunni and Shi'a Muslims, with the former against and the latter for it. The proponents adhere to the practice being legal during the time of Prophet Muhammad (peace and blessings be upon him). However, the opponents, mostly Sunnis, say the practice was abrogated and, therefore, prohibited.

Temporary marriages may be a solution to some changes in the modern world. As the traditional kind of permanent marriage has come under literary, legal, and social criticism, various temporary arrangements are considered legitimate from the religious perspective and is even recommended in certain circumstances.

While temporary marriage is practiced by some Shi'a Muslims, the practice is shrouded in stigma, and women are discouraged from involvement. Permanent marriages require a written, signed contract that is witnessed. Temporary contracts require none of that. Consequently, the practice can be abused. Countless women have fallen in love with a man who only used them for his own physical needs.[2] However, temporary marriages can give women agency over their sexuality with respectability.

In addition to my reading on temporary marriages, I also spoke to other Muslim chaplains. I recounted my conversation with Bilal to their amazement and wonder. Several reminded me that my responsibility was to Bilal, not his wife. My job was to guide him. If a temporary marriage was his choice, my professional responsibility was to help Bilal be the best husband and student for the duration of his contract, all judgment aside.

That guidance forced me to reflect on my thoughts and actions during that initial conversation. Although Bilal was a Howard student, I connected immediately with his wife and what I saw as the vulnerability of her position. Therefore, I wondered: What did she know about her marriage? What did her parents think? What about her friends? Such questions had skewed my thinking. I had not been professional as a chaplain. Clearly, I had been in "mother mode."

My research was rewarding. I felt prepared to continue the conversation. Several weeks later, Bilal found his way back to my office. I wanted this meeting to be smoother than that first conversation, which had been so full of my angst. I wanted to be the chaplain I had been trained to be.

This time, as Bilal entered my office, I smiled and greeted him: "As-salaam alaykum." "Wa alaykum salaam," he replied. "How are you?" I asked. "I'm fine," he said. "How's your wife?" (Bad move, I said to myself. Come on, Nisa! Get it together.) Bilal looked at me blankly. "Is this about my marriage? I'm a little uneasy talking to you about that." I smiled. "Forgive me. Our meeting is not about your marriage unless that's what you want to discuss. (I was hoping it was.) It's all about you and how I can help you." He looked relieved. "I was surprised at how far to the left our first conversation went," he said; "It almost felt like I was talking to my mom." I resisted the urge to ask what his mom thinks about his marriage. I simply said, "You're right. In some regard, you *were* talking to a mom; but that was my fault. That's not my role here. How can I help you?"

I was ready with tips from my research on the best things Bilal could do in his temporary marriage. Here are the top three recommendations I was prepared to make, based on the advice given by Shereen Yousuf and Nousheen Yousuf-Sadiq in a recent essay on *mut'a*:[3]

1. Focus on your marriage and not the temporary part of it.
2. Be honest with yourself as to what you hope to achieve through *mut'a*.
3. Do NOT be pressured to continue or pressure her to continue.

I sat poised, wondering what questions or concerns Bilal would bring up about temporary marriage. He shifted in his chair and spoke: "I contacted you because I need a reference for a scholarship program. Can you help me?"

I was stunned! Shocked! What did he just say? I smiled, then replied warmly, "Of course. Tell me more about the program you're applying to and what you need from me."

***

This was a painful "intrafaith" conversation. Yet, significantly, "interfaith" relationships helped me find a way forward. By imagining how this situation would appear in the eyes of my Christian chaplain colleagues, I could take a more precise look at it myself. Taking a good look at my response to Bilal caused me to remember other times when I strongly reacted to someone's offhand remark—other moments when, in horror, I've wondered, "What did that person just say?" These situations are difficult, whether they involve interreligious misunderstanding, religious bigotry, or intrafaith differences. To address them well, we need to make a quick and a critical assessment: Who are we supposed to be in this scenario? The parent? The spiritual caregiver? The career counselor? Somebody else? Getting that answer right will be easier if we remember to ask a clarifying question: "What brings you to my office today?"

Notes

1. Specifically, I read Khalid Sindawi, *Temporary Marriage in Sunni and Shiite Islam* (Weisbaden: Harrassowitz Verlag, 2013); Sammy Badran and Brian Turnbull, "Contemporary Temporary Marriage: A Blog-analysis of First-hand Experiences," *Journal of International Women's Studies* 20, no. 2 (January 2019): 241–45; Shereen Yousuf and Nousheen Yousuf-Sadiq, "Temporary Pleasure, Permanent Effects: Practical Advice on Mut'a Marriage," in Kecia Ali, ed., *Tying the Knot: A Feminist/Womanist Guide to Muslim Marriage in America* (Boston: OpenBU, 2022), 43–54; and Vicki Larson, "A Temporary Marriage Makes More Sense than Marriage for Life," *Aeon* newsletter (November 16, 2015), https://aeon.co/ideas/a-temporary-marriage-makes-more-sense-than-marriage-for-life.

2. Yousuf and Yousuf-Sadiq, "Temporary Pleasure," 43–54.

3. Yousuf and Yousuf-Sadiq, "Temporary Pleasure," 49–50.

Chapter 18

Radical Interdependence
Making Meaning through Difference

Anthony Cruz Pantojas

I had always wanted to become a chaplain, so here I was, a queer-identifying humanist, at a hospital, taking an experiential course called Clinical Pastoral Education (CPE). In this rigorous program, aspiring chaplains and spiritual care providers work in an interreligious cohort to learn the skills, competencies, and reflexive processes to attend meaningfully to others. As part of the CPE formation process, we would be required to complete two "Spiritual Renewals." These events would be held at the hospital's interfaith chapel. Their purpose was to provide an experience of respite and healing, available to anyone who entered the space. They were also an opportunity to create a meaningful experience for others. Each CPE student would be given a partner with whom to develop these presentations. I was looking forward to the prospect of creating something meaningful with my colleague.

I had come to this CPE program with plenty of apprehensions about how I might be perceived—and now, it seemed to me, for good reason. My partner, I learned, was going to be Tim (a pseudonym)—a male-identifying Roman Catholic priest in his fifties who had grown up in Africa. His booming voice and venerable manner were slightly intimidating to me. Furthermore, there was a clear power dynamic: Tim was a resident chaplain, an established leader; I was a twenty-something-year-old who was trying to find my way into the profession of spiritual caregiving. Surely, I had my own assumptions and apprehensions when I started this program—but now, I wondered: how would Father Tim perceive me as a humanist? Would my queer identity and unconventional orientation and trajectory to this work be too legible? Would I be too much? An enigma? Would I be misunderstood? How would I misunderstand him? What would common ground between us look like?

My trepidation about working together was only heightened when Tim volunteered us to go first. Immediately, I had a bodily aversion to that idea! Was I simply not prepared? No. I just wanted to create some rapport first. I wanted a chance for us to discuss what it meant for both of us to reckon with our philosophical differences. After all, a working assumption I had was that in order to work toward healing and to facilitate meaning-making, especially with our clients collegiality meant to wade in the deep and not stick to cosmetic pleasantries.

Our initial meeting to prepare for the Spiritual Renewal session was frustrating and difficult. It didn't help that it was over the phone. I would have preferred for us to establish the relational space to deepen our understanding of each other and to locate our emotions and our bodily comportments. However, I wanted to display adaptability; so, I reluctantly sat in my hot room attempting to make my ideas cohere with Tim's.

During our conversation, we broached a number of potential subjects to orient our session. Tim was most interested in the formation of consciousness, God the creator, and the purported consequential connection to obedience and the good life. I was intrigued, yet doubtful, about how this topic would resonate with a broader audience. I wondered how it would contribute to a session on spiritual renewal. Still trying to be receptive and cordial, I knew I had burning questions; I knew that I needed to ask Tim for clarification, perhaps to expand my worldview—questions like, Why was this significant? What type of consciousness were we talking about? Does this God have to be the ultimate mediator of reality, regulating our sense of what is right and wrong? How about our sense of agency? Yet, I didn't ask! I deferred to Tim—maybe because I was fatigued, maybe because I did not want to overstep his authority. These questions and conflicts consumed my thinking and ultimately led me to consider the larger implications of the work.

When I look back, I think about how I did a disservice to this collaborative project by not openly sharing what informed my everyday life and professional praxis. Acquiescing to what was comfortable created more of a unilateral, expert-learner binary, which was ultimately reflected in the session. We agreed that Tim would go first, and I would follow suit with some insights from my humanist/freethinker lifestance and interests—namely, that of radical interdependence, or the ways we come together through difference that builds coalitions for social change. Perhaps my independent path eclipsed this radical interdependence in action for the project.

The day of the session, I felt resentful. I sat behind Tim, awaiting my part of this supposed coconstructed effort. Tim offered an incisive lecture on conscience and consciousness, and the formation of ethical beings through the providence of God. As I scanned the space, the audience of CPE interns, resident chaplains, and supervisors were carefully listening, some with furrowed brows. After Tim's lecture, I shifted gears. With visible annoyance, I declared to the group that I wanted to take the session in a different direction, in order to underscore the purpose of renewal. I led a contemplative practice, played a song from *The Greatest Showman* about being unabashedly our whole selves, and facilitated a discussion on expanding the capacity for embodied joy. While the audience's gesticulations and dancing indicated that they enjoyed my presentation, I did feel bad that my portion of the session wasn't integrated with Tim's. I was left dissatisfied by the entire experience, feeling as if we could have displayed, again cohesively, the fullness, range, and diversity of our lived experiences.

My conundrum throughout this process—and something that I am consistently working on as a growing edge—is how to engage in dialogue through difference. Interreligious work requires us to be present with and to probe the uncomfortable, the unfamiliar, and messy terrain of difference. A practice of interreligious fellowship requires us to be challenged and to be willing to be changed, even slightly. It is only through acknowledgment of our partiality in understanding this life that meaningful encounters can occur.

Chapter 19

Why Did I Not?

Reflections on a Challenge to Celebrating Diwali

Nikky-Guninder Kaur Singh

I grew up in the Punjab. Diwali, the Indian festival of lights, was a major annual celebration. Everyone in my family would be excited for weeks in advance. Huge amounts of sweets were prepared; gifts were bought; clothes were tailored in fancy designs; houses were decorated. When the festival arrived, candles and earthenware lamps with oil and cotton wicks shimmered in and around each home. Relatives and friends got together for conversations, meals, and songs. Sights and sounds of sparklers, firecrackers, and fireworks filled the air.

When I arrived in America in the 1970s, there was no such festivity. I was the only South Asian student at Stuart Hall, a girls' preparatory school in Virginia. Even during my undergraduate studies at Wellesley College, I was one of very few South Asian women in the student body. The timing of Diwali is determined by the Hindu lunar calendar. It takes place in October or November, depending on the cycle of the moon each year. Every fall, the lack of festivity at Diwali time hit hard. So, when I landed a teaching position at Colby College, a liberal arts college in Maine, I decided to celebrate the Festival of Lights with the campus community. Diwali is a pan-Indian festival celebrated by Hindus, Jains, Buddhists, and Sikhs. Each religious tradition may have its own motivation and method of celebration—with regional variations as well. Diwali reveals a universal human pattern: as the days get shorter, we honor light. (Hanukkah and Christmas are additional examples.)

I put in a lot of effort and thought so I could share the collective effervescence with my Colby College community and the city of Waterville as a whole. The forty-some students in my religions of India class enthusiastically took the lead in organizing. Typically, the event featured

- presentation of a portion of the *Ramayana*, adapted and performed by several of my religions of India students;
- performance of Indian dance (during which the dancer's movements flowed like waves in a sea);
- performance of a Diwali song by Colby Eights (the college's male *a cappella* group);
- readings by faculty and students of passages from their sacred texts that pertained to light;
- preparation and serving of Indian desserts (hundreds of samosas and baklavas) with Colby students in my tiny apartment;
- guests greeted by students wearing saris and carrying platters holding fruit, flowers, incense, and lights.

Since there were barely any South Asians in this part of Maine, most of these participants—hosts, performers, and guests—were mainstream "White" Americans! Colby's Diwali celebration became a very successful, annual all-college event. Townspeople found it an informative and entertaining evening, so they attended it in great numbers.

Then, one year, a Colby student—a recent convert to Islam—complained to the dean. This student described Diwali as a "polytheistic" event—therefore, something inappropriate for the college to sponsor. That complaint, and the reasoning behind it, came as an utter shock to me. All the joy dissolved. I went numb. I did not want to face the student. I did not want to organize Diwali on my campus ever again. And to this day, I have not. For all these decades, I simply kept the incident locked inside me. Nowadays, we have many South Asian students. They take their own initiative to organize Diwali celebrations, which I happily promote and attend.

Thirty-some years later, I have an opportunity to examine my response to a student's complaint. I now see that the incident had offered me a vital interfaith dialogue opportunity–and I missed out on it. And so, I am engaging in long-overdue self-reflection. I have questions for my younger self: What made me so upset? Was it anger? Was it fear of theological conflict? As I ask myself such questions, I feel guilty. After all, I was then and am still a professor. It is my duty to engage with students and to encourage them to think critically. Why did I not carry out my responsibility? I allowed a potentially transformative interreligious encounter to slip away. I should have met with the student. I should have asked them what they were thinking, what they were feeling. I could have asked them to share their understanding of polytheism, of monotheism. I could have asked what specific sights or sounds bothered them. I could have explained to this new monotheist that, as a Sikh, I also belong to a monotheistic tradition.

Upon reflection, I now wish that this student and I had sat together and studied the scripture passages that would have been read on stage during the Diwali event. I wish that, together, we had analyzed those beautiful and powerful symbols of light. We also could have read together from Holy Qur'an: "O humanity, We have created you male and female, and appointed you races and tribes, that you may know one another" (49:13).

I could have encouraged this student to read about Nur Jahan–the generous Muslim queen who did so much for Hindu women. I could have told stories about the famous Mughal emperor Akbar. We could have discussed the avowedly pluralistic Akbar's celebration of Hindu festivals; his wonderful *Dīn-i-Ilāhī* with dialogues among Hindus, Muslims, Jesuits, Jews; his kissing of the Bible. I take delight in remembering those remarkable interfaith moments! Our world needs to remember them desperately.

Likewise, we could have discussed Sikh emperor Maharaja Ranjit Singh. Having lost an eye, the king used to joke "God gave me one eye so I could see everybody with the same eye." The maharaja is remembered for contributing expensive silver doors at the temple of Hindu Goddess Kali, and for paying an inordinately high price for a manuscript copy of the Holy Qur'an.

I realize now that I also missed facilitating peer-to-peer learning. I, a Sikh, could have introduced this new Muslim to a fellow student who was Hindu or Buddhist. Both could have gained new insights. Indeed, our most deeply held perspectives come into question in conversation, and lead to deeper communions, more integrated and more encompassing ways of knowing ourselves and the world we live in.

When informed by the college's dean that a student had objected to a celebration I was planning, I could have done such things. *Why did I not?* I may never be able to answer that question. I may never be able to say precisely why these responses did not occur to my more-than-three-decades-ago self. However, I am quite certain that, were a similar incident to occur this year, I would not hesitate to invite the reluctant student into a conversation.

Part IV

COMPETING VALUES

Chapter 20

ASHES ON THE FOREHEAD

Appreciation as an Approach to Religious Difference

PREETA M. BANERJEE

It was a rare conjunction. In 2022, Maha Shivratri (Great Night of Shiva) and Ash Wednesday fell just a day apart. This is not usually the case. The timing of the observance of each cherished holiday—one Hindu, one Christian—is determined by reference to the cycles of the moon. Their processes of that determination are different, however. So, their position on the secular calendar, and in relation to each other, can vary by many days or weeks. Yet, some years, Maha Shivratri and Ash Wednesday occur close together; and I—when a Hindu child growing up in Overland Park, Kansas—had taken note. Why? On both holidays, those observing are marked with ash. When, in my youth, I saw ash on foreheads of both Christians and Hindus, I assumed that these two holidays were, therefore, linked somehow. In fact, in India, a holiday's timing and customs can vary significantly from one region to the next. For example, the celebration of Shakti's victory over evil (as recounted in the *Devi Mahatyam*, part of the *Markandeya Purana*) is celebrated as Navratri over nine days in the west of India and as Durga Puja over ten days in the east of India. In my childhood mind, any difference between Maha Shivratri and Ash Wednesday appeared similarly situated.

Over time, through both academic study and careful observation of practices, I have come to appreciate the differences. On the Maha Shivratri, some Hindus apply *Tripundi Vibhuti* (three horizontal lines of ash) on their forehead to honor Shiva, who covers his body in ash and symbolizes the ultimate truth of the mortal, physical body. *Vibhuti* is made from the white ash of wood burnt in the *homa* (sacred fire). The three lines are said to represent the three *gunas* (qualities of human nature)—namely, *Rajas* (passion/action), *Tamas* (laziness/inaction), and *Sattva* (peace/balance).

107

Christians who observe Ash Wednesday may use ashes resulting from burning blessed palm fronds saved from the previous year's Palm Sunday celebration. The ashes are applied by a clergyperson to the forehead of each worshiper as a reminder that death is inevitable for each of us. However, that is where the similarity to Hindu practice and theology ends. For many Christians, Ash Wednesday begins the time of Lent, recalling the forty days Jesus spent fasting in the desert.

When I was a child, I saw a practice—marking the forehead with ash—that resembled one I knew. I was mistaken in my naïve interpretation of it. Yet, advanced questions arose from this starting ground, and I personally believe that this is a very sacred place between a question and an answer. It is a time of not knowing, when we can look at all the possibilities, wonder at the complexities of life, and sit with the expansiveness before coming to our own conclusions.

Thus, this reflection explores the question: can harm be caused by not rectifying such mistakes, as I made in childhood, in only looking for similarities in traditions? In what follows, I share thoughts on the spectrum of impact in not honoring the differences from respectful exchange to harmful extraction.

Appreciating the Nuances

Jennifer Howe Peace has developed a framework for analyzing responses to similarities and differences.[1] One of her categories is "sameness as assumed." That is where this reflection locates itself. The challenge of this posture is that it may be experienced as a form of assimilation or annihilation. Thus, I want to acknowledge how many of us might be weary of the amalgamation or attempted amalgamation of different religions, cultures, or schools of thought in the name of "we are all one." It can even be worse when one's traditions are taken without consent and capitalized upon. Richard Rogers, in the exploration of cultural appropriation, finds nuance between the exchange, the dominance and exploitation, and the transculturation.[2] In this reflection, I will look specifically at the exchange that leads to adaptation and in many cases assimilation as synonymous with *syncretism*; the dominance and exploitation as synonymous with *appropriation*; and *appreciation* as the transculturation that occurs organically in the realms of the interreligious and interspiritual.

While we may wish that exchanges had involved the reciprocal sharing of symbols, artifacts, genres, rituals, or technologies between religions with symmetrical power, this is rarely the case. Examples of such equitable sharing might include the reciprocal borrowing of linguistic words and phrases, mutual influence on religious beliefs and practices, technological exchange, and two-way flows of music and visual arts. In its ideal form, cultural exchange involves a balance of this reciprocal flow, which is generally voluntary, with the choices involved being at multiple levels, including individual and/or cultural.

Syncretism is often a factor in the assimilation of marginalized and colonized cultures and in the survival of subordinated cultures and their resistance to dominant cultures. This may be exploitative. It may benefit the colonized culture in subversive ways. An example, as described in a remarkable dissertation by Erica Washington, is the Ring Shout. She writes: "Although African retentions were apparent in the Ring Shout, variations occurred in the translation and re-creations in a new land and culture. Because the enslaved West Africans and their descendants were in the New World where Christianity dominated, songs became more outwardly connected to the Trinitarian structure of Christianity than with the structure of West African spirituality."[3]

This is currently occurring in response to the Theosophical Society, founded in 1875, with the aim of advancing the ideas in continuation of previous theosophists, especially the Greek and Alexandrian Neo-Platonic philosophers dating back to the third century CE, encompassing wider religious philosophies like Vedānta, Mahāyāna Buddhism, Qabbalah, and Sufism. It has been argued, Siv Ellen Kraft notes, that the Theosophical Society started out as a hyper-syncretistic religion, while at the same time promoting anti-syncretism on behalf of other religions through its practices of appropriation.[4]

On the other hand, the worst of appropriation is commodification. Commodification, by abstracting the value of a cultural element, necessarily removes that element from its native context, changing its meaning and function and raising concerns about cultural degradation. Such commodification creates a pendulum swing of protective behaviors. We see this in present-day Western yoga studios that teach only the *asana* (or physical practice) of the eight limbs of Raj yoga. They decline to acknowledge roots in Eastern practices. We see this also in the use of the word *yoga* to sell anything from expensive clothes to fancy foods.

Given that mutual consent and reciprocal sharing has not been the historical truth of many, where we all hope to be currently is in the category of *appreciation*. Appreciation includes concepts such as "holy envy"— an approach to religious difference put forth by the great scholar Krister Stendahl in 1985 and advocated by many in the decades since. By "holy envy," Stendahl meant the honoring of beautiful elements in faith traditions other than one's own.[5]

The phenomenon of appreciation can also be termed "religious manyness," "religious pluralism," "religious multiplicity," or "spiritual fluidity" and has been increasing in recent years, due to intermarriage and mystical seekers who find more similarity with fellow journeyers in peak experiences than in the long lineages of the past.[6] Elements created from and by multiple religions create "in-between" spaces ripe for hybridity.[7] Pluralistic, hybrid spaces encourage celebration of differences rather than emphasis on dichotomies—and that has the potential to usher in a new paradigm for religion in the modern age.

In closing, I offer descriptions of three ways of being with sameness that vary in their means of approaching differences:

1. Syncretism: the amalgamation or attempted amalgamation of different religions, cultures, or schools of thought; where the term *religion* refers to the distinctive set of rituals, beliefs, doctrines, institutions, and practices that enable members of a particular tradition to establish, maintain, and celebrate a meaningful world.[8] This blending of the belief systems and practices of two or more religions, such that a whole new religion (or at least a distinctly new sect of one of them) emerges, recognizes differences but incorporates them into a type of sameness.
2. Appropriation: the act of taking something for one's own use, typically without the owner's permission. This harmful act of knowingly or unknowingly utilizing another's traditions, rituals, practices, faith without respectful acknowledgement (and often without consent) blatantly ignores difference and entitles sameness as a privilege that overpowers the nuances that make humanity so beautiful.
3. Appreciation: the recognition and enjoyment of the qualities of someone or something. This is where I hope we can all come to rest together, finding ourselves in asking questions about one another's traditions, rituals, practices, and faiths with respect, curiosity, and humility.

I prefer the third approach. It often happens that when we encounter something, we try to understand through what we know. Dr. Lucinda Mosher, in her description of religious manyness and pluralism, says that "we can't help but view, hear, and understand the religious other from our own religious perspective. We always stand somewhere when we meet; we always start at a location when we move. No matter how openminded we are, we assess the truth and beauty of another religion according to our (rather than its) criteria."[9] Yet we each have a choice as to *how* those comparisons are made—by form or by function. In my youth, I just looked at the form of ashes; as an adult, I learned to look at the function. As Valarie Kaur, Sikh activist and author of *See No Stranger*, urges us, we always can turn to wonder.[10] May we take the time to ask questions and understand on a deeper level.

Notes

1. Jennifer Howe Peace, "Responses to Sameness and Difference in Interfaith Relations," in Lucinda Mosher et al., *Deep Understanding for Divisive Times* (Newton Centre, MA: Interreligious Studies Press, 2020), 6–11.

2. Richard A. Rogers, "From Cultural Exchange to Transculturation: A Review and Reconceptualization of Cultural Appropriation," *Communication Theory* 16, no. 4 (2006): 474–503.

3. Erica Lanice Washington, "'Shabach Hallelujah!' The Continuity of the Ring Shout Tradition as a Site of Music and Dance in Black American Worship" (PhD diss., Bowling Green State University, 2005), 36–37.

4. Siv Ellen Kraft, "To Mix or Not to Mix: Syncretism/Anti-Syncretism in the History of Theosophy," *Numen* 49, no. 2 (2002): 142–77.

5. For one explanation of Stendahl's notion, see Barbara Brown Taylor, *Holy Envy: Finding God in the Faith of Others* (New York: HarperOne, 2019), 64–67.

6. Duane R. Bidwell, *When One Religion Isn't Enough: The Lives of Spiritually Fluid People* (Boston: Beacon Press, 2018).

7. Michaela Pfadenhauer, "In-Between Spaces: Pluralism and Hybridity as Elements of a New Paradigm for Religion in the Modern Age," *Human Studies* 39, no. 1 (2016): 147–59.

8. H. Byron Earhart, *Religious Traditions of the World: A Journey through Africa, Mesoamerica, North America, Judaism, Christianity, Islam, Hinduism, Buddhism, China, and Japan* (New York: Harper, 1992).

9. Lucinda Allen Mosher, "Public Theology: Characteristics from the Multireligious Neighborhood," *Anglican Theological Review* 102, no. 2 (2020): 251–62.

10. Valarie Kaur, *See No Stranger: A Memoir and Manifesto of Revolutionary Love* (New York: One World, 2020).

Chapter 21

ADAPTIVE FACILITATION

A Requirement for Interfaith
Discussions of Israel/Palestine

YEHEZKEL LANDAU

The "Conflict Spectrum" seemed like an ideal exercise to include in the schedule for "Building Abrahamic Partnerships"—an intensive, weeklong interfaith training for Jews, Christians, and Muslims. This activity called for participants to convey through their bodies, positioned along a diagonal line in a large classroom, how they apportioned responsibility for the ongoing conflict in Israel/Palestine. Those who held the Israelis wholly or primarily responsible for the conflict were to gather in one corner, while those who believed that the Palestinians and their Arab allies were solely or mainly responsible for fueling hostility were to congregate in the opposite corner. Those who felt that the two sides were equally responsible for the conflict would stand in the center of the room, while those (usually the majority) who apportioned responsibility inclusively but not equally would choose a spot between the two poles reflecting the degree of responsibility they felt each side had. Having explained this procedure, my cofacilitators and I asked the group members to step onto the line. To our surprise, almost everyone in the group refused our invitation!

As a religious educator and peacebuilder with decades of experience facilitating interfaith interactions in both Israel/Palestine and North America, I am acutely aware that the ongoing Middle East conflict is a fraught subject for conversations among Jews, Christians, and Muslims. For this reason, facilitators of interfaith, as well as *intra*faith, encounters often avoid the subject entirely, lest it create or exacerbate intergroup tensions. They know that participants can be left grappling with hurt feelings, without any broader context for processing those feelings or the precipitating issue.

I find it preferable to address this divisive issue intentionally, as part of a process of building trust and empathy. Better to take a pro-active stance than a reactive one aimed at damage control once a bitter argument

112

breaks out. Trained facilitators can model how to engage in constructive dialogue on such an emotionally charged subject. For anyone preparing to be an interfaith leader, such experiential learning is essential. Yet, even if our intentions are positive, problems can arise. What follows is a descriptive analysis of three distinct challenges.

The Context

The incidents described here occurred during sessions of an interfaith capacity-building program that I designed and directed for fourteen years at Hartford Seminary (recently renamed Hartford International University for Religion and Peace) in Connecticut. Called "Building Abrahamic Partnerships (BAP)," the primary aim of this eight-day intensive course was to help some twenty-four to thirty participants from the three traditions, in roughly equal numbers, develop concepts, skills, and sensitivities for interfaith engagement and leadership. The teaching team consisted of academics and "pastoral adjuncts" (leaders of local congregations).[1] As a general principle and practice, we tried to ensure gender balance on the teaching team across all three traditions. My cofacilitators and I also designed BAP II, an advanced training program that was offered three times at the seminary. More practical and less theoretical than the basic course, BAP II focused on concrete skills, techniques, and methodologies for interfaith leadership. For each iteration of the advanced course, the facilitation team was supplemented by professional trainers enlisted for their expertise in specific areas.

From 2004 to 2016, several hundred people took part in twenty-two rounds of BAP. At both the basic and advanced levels, the pedagogical approach was holistic, combining academic study with experiential learning: interactive exercises, small-group text study, sacred music from the three faith traditions, shared *kosher/halal* meals blessed by representatives of all three traditions, designing interfaith worship, and weekend visits to local synagogues, churches, and mosques. The educational process was meant to model at the micro-level—with course participants serving as an experimental learning community—the spirit and the practice that we facilitators envisioned as normative for our wider society. Yet, in spite of careful planning, unanticipated challenges with regard to Israel/Palestine arose.

Missteps: The Importance of Having a "Plan B"

In the first round of BAP II, on the day devoted to exploring conflict transformation, our facilitation team wanted participants to address the Israeli-

Palestinian dispute by using the "Conflict Spectrum" exercise described above. We took it from *The Little Book of Cool Tools for Hot Topics* by Ron Kraybill and Evelyn Wright.[2] Its goal is to make visible a continuum of perspectives between two opposing viewpoints in order to generate discussion.[3]

Usually, the "Conflict Spectrum" is an effective pedagogical tool. However, on this day, most of the cohort of interfaith practitioners resisted our invitation to participate in it. They feared that the exercise would reveal fault lines in the group, create animosity, and jeopardize the friendly relations forged over several days. We three facilitators—experienced interfaith educators from the Jewish, Christian, and Muslim traditions—tried to reassure them that we had already created an emotionally safe "container" for handling conflict. Still, the group balked, even though conflict transformation was the topic we had all agreed on for that day. This was an unanticipated situation, and we needed a "Plan B" quickly. We facilitators came up with an alternative: a simulation exercise in which three multifaith subgroups would represent the Israeli, Palestinian, and American government positions on the conflict. The participants embraced this suggestion, and the simulation went smoothly—too smoothly from our vantage point as facilitators.

Opting for the "safer" option had a less-than-optimal consequence: it ensured that no one would be seriously challenged and stretched, either cognitively or emotionally. My colleagues and I came away from this experience with some concrete lessons:

- Even for experienced interfaith practitioners, a willingness to explore new emotional territory can be superseded by aversion to interpersonal conflict.
- Facilitators must adapt to unforeseen challenges by having a range of techniques and methodologies in their professional "toolkit."
- Facilitators should verify their assumptions about a group's response to conflict before proposing particular exercises or activities.
- There are times when it is appropriate to give the group a say in choosing an external conflict that is likely to engender disagreement among participants.
- An endeavor that seems, at first, to go awry can become an opportunity for deeper learning.

The Need to Create a Level Playing Field

A different sort of problem arose in the initial rounds of the basic BAP course. That eight-day program began with a Sunday night dinner and concluded with dinner on the following Sunday. The first three days were devoted to introductions to each of the three Abrahamic religions, in chronological order—Judaism on Monday, Christianity on Tuesday, and Islam on Wednesday. We would have morning presentations, a long lunch break for informal socializing, and afternoon discussions. At around 4 p.m. each day, we shifted from a traditional academic mode to another evocative exercise from Kraybill and Wright. In this activity, called the "Fishbowl," "one group sits in a circle and has a conversation, surrounded by a larger circle of listeners. Only people in the inner circle can speak (in our case, in response to a prompt); the surrounding group listens in silence."[4] Kraybill and Wright say it is "a simple, sturdy, flexible tool that can serve dialogue, analysis, or decision-making." True. Yet its simplicity belies a deeper challenge: taking on the discipline of active, compassionate, nonjudgmental listening.

On Monday, after the group explored Jewish beliefs and practices, the Jewish participants formed the inner Fishbowl circle. On Tuesday, the Christians in the group sat in the center; and on Wednesday, the Muslim participants had their turn. At the start of the exercise, we facilitators invited members of the inner circle to speak for up to three minutes each in response to a question. Each participant had one chance to talk and three opportunities to actively listen—once as a member of the inner circle and twice when seated on the outside. On Thursday evening, after a degree of mutual familiarity, vulnerability, and trust had developed, we three facilitators led a group discussion processing what had been learned in the three Fishbowl sessions. Those debriefings were usually a highlight of the course, with deeper insights emerging through the exchange of experiences, feelings, and perspectives.

When we launched our basic BAP course, our Fishbowl prompt was a general, politically neutral question about Israel/Palestine. Our aim was to elicit genuine feelings on a neuralgic issue within a supportive, trustworthy setting. To our dismay as facilitators, a problematic pattern emerged in which Jews and Muslims tended to open up emotionally, sharing fears and hopes for their coreligionists in the Holy Land, while most of the Christians expressed concern for those caught up in the conflict—but they had no emotional investment in the subject themselves. Some Christians even shared a sense of guilt over their minimal awareness of events in Israel/Palestine and their lack of emotional connection to either side of the conflict.

After the second round of BAP, it was clear to us facilitators that the prompt we had chosen for this exercise was inappropriate, since the three subgroups were not on a cognitively or emotionally level playing field. So, for subsequent rounds we used this Fishbowl prompt: "What would you need to experience from the other two faith communities in order to trust them more?" This question proved to be a much better stimulus for inclusive sharing of both thoughts and feelings. Some of those feelings were intense, evoking tears of pain in the speakers and tears of empathy and compassion in the listeners.

The Fishbowl was an effective activity for deep learning by our participants. However, we facilitators also needed to learn how best to use it. Here are three lessons gleaned from our experience with it:

- Jews, Christians, and Muslims do not relate to the conflict in Israel/ Palestine with comparable knowledge or emotional investments; hence, the choice of prompts for a Fishbowl exercise must reflect sensitivity to the experiential backgrounds of the participants.
- Fishbowl facilitators need to select prompts that all participants can relate to.
- As in the case of the Conflict Spectrum exercise, Fishbowl facilitators should have a "Plan B" in case the initial approach does not produce the intended results.

The Need for Agility in Responding to Real-World Challenges

What happens when interfaith concepts and practices are tested in the "real world," outside the BAP bubble? Our third case study explores that challenge.

As an integral part of the basic BAP course, arrangements were made with local houses of worship to host participants for *Jum'ah* prayers on Friday, *Shabbat* morning prayers on Saturday, and Christian worship on Sunday mornings. Those nonclassroom learning opportunities, coming at the end of an intense week of shared study and conversation, were a highlight of the course. They helped to develop what the late Krister Stendahl called "holy envy"—soulful appreciation for a spiritual practice in another tradition that is not part of one's own faith.

In 2007, a painful but educationally powerful incident occurred at my Modern Orthodox synagogue in West Hartford. During the light meal following *Shabbat* morning prayers, the rabbi of the synagogue conducted a question-and-answer session for BAP participants and some members of the congregation, as he had done several times before. This time the Middle East conflict became the focus of intense and increasingly bitter exchanges, sparked by a question from a BAP student. A few Jewish congregants got defensive and made some bellicose statements that were hurtful to the Muslim students, among them four women from Syria. The safe learning environment we had sustained all week was shattered.

Later that afternoon, the BAP group reconvened in our classroom to process what had happened. My Christian cofacilitator led that conversation. Her pastoral presence helped to ease the raw feelings. Many tissues were consumed as students and teachers shared their pain over the verbal assault, along with their mutual affection and care. Despite the shock and hurt, the experience proved cathartic for the group, taking it to a deeper level of empathy and solidarity. It also challenged me to engage more deliberately in intrafaith work, especially with my rabbi, before other BAP groups visited that synagogue.

A similar incident, in reverse, happened in the major Hartford-area mosque two years later, when the hosts invited a Palestinian-American speaker to present a partisan viewpoint on Israel/Palestine over the lunch that followed their Friday prayers. Our BAP students were visitors, yet they felt that our safe, politically neutral space had been violated, along with the consensual ground rules governing our communications. Like the incident at the synagogue, this unanticipated situation demonstrated the necessity to sensitize host communities before interfaith groups are brought to their places of worship for a discussion.

After these unpleasant, but instructive, experiences at the synagogue and mosque, the facilitation team decided that, following their visits to houses of worship, BAP subgroups should be brought back to the seminary for debriefing sessions over catered meals. We realized that this was a trade-off. It meant that congregants were deprived of an opportunity to share in a multifaith conversation. Yet, we understood that, without prior preparation and adherence to agreed-upon guidelines for interaction, those congregants might give voice to grievances and animosities that posed a serious risk to what we were trying to accomplish through BAP. We course leaders impressed upon participants that the safe and supportive atmosphere in the program was atypical. Constructive intentionality and competent facilitation are needed to replicate it in local communities, especially if volatile issues like Israel/Palestine are made part of the agenda.

The incidents in the synagogue and mosque—and our adaptive responses to them—yielded these lessons:

- Having Israel/Palestine as a discussion topic with interfaith groups is, indeed, a risky undertaking, requiring thoughtful planning.
- *Intra*-faith conversations are needed to prepare the host congregations before such interfaith encounters.
- Apply the BAP ground rules for respectful dialogue in conversations that include non-BAP participants.

- If the facilitators are well trained, a group's painful experiences can become catalysts for emotional catharsis and positive transformation.

Setbacks Can Be Edifying

As an educational program, "Building Abrahamic Partnerships" enjoyed a long and fruitful run because the combination of academic and experiential learning modes generated a holistic and transformative approach to interfaith engagement. It also benefitted from the willingness of the facilitators to learn and adapt to unforeseen circumstances. The few setbacks described here were edifying, even if they were unpleasant when they occurred. These missteps and corrections confirmed that the subject of Israel/Palestine is the most challenging issue for Jews, Christians, and Muslims to talk about constructively. Nevertheless, I still maintain that, since we cannot avoid the subject, it is better to address it pro-actively within settings that ensure the emotional well-being of participants as they explore the multiple dimensions of this tragic conflict. Ultimately, we should all be corrective mirrors for one another as we commit ourselves to healing the legacies of fear and pain that we all carry.[5]

Notes

1. I owe a debt of gratitude to my cofacilitators, who included Rev. Dr. Karen Nell Smith, Rev. Dr. Brita Gill-Austern, Imam Abdullah Antepli, Imam Sohaib Sultan, Rabbi Amy Small, and Rabbi Debra Cantor.

2. Ron Kraybill and Evelyn Wright, *The Little Book of Cool Tools for Hot Topics: Group Tools to Facilitate Meetings when Things Get Hot* (New York: Good Books, 2006), 49–51. This is a volume in the Little Books of Justice and Peacebuilding series. From that series, see also Lisa Schirch and David Campt, *The Little Book of Dialogue for Difficult Subjects: A Practical, Hands-On Guide* (New York: Good Books, 2007), esp. chap. 6, "Facilitating a Dialogue," 58–64.

3. An effective technique to supplement the "Conflict Spectrum" is a "Samoan Circle." See Kraybill and Wright, *The Little Book of Cool Tools,* 51–53.

4. Kraybill and Wright, *The Little Book of Cool Tools,* 54.

5. For a downloadable discussion guide on *How to Talk about Israel/Palestine with Just about Anyone,* which I cowrote with Joyce Schriebman, see www.MyBrotherFromAnotherMother.org. For a U.S. Institute of Peace research report on efforts by faithful Jews, Christians, and Muslims to transform the conflict, see Yehezkel Landau, *Healing the Holy Land: Interreligious Peacebuilding in Israel/Palestine,* at www.usip.org.

Chapter 22

Bach and the Indelible Stain
When a Cultural Project Exacerbates Old Tensions

Christopher M. Leighton

Back in 1990, the Institute for Christian & Jewish Studies (ICJS), of which I was executive director, was wedged into the third floor of Baltimore's Brown Memorial Presbyterian Church office building. One afternoon, Tom Hall, director of the Baltimore Choral Arts Society (whose offices were directly beneath ours), knocked on our door with a vexing dilemma. He had submitted a request to a Jewish philanthropic foundation known for its support of cultural programming to help underwrite a performance of Johann Sebastian Bach's masterpiece the *St. Matthew Passion* at the Meyerhoff Symphony Hall. Significant support would be needed in order to conduct a work lasting nearly three hours and featuring two choirs, a double orchestra, and several soloists.

The funding appeal had gone to David Hirschhorn, the head of the philanthropic foundation, who was also one of the founding board members of the ICJS. He was well aware that the Passion narratives had enshrined a noxious portrait of the Jewish people, and he wanted to know how the Choral Arts Society was going to handle the polemical material. He urged Tom to consider with me the extent to which these choral works continue to perpetuate negative views of Judaism—a concern long ignored, cavalierly dismissed, or resolutely avoided. Our conversation launched a collaboration that would lead to the first community-wide symposium on the legacy of anti-Judaism in the music of J. S. Bach and a partnership that would continue for the next two decades.

In terms of its historical context, Bach composed this devotional music in 1727. The work was first performed in Leipzig at the St. Thomas Church on Good Friday. In addition to texts drawn from Martin Luther's German translation of the Gospel of Matthew, the composition featured the poetry of Picander (the pen name of Christian Friedrich Henrici). These commentaries opened and closed most scenes in the narration, adding to the devotional depth of this musical meditation. The dramatic centerpiece retraced the narrative flow of the Passion, moving from the arrest of Jesus to his burial and the sealing of the tomb.

As we considered performing these masterworks, guidance came from Bach scholar Michael Marissen, now a professor emeritus of music at Swarthmore College. The good news, he explained, is that Bach incorporates commentaries into his compositions that moderate the anti-Jewish tenor of the Passions. The bad news is that his settings include biblical texts that amplify the violence and heighten the drama of an already-damning portrait of the Jews.

While our efforts broke new ground, there was considerable pushback, indeed outrage, in response to the proposed performance of Bach's *Passion* by Baltimore's Choral Arts Society. At one end of the spectrum, a prominent Reform rabbi in Baltimore denounced the entire enterprise as an empty gesture. He claimed a great deal depended on the location of the performance. It is one thing to integrate Bach's *Passions* into the church's liturgical calendar and keep the performance bounded within the confines of sanctuary; it is an altogether different matter to perform these works in a public venue. As he saw it, the stain of antisemitism was indelible, inextricably embedded in the music. No matter what verbiage we used to surround the production, words of explanation could not compete with, much less annul, the damage. The conspiratorial role assigned to the Jews was integral to a plot powered by music that would overwhelm the audience's rational faculties. From his perspective, audiences feasted on an aesthetic masterpiece without acknowledging—much less reckoning with—the poison they ravished.

Of particular concern was the moment in Matthew's Gospel when Jesus is brought before the Roman procurator Pontius Pilate. Having found no justification for Jesus's death sentence, Pilate declares Jesus innocent. Invoking a custom of releasing a prisoner, Pilate invites the assembled crowd to make a life-and-death decision. Who should live: Jesus or the notorious criminal Barabbas? The crowd reveals the depth of its depravity in its rejection of Jesus and the demand for Barabbas's release. When Pilate asked what they want done with "Jesus who is called the Messiah," the Jewish multitude clamors for his crucifixion. Pilate washes his hands of this sordid affair, while the people proclaim, "His blood be on us and on our children."

This passage is arguably the most pernicious text in the entire New Testament, because the alleged crime becomes the basis for the deicide charge—the evil of attempting to murder God. The assembled crowd is presented as willfully and knowingly responsible for this transgression—and even more significantly, they have enmeshed their children in their wickedness. The iniquity mirrors, indeed magnifies, the sin of Adam insofar as this crime implicates future generations.

The Gospels' depiction of Pilate as an indecisive and magnanimous arbiter of Roman justice conceals his true character. The Jewish chronicler Josephus presents a picture of a brutal ruler who evidently had little difficulty getting a good night's sleep before or after a busy day of state-sponsored murder. He enlisted the muscle of Rome to crush dissent and savagely imposed civic order on an oppressed and aggrieved population. His practice was to execute slaves and revolutionaries utilizing a distinctive form of execution, a public spectacle to underscore Roman domination—namely, crucifixion. His exercise of power was excessive, even by Roman standards; and the gruesome displays that he choreographed to intimidate the masses were conducted with such brutality that he was ultimately relieved of his duties by his Roman superiors.

The discrepancy between the historical evidence and the sympathetic rendering of Pilate in the Gospels offers vital clues about the precarious conditions of the early followers of Jesus. Without an adequate appreciation of the political pressures under which the early church labored, we will fail to understand why the Gospels delivered such a negative portrait of the Jews while offering a relatively sanguine image of the actual powerbrokers, the Roman occupiers. Crucifixion was a Roman form of execution associated with sedition, and Jesus's death locates his followers in the shadows of political revolution. In the midst of the First Jewish War, from 66 to 73 CE, the messianic dreams of the Jesus movement would have engendered suspicions and prompted the early believers in this messianic figure to distance themselves from Jewish insurgencies.

To redirect the watchful eye of Rome away from the early church, the Gospel writers made two decisive adjustments. First, they insisted that the Kingdom of God transcended the power politics of Rome. Jesus insisted, "My kingdom is not of this world" (John 18:36). Second, they whitewashed Roman culpability for Jesus's execution and thrust Jews, already perceived as rebellious subjects, into the spotlight. In this historical inversion, the oppressive Roman conqueror is reconstructed as a feckless defender of the innocent, while the oppressed Jewish populace is transformed into the murderous enemy. What began as a politically expedient tactic of survival was read by subsequent generations of Christians as a faithful and accurate account of a malicious Jewish disposition, an essential character trait of a politically and theologically disobedient people.

Anti-Jewish legislation was repeatedly framed as a defensive measure to counter the diabolical plot to overthrow Christendom, and this lethal conspiracy theory pulsed through the veins of churches until it was officially condemned by a number of mainline Protestant churches at the World Council of Churches in 1961 and most especially in the landmark declaration *Nostra Aetate* promulgated by the Roman Catholic Church at the Second Vatican Council in 1965.

Tom Hall has observed that, in Bach's setting, the Gospel text in which the Jewish crowd calls for Jesus's execution occupies less than two minutes of a three-hour performance. More significantly, Bach avails himself of a devotional discipline that goes a long way to deflect the antisemitic thrust of these Passion settings. Drawing on a potent current of Lutheran theology, Bach underscored the doctrinal claim that all of humanity bears the stain of original sin. One and all are guilty. One and all stand in need of redemption, not least the German Lutherans who claimed to have emancipated the gospel from Roman Catholic captivity. Bach's *Passions* do concentrate on the redemption of the world from sin, not the so-called villainy of Jewish deicide.

A fundamental problem nevertheless persists. Since the scope of sin and redemption is universalized, Jews are incorporated into a story that expunges their own distinctive calling, their divine election, and their covenantal integrity. They do not recognize or appreciate the necessity of Jesus's redemptive death, nor do they understand and accept the expanded dimensions of salvation now open to them along with the rest of humanity. The Christian missionary's dream of the Jewish conversion perdures, and their access to the heavenly kingdom depends on their willingness to be loved out of their communal existence.

Those who occupy a comfortable seat in the dominant culture are generally unaware or indifferent or hostile to efforts to contend with the vulnerability of all those who live on the edges of our society. My initial reaction to the criticism of the Reform rabbi was a mix of disappointment and exasperation. Now I am not so certain about my dismissal of his reservations.

My rabbinic colleague suspected that Bach's *Passions* continue to cultivate the seeds of contempt. Although I found myself at odds with his conclusions, I could not easily write off a man who took great risks to march on the front lines in the early days of the civil rights movement. What my rabbinic critic helped me to grasp is the fact that our most celebrated cultural achievements shape the social imagination and inform the ways in which we inhabit the world. Any and every artistic artifact that degrades and dehumanizes others—whether rooted in anti-Judaism, racism, Islamophobia, sexism, or gender discrimination—needs to be critically engaged and potentially removed from the public eye. These works operate beyond the confines of reason and exert a power that rational discourse cannot tame. There are boundaries of propriety that are under constant negotiation, and they constantly shift. Yet, the guardrails are consequential because they safeguard norms essential for a decent society.

The pushback from the other end of the spectrum was even more strident. We were repeatedly admonished by devotees of Bach that our educational efforts were besmirching the reputation of one of the world's greatest composers. The idea that this exquisite choral music, which elevated audiences to great aesthetic heights, contained an anti-Jewish bias struck them as a nefarious allegation. Not only were they incensed by the apparent assault on Bach's reputation, they reacted as though their enjoyment of this music was enough to implicate them in the dissemination of hatred. Their reaction reflected outrage and resentment: they were simultaneously being condemned and robbed of an incalculable treasure.

Time and again, we heard concertgoers contend they paid no attention to the words. The overwhelming majority of them insisted that they did not understand German, and they did not dwell on the translations in their printed programs. From their perspective, we were magnifying, if not creating, a problem better ignored. Indeed, the interjection of our concerns into the program was not only an unwelcome distraction but an infringement ruining the pure joy they had once innocently relished. The inquiry amounted to a defilement of the sacred.

Yet another position was staked out by one of Baltimore's distinguished lawyers, a devout Christian, who maintained "our interrogations" led to the defamation of Christianity. If the Passion narratives are laden with anti-Jewish animus and should not be aired in a public venue, shouldn't they also be banned in church settings? He argued we were greasing a slippery slope: our critiques of Bach's *Passions* would logically culminate in a summons to cancel Good Friday services. Since there can be no Easter celebration of the resurrection without the ignominious death of Jesus, our efforts to educate the public were undermining—wittingly or unwittingly—the moral and theological foundations of the church. He declared that he was "embarrassed and ashamed for me, an ordained minister."

As the range of reactions makes painfully clear, our inquiry into Bach's *Passions* had landed us at a hazardous intersection where religious, political, and cultural allegiances collide. How can anyone adjudicate such vastly conflicting viewpoints? Who is vested with the authority to determine the acceptability of aesthetic works displayed in museums or performed in public spaces? And when does critical engagement swerve into repressive censorship?

I believe the resolution of these conflicting viewpoints is not possible. My rabbinic colleague articulated a position that I suspect is shared by others who are convinced anti-Jewish bias lives in the marrow of the Christian tradition. My aesthetically minded compatriots argue for a boundary that insulates the work of art from political and theological meddling. For them, every effort to contextualize Bach's masterpieces detracts from the purity and beauty of the performances, transmuting an experience of artistic transcendence into an object for rational analysis. This educational intervention amounts to surgery that murders the patient. Meanwhile, my pious lawyer maintains the truth of Christianity is bound to offend those who are at odds with the tradition. These individuals need not patronize the concert hall or visit the church. If anyone is scandalized or affronted by the proclamation of the Gospel, that is their misfortune—but the potential for bruised feelings should not induce compromise or censorship. A preoccupation with anti-Judaism tarnishes Christian confidence and undermines trust in the revelation made known through Jesus Christ. No wonder the next generation is growing disenchanted and estranged from their religious communities!

Was it a mistake to mount a civic performance of Bach's *Passions* in Baltimore? I think not. However, I do not wish to minimize the sense of threat or dismiss the profound experience of loss that our efforts sometimes precipitated. The experience we orchestrated underscored the fact that interreligious education comes with a cost—and it is not always clear whether the gains outweigh the heavy price. Whether our ancestors' gifts are etched into our sacred scriptures or find expression in sublime music, the bequest bears both the blessings and curses of the culture that gave form to our most hallowed treasures. I believe that, sooner or later, there comes a reckoning with the past, an inescapable imperative to contend with the flaws—our own as well as those our ancestors passed down. Each generation is called upon to redeem the inheritance; and future generations will discover that the work of rehabilitation remains unfinished. In the jumble of the dance, we get close to one another. I do not know how to avoid mangled toes.

Chapter 23

Toward Strengthening the Civic

Interfaith Work in an Era of Competing Concepts of Justice

Eboo Patel

In the spring of 2008, at the height of the war in Iraq, I met the prime minister of the Kurdistan region of Iraq, Nechervan Barzani. I shook his hand and immediately apologized for the American invasion of Iraq and the destruction it had caused his country. Barzani was rendered speechless for a moment. I thought his English was bad and that I had spoken too quickly, so I repeated myself. "I am so sorry for America's war in Iraq and what it has done to your nation and your people."

Turns out that Barzani had understood me perfectly well, he just did not like what I had said. When he finally spoke, he said through clenched teeth that the only thing unjust about the war in Iraq was that it didn't happen sooner. He was a Kurd, and Saddam Hussein had murdered his people for decades. To him, any reasonable definition of justice meant ridding the world of Saddam Hussein. My conversation with Prime Minister Barzani underscored the most common mistake that I have made in interfaith work: assuming others have the same definition of justice that I have.

Here is another example. It was January 2017, and I was at a hotel in Washington, DC, where I was giving a talk to the presidents of the Consortium of Christian Colleges and Universities. Over breakfast that morning, I had seen groups of high school and college students gather excitedly around pancakes and omelets, some with Bibles in hand. They wore t-shirts advertising their various faith communities: Mormon, evangelical, and Catholic. Finally, my curiosity got the better of me. I approached one of the tables to ask what was going on. "We're here for the most important March for Life in history," one of them told me. "This is the first time a sitting vice president is addressing the event."

"It's a big moment for justice and life," another student said to me. I almost had to do a double take. For twenty years, I have run in mostly progressive circles. The vast majority of my friends and colleagues are pro-choice, and they invariably use justice language to justify their view. This is absolutely the case in interfaith work. The Reform Jews, progressive Muslims, liberal Christians and secular humanists who dominated the interfaith movement that I was part of frequently spoke of women's rights and being pro-choice as a justice position.

While I certainly knew some pro-life people, I don't think I had ever heard them state their views in justice terms. Or, perhaps I had just not listened closely enough. In any case, here I was, standing in front of a religiously diverse group of young people—Mormons, evangelicals and Catholics—who were speaking about the pro-life cause in the terms I normally heard progressives employ. Yet, did these religiously diverse people gathering to advance their cause not have a claim to being an interfaith movement for justice?

I think it is useful to separate the mistake I highlight in the stories above into two parts, one leading right into the other. The first part of the mistake is personal in nature: assuming that people have the same definition of justice that I have. This leads to some embarrassing moments, like the one with Nechervan Barzani. It also leads to a too-simplistic mental model of the world.

The second part of the mistake is connected to the first. The interfaith events I have organized have been a reflection of my mental model of the world. In my mental model, people share my definition of justice, and so the interfaith events I have organized generally include people with whom I generally agree.

But as the examples above illustrate, the world is far more complicated than my mental model of it. A quick glance beyond my biases shows that people differ in their definitions of justice—and those definitions are shaped by their interpretations of religious traditions and their belonging to particular religious and ethnic communities. There are Catholics and evangelicals who believe the most important justice issue in the world is a pro-life view on abortion; and there are religious and secular people who believe that a pro-choice position is an equally important justice issue. There are Muslims who believe the most important justice issue in the world is supporting the Palestinian cause, and Jews who believe the most important justice issue in the world is a secure Israel. In these cases and many more, different religious convictions profoundly shape political positions.

I believe the key question here goes to the heart of interfaith work. Is interfaith work principally about bringing together religiously diverse people who share a perspective on justice? Or, is interfaith work principally about bringing together religiously diverse people with *different* definitions of justice? I think it should be about the latter. The reason for this is simple: *the former is already being done.* Well-established organizations already mobilize diverse religious groups for their various causes. There is a religiously diverse movement *for* same sex marriage, and one *against* it; a religiously diverse movement *for* access to abortion, and one *against* it; a religiously diverse movement that supports the Palestinian cause, and a religiously diverse movement that supports Israel.

In fact, movements advancing opposing ideas of what qualifies as "fundamental" or what constitutes "justice" are one of the signature features of our times. In their book *American Grace*, Robert Putnam and David Campbell point out that the most polarized areas in America are around political positions that are connected to religion.[1] Moreover, people with different views on core issues increasingly run in different circles. It is so easy, in this situation, to demean the other side.

Let me be clear: I am a political person. I use the term *justice* frequently. My convictions are rooted largely in a progressive interpretation of Islam. I have sharp opinions on the affairs of my nation and the world. Nevertheless, I do not think the primary task of interfaith work is to circle religiously diverse wagons more tightly around particular views of justice—however strongly I might hold some of those views. I do not believe it is the primary purpose of interfaith cooperation to widen what are already deep and dangerous divides.

The central problem interfaith work seeks to solve is this: how are all of us, with our differences, to share a nation and a world together? The central task of an interfaith leader, in my view, is to help build relationships between people with profoundly different views of what is just. How else do you have a diverse democracy unless people who have deep disagreements on some issues are able to work together on other issues?

I call this civic work—and we need more people doing it! "The civic" is that layer of our democratic life together—defined by common activities that guide cooperative relationships between people with different doctrines, political points of view, and definitions of justice. Schools, hospitals, basketball leagues, well-run companies, nonprofit organizations: all of these make up the civic. Strengthening it is what interfaith work needs to be about!

Notes

1. Robert D. Putnam and David E. Campbell, *American Grace: How Religion Divides and Unites Us* (New York: Simon & Schuster, 2010).

Chapter 24

BREAKING BREAD

A Breach of Intra-Religious Boundaries

JENNIFER HOWE PEACE

> While they were eating, he took a loaf of bread, and after blessing it he broke it, gave it to them, and said, "Take; this is my body." Then he took a cup, and after giving thanks he gave it to them, and all of them drank from it. He said to them, "This is my blood of the covenant, which is poured out for you and for many." (Mark 14:22–24)

Walking into the church, what I noticed first was the quality of light streaming through the massive windows lining both walls. Pine wood boards separated one layer of windows from a second row of equally large panels reaching to the roofline. Great wooden beams with black metal brackets and truss cords supported a vast open space. The windows opened to thick foliage, slanting sunlight, and the soft rush of a cool breeze. The architecture seemed to blur the boundaries between inside and outside as if the church had flung its arms wide to the world. I sat near the back of the church in an empty row and looked toward the altar and beyond to the wrought-iron bars of the monastic grille. Separated from the choir stalls where the nuns would soon assemble, I waited in silent anticipation.

The nuns filed in from doors leading to their enclosure behind the grille. The warm tones and smooth syllables of the Latin chant filled the air. As the service unfolded, I tried to follow along, flipping back and forth through the Daily Missal. I imagined the nuns would view the simple folded programs handed out in my Congregational church like the *CliffsNotes* version of this book-length guide for navigating the chants, prayers, and responses of this pre-Vatican II Latin Mass.

Once the brief sermon ended (mercifully delivered in English), there was a shift in tone. Now we were preparing for the encounter at the Communion table. "Mass" is both the word for the whole service and for that moment when we share the bread and wine of the Eucharistic meal. I have always loved taking Communion in my church, where it is a monthly event. Passing the special silver plate, breaking off a piece of bread offered by my neighbor, and sipping the wine with my whole congregation never fails to move me. It is such a tangible expression of being community—of being One Body in the theological sense. I was a little jealous that the nuns got to take Communion daily.

Now Father Andrew was facing the altar. "This is my body, broken for you." He held up a perfectly round, smooth wafer, and abruptly broke it in two with a snap. Then he took the cup. He held the wine toward the beams and trusses. I heard an echo of the words from his sermon: "Because of the Incarnation, because the Divine Word of God has become flesh it changes how you look at all flesh and the world." Mass is the central ritual enactment of Divine Presence in human form. It is a reminder of God's radical, improbable decision to join our human story, creating a profound connection between the Infinite and the finite. This stirs my imagination. Communion is an invitation to bridge the gap; to participate for a moment in a convergence between my community, myself, and the Divine.

I was completely absorbed in the pageantry and ritual power of what was unfolding. When everyone lined up and walked to the altar to receive the wafer and sip the wine, I joined right in. Never mind that I was in a Catholic Church—where "other Christians" were expressly not invited to take Communion, where taking Communion was reserved for baptized Catholics in good standing with the church. Never mind that what for me was a symbolic act of remembrance was for the faithful Catholics around me an act of *transubstantiation* when bread and wine *became* body and blood. As Mother Placid would explain it to me, "the problems of this world are far too great for us to do with anything less than the actual body and blood of Christ." None of this occurred to me as I walked forward with the others.

In fact, I didn't recognize my blunder until after Mass, when I had a one-on-one session with Mother Placid—a nun everyone called "the bartender" for her ability to get people to talk. After some softball openers she looked at me directly. "Are you Catholic?" she asked. "No," I confessed. "I knew it!" she said, slapping her knee as if she had just won a bet with her fellow nuns. She never mentioned my walk to the altar directly. I was never openly reprimanded. But we both understood my breach. I was operating from a Protestant theology of the "open table." In my church, anyone can freely choose to come to the Communion table and partake according to their own conscience. The familiarity of the ritual, my identification as a fellow Christian, the meaning of Communion for me personally had overridden my practice of trying to follow the norms and boundaries established by my host community.

I continued visiting the Abbey of Regina Laudis in Connecticut periodically over three years as part of doctoral research. I explored the ways liturgical chanting functions in this Benedictine community in contrast to the role of chanting in a Hindu context at the Sri Lakshmi Temple in Massachusetts. But never again did I walk up with the nuns to take Communion.

As a Christian, the lines between insider and outsider, participant and observer, were far clearer to me when I was visiting the Sri Lakshmi Temple. This is why I found it ironic that, the first time I went to the Sri Lakshmi Temple, the priests urged me to take and eat a portion of the *prasad*—food that has been ritually blessed as an offering to the Divine before it is returned to and shared with the people present as an act of grace. When the *prasad* was offered, I hesitated. What did it mean for me as a Christian to receive this sacred offering in a Hindu temple from a Hindu priest?

My intrafaith blunder was a reminder of the complexities that arise from the constant negotiations among religious adherents as we navigate one another's spaces and witness or participate in one another's ritual practices. Each of our traditions has obligations and expectations that are distinct. Each has theological and physical boundaries that distinguish and set it apart from other traditions. Each of us with our beliefs, practices, and obligations occupy a distinct relationship to our own and other traditions. Sometimes the lines of division are as stark between branches within a particular tradition as they are across different faiths. Sometimes the lines are faint or porous. My own sense of theological proximity to Catholicism did not automatically entitle me to join the nuns at the abbey for Communion. My sense of theological distance from Hinduism did not necessarily exclude me from accepting the *prasad* at the Sri Lakshmi Temple. This is why I could never create a simple guide to interfaith or intrafaith engagement. What makes this work rich and fascinating as well as challenging and complex is all the nuances of our relative positions as we sort through our relationships to one another and to our diverse philosophical and religious perspectives.

For the remainder of my doctoral fieldwork, I abstained from Communion when I visited the abbey and accepted the *prasad* when I visited the temple. That is, I followed my ethic of privileging the perspectives of my hosts. But I couldn't help feeling left out as I watched the nuns and their Catholic guests walk up to the altar and enact their membership in the "One Body" I also claimed. And I continued to feel slightly uneasy about what I was signifying by sharing the *prasad* at the Hindu temple. Ultimately, the gift of this work is a deeper and more nuanced understanding of both myself and others—with all of our irreducible differences and all of our undeniable similarities. I will continue to make mistakes and I expect others will too. But the learning, the connections, and the grace that can arise from reflecting on these blunders in the company of others keeps me coming back to the table.

Chapter 25

RECALLING THE BOSTON UNIVERSITY CONFUCIAN ASSOCIATION
Bittersweet Stories, Lessons Learned

BIN SONG

I grew up in a country haunted by political and familial authoritarianism. I worked for its academy for quite a while before I fled to the United States. I may be lucky in this, considering how few people in a similar situation to mine have been able to do so. Even so, the luck has left—not joy—but rather, the feeling one would have when one finally has escaped an enduring relationship of narcissistic abuse.

However, every disruption of life betokens new possibilities. The wild field of religious freedom promised by the American constitution immediately compelled me to proclaim who I shall be in this brave new world of religious diversity. During my first semester of PhD course work in religious studies at Boston University, I received an email from the university chaplain inviting me to form a student faith group focused on Ruism (Confucianism) and register it with the chaplain's office.[1] The benefits for doing so, according to the chaplain, would be abundant: our group would have a reserved space for activities, an official bank account to accept donations, and other supporting facilities. This was the starting point of the Boston University Confucian Association (BUCA)—allegedly the first campus faith organization in America dedicated to Confucianism.

BUCA was active from 2014 to 2018, the years during which I completed my PhD. Its funding came from anonymous donations, plus gifts from larger Confucian organizations based in East Asia. Its activities included weekly reading and meditation gatherings open to students and residents in the greater Boston area, a summer retreat, scholarly conferences and speeches, and so on. Indeed, during its short life, BUCA made or witnessed interreligious missteps and mistakes. Here are three.

Is Confucianism a Religion?
An Outside Perspective

Once it was registered under the office of the university chaplaincy, BUCA was automatically seen as a "religious" group, and Confucianism was therefore treated as a religion. No matter how the Ru tradition historically organized its own spiritual life, it now coexisted with other religious groups and had to succumb to all conceptual and institutional assumptions about religion in the United States. In my scholarship, I am dedicated to studying what these assumptions are and how they are formed and evolve in the Western history. The story I tell here demonstrates how, under these assumptions, the religiosity of Confucianism may be drastically misconceived.

In fall 2015, just as in each fall semester at BU, I received another email from the chaplain's office, inviting BUCA to join a "show day" for all BU religious groups. I was told that a table and a tent would be provided. It would be set up in a circle in Marsh Plaza (in front of BU's Marsh Chapel), and the members of each group could bring their own materials to promote their own religions. Never before had I done anything to "sell" Confucianism overtly in a market-like public space; but since the email was so enthusiastic, I thought I might just give it a try. I had no "materials" to bring other than a few books I used in the weekly gatherings of reading and meditation. I did have a few sheets of paper on which BUCA's schedules and logo appeared. I did not want to bother the "members" of our group. In fact, I did not keep any record of BUCA membership. Apart from sending a message to a couple of my close friends, I did nothing to inform BUCA participants of such an event. What shocked me was that all other religious groups were very organized—even to the extent of being professional—for their shows! Since BU had a very diverse student body, all sorts of religious professionals took part in this event: Catholic, Methodist, Lutheran, Baptist, Muslim, Jewish, Buddhist, to name a few. And they all brought their extremely colorful and delicate assisting materials such as banners, brochures, and statues. Some of them wore special regalia. Clearly, each of these student religious groups was backed by a huge religious organization, like a church or temple; and these groups treated this event as a yearly opportunity to passionately promote their religions to newcomers.

A couple of my Bostonian friends did visit the table of BUCA with me sitting behind it alone—by which I mean literally "alone," with barely any decoration accompanying me. Some of them laughed at me when they found I was so cool-minded in the midst of such religious fervor; but after a while, we just sat down and started to chat about our daily life.

Indeed, some students did walk up to our table and picked up a schedule and books. My friends and I cordially introduced our activities. However, apart from these sporadic encounters, my main activity throughout the day was just watching everything that was happening on the plaza, like a baffled stargazer staring at the beautiful sky over another planet.

The reason I did not keep any record of BUCA membership is that Confucius once taught that a noble-minded person (君子, *junzi*) should be "sociable without being sectarian" (*Analects* 15.22), be "broad-minded without being partisan" (*Analects* 2.14), and aim for "harmony without uniformity" (*Analects* 13.23).[2] These ancient teachings imply that originally, the purpose of Confucius, who opened the first private school of ancient China, was to promote the coflourishing of all individuals involved in varying situations while still respecting the uniqueness of each of them. This implies that the tradition Confucius helped to transmit is not meant to operate within a parochial framework in which insiders separate themselves from and compete with outsiders. Nevertheless, the constraint of "religions" into private institutions that stand alongside one another to interact in a public space is exactly what the modern principle of the separation of church and state assumes. It is also the underlying principle of the aforementioned show day.

Regarding the way to promote a tradition, the *Classic of Rites* clearly states, "It abides by ritual propriety to have someone come to learn, rather than going out to teach." In other words, the taught way of spreading Confucianism is that some noble-minded person is dedicated to learning and self-cultivation in the first place, and then, in reliance upon the felt impact of this person, students are attracted to come to learn with them as a teacher. A show booth in a market seems to be quite far away from this Confucian teaching. My loneliness during that day of promotion of campus religious organizations clearly resulted from the contrast between the traditional Ru way of life I believe in and how a religion is supposed to function in American society. Because of this mismatch, I never again participated in BU's fall "show day" for campus religious organizations. I think my readers can understand.

Is Confucianism a Religion? An Inside Perspective

The fact that Confucianism traditionally did not organize itself along the model of separation of church and state in modern America does not imply that it has no sacred dimension. Likewise, that it has a sacred dimension does not mean that, conceptually, the sacred can be separated from secular moments of everyday life. Again, in my scholarship, I am dedicated to parsing out all the intricate concepts in the last two sentences. For now, let me tell a story about how performing a sacred ritual in a Ru way can cause misunderstanding or even discomfort for its participants.

During the summer of 2016, BUCA organized a retreat open to friends nearby and from afar.[3] Besides activities such as reading, discussion, and meditation, we organized a special event of ritual performance, since most participants of the retreat cared more about what to do than what to think. In the Ru tradition, there is a system of "three sacrificial rituals," which are performed respectively to ancestors, to Confucius and other exemplary teachers, and to *Tian* (天, heaven or universe). The sacrificial ritual honoring one's ancestors takes place within one's extended family; the one honoring Confucius is conducted in a Confucian temple and is usually hosted by a school or academy; and the one honoring *Tian* can only be performed by an emperor in the imperial court. Since there is no emperor anymore, friends in BUCA decided to combine the latter two sacrificial rituals together. We put a statue of Confucius together with a beautiful traditional Chinese landscape painting that symbolizes *Tian*; and then, we held incense-sticks as we bowed to both.[4] The ritual was simple and solemn, and most of the participants felt quite content after that. However, one participant stood by during the entire session without actually performing the ritual. He came to me afterwards. Explaining that he felt uncomfortable, he said he had to leave. He never returned to the retreat, or to other BUCA activities.

This young man was a BU undergraduate student who majored in engineering. He was a White, male American. He looked quite strong. Clearly, he was a gym-goer. He had joined us in our weekly reading group for a long time. He liked to discuss Ruism with us and enjoyed the food we offered. I saw him as a friendly Ru learner until that retreat. Now, I saw that the fact that a learner of Confucianism would want to conduct a ritual to venerate their prominent teacher (Confucius) and to express their awe of ultimate reality as expressed in Ru thought (*Tian*) was clearly beyond the pale for him. The weekly groups in which he had participated regularly might have led him to misunderstand that Ruism is merely a philosophy, a way-of-life sort of philosophy, which someone can freely study and selectively practice according to their own individual taste. Yes, Ruism is this sort of philosophy; but it is also more than that. The practice of Ru philosophy includes ritual and ceremony.[5] To perform those sacrificial rituals, one clearly needs a higher level of commitment to the tradition, while anticipating a more holistic and intense degree of personal transformation via the rituals.

If I organize a similar retreat in the future, I'll make sure to explain the sacred dimensions of Ruism more carefully to all participants. I'll then let them decide whether to participate or observe ritual performances.

The Tie of Confucianism to China

Since Ruism's sacred dimension transcends culture-specific discourses and symbols, I have always tried, during my teaching of it, to explain its transcendent dimension via its original embeddedness in ancient Chinese culture on the one hand, and to decouple it from China on the other. This could engender serious misunderstanding, particularly when the activities of BUCA involved international politics. This brings me to my third story.

In the greater Boston area, many universities hosted a Confucius Institute. Since some Confucius Institute cultural activities overlapped BUCA's to a certain extent, a Confucius Institute head asked me to help them organize public lectures. I was asked to invite American scholars to give speeches on Confucianism and ancient Chinese culture. I was willing to do it as long as the lecture series could be conducted freely, without any strings attached. However, the Confucius Institute head demanded two conditions: first, invited scholars must have a positive view toward the current regime of China, and second, they must have great confidence in a bright future for China. Obviously, I had no intention to attach Confucianism to the current government of China in such an inseparable and egregious way; hence, I declined the opportunity of cooperation between the Confucius Institute and BUCA.

In fact, during the years of BUCA's activity, Confucius Institutes as a whole system had great troubles with the American higher education and government because of their potential violation of intellectual and academic freedom. The aforementioned branch of the Confucius Institute was experiencing increased need of the BUCA in order to improve its relationship with the American public and its rapport with the American academy. Therefore, in 2017–2018, BUCA finally agreed to organize several public events focused on Confucianism—with no strings attached! These well-attended and widely reported academic events were designed as workshops, each of which consisted of a speaker and a couple of commentators. All of them were professors from American universities and colleges. The themes of these lectures were global and comparative, touching Indonesian, Japanese, and American Confucianisms, as well as global higher education.

Unfortunately, it was too late for Confucius Institutes to realize that they needed to do things like this. The damage done to public relationship through their previous malpractice of academic freedom caused them to be mired in great political troubles in the United States, from which they could barely escape. For example, during one public lecture co-organized by BUCA and the Confucius Institute at Boston University, a local American religious group simultaneously showed a documentary called *In the*

Name of Confucius on the BU campus. The major motif of the film was to protest against the infiltration of Communist ideology of China into the United States via the Confucius Institutes. The head of the Confucius Institute cooperating with BUCA for that lecture was extremely worried that people protesting the documentary might intrude into the lecture and disrupt it. Fortunately, this did not happen. Even still, this Confucius Institute branch soon was closed permanently, and the head was let go.

I am happy that BUCA was able to maintain and highlight the spiritual transcendence of Confucianism over varying cultural and national expressions. I think this is the exact reason why BUCA did not get into the sorts of troubles that trapped Confucius Institutes. I can foretell, however, that any kind of Confucian organization wishing to establish itself in the United States and aiming to thrive here will have to overcome the misconception that Confucianism is inseparable from China.

BUCA's Legacy

BUCA has been taken as a case of global Confucianism to be studied carefully by sociologists of religion.[6] One of these studies analyzes whether Confucianism has been "Protestantized" in the United States, as many other migrated traditions have been. The term "Protestantization" in this study has implications with regard to the separation of church and state as the fundamental principle of religious freedom conducted and constrained in a public space, as well as many assumptions regarding religion vis-à-vis education and politics accompanying such a principle. My three stories illustrate the struggles of Confucianism within a Protestantized public space. In light of all these struggles, I am exploring how to live a Ru way of life in the United States that transcends the constraint of Protestantization without overstepping appropriate boundaries set by it. My hope is that the continually growing field of interreligious, interspiritual, and comparative studies of religions can furnish inspirations and energies for my exploration. I continue to search for the best Way (*Dao*) to fit and encourage the flourishing of the Ru way of spirituality in the United States.

Notes

1. Because of the colonialist origin of the name "Confucianism," I have been consistent to replace it with "Ruism" in my other publications. However, since the institution in question (BUCA) retains "Confucian" in its title, I employ the terms Confucianism and Ruism, Confucian and Ru, interchangeably and indistinctly in this essay.

2. English translations of quoted Confucian classics are my own.

3. Its schedule can be checked at Bin Song, "The First 'Ruist (Confucian) Friends from Afar' Retreat in North America," HuffPost, April 21, 2016.

4. See Bin Song, "Introducing a New Ruist (Confucian) Ritual: Tian-worship and Confucius-veneration," HuffPost, October 12, 2016.

5. I explain the intertwining of philosophy and ritual-performance in Ruism in Bin Song, "'Three Sacrificial Rituals' and the Practicability of Ruist (Confucian) Philosophy," *The APA Newsletter on Asian and Asian-American Philosophers and Philosophies* 17, no. 2 (April 2018): 2–5.

6. See Anna Sun, "To Be or Not to Be a Confucian: Explicit and Implicit Religious Identities in the Global Twenty-First Century," in *Annual Review of the Sociology of Religion (Volume 11): Chinese Religions Going Global*, ed. Nanlai Cao, Giuseppe Giordan, and Fenggang Yang (Leiden/Boston: Brill, 2020): 210, 225; and Lawrence A. Whitney, "Way-Making: Portability and Practice amid Protestantization in American Confucianism," *Religions* 13, no. 4 (2022): 291.

Chapter 26

Coexistence Wasn't Good Enough

Learning from Blunders in Interfaith Spaces

Jaxon Washburn

Across the rich cultural landscape of the United States, expressions of religious diversity can be found in many places, especially in domestic arrangements. With regard to interfaith marriages, the tradition with the lowest rate would be my own: Mormonism—or specifically, The Church of Jesus Christ of Latter-day Saints. Given its immense communal and theological prioritization of marriages sealed to last throughout the eternities—a ritualized arrangement between two Latter-day Saints in good standing, ratified inside our sacred temples—many members seek out and restrict marital opportunities to other members of their faith. This was certainly the case for my family. My siblings and I were raised in a standard Latter-day Saint household where both parents came from a multigenerational Mormon background. Idyllic in many respects, this dynamic was dramatically changed for all of us when, shortly after my twelfth birthday, my mother departed from the faith of her upbringing and became a nondenominational Christian. This was my earliest and most formative encounter with the concept of "interfaith."

I had always been raised in a household that respected the religious decisions of others. I recall multiple occasions when both my parents would instruct my siblings and me that, although we were Latter-day Saints, should any of us choose something different down the road, our family relationships and love for one another would remain intact. This foundational commitment was tested, of course, when my mother found new faith outside of Mormonism. My parents stayed married. My siblings and I began to be raised in an interfaith household. With no prior experience to what such a familial arrangement like this entailed, all of us mutually embarked on a new, at times tenuous, effort to support one another, even as it brought plenty of new growing pains.

My introduction into the world of interfaith was a bit of a crash course, in which all of us were required to learn on our feet, with mistakes or blunders seeming to carry potentially higher consequences. As a family, we had new questions to answer. What would this mean for our established practice of family scriptural study? How would we approach church attendance? What was appropriate to say with both parents present (as opposed to one of them in private)? The rawness of my mother's faith transition made these difficult topics to navigate at times.

My parents' early efforts to sustain our practice of reading and discussing the scriptures together as a family attempted to center our devotional readings on the Christian Bible as a place of common ground between their two faiths. However, in the act of interpretation, differences abounded to the point of frustrating both of them enough to give up their simultaneous spiritual instruction. Instead, each parent attempted to lead their own studies with us children individually. These early impressions of what "interfaith" entailed were personally associated with fragility, good intentions, yet limited success.

In this sense, it is also safe to say that my interfaith exposure both preceded and catalyzed my interest in interfaith and religious studies. As my parents gave me the option to switch off between churches week to week, I often chose to attend both on any given Sunday—an experience that provided me a close contrast between their respective modes of worship, community, and beliefs. Although my parents made sure not to place any undue pressure on my siblings and me with respect to our religious choices, this experience of simultaneously participating in two different religious communities often caused me to feel a bit stretched within my own skin. In Latter-day Saint (LDS) spaces, I was implicitly reminded of the difference of my family compared to all the other "model" Mormon families, which fully practiced and shared their faith together. Any messaging I encountered concerning people who left the faith, having doubts, or the importance of maintaining temple marriages would bring my own family circumstances to the forefront of my mind. Similarly at my mother's nondenominational church, I was met with dynamics and realities, both chosen and given, which lent themselves to making me feel othered. Where the other youth wore casual dress, like jeans and t-shirts, for worship, I attended in my Sunday best—dress shirt, tie, and slacks—as I would to a Latter-day Saint sacrament meeting. Where the other youth raised their arms, approached the stage, and swayed during musical worship of the Christian rock variety, I often remained stiff, uncomfortable, and unsure of how I was to engage in a form of worship I found spiritually unfamiliar, given the notions of reverence I was used to in LDS contexts. Socially, I quickly received the nickname of "the Mormon," also reflecting my difference among a community that understood the same to mean "not Christian."

From attending two different religious spaces, albeit two that both focused and revolved heavily around the person of Jesus Christ, one of my first lessons had to do with the differences in their shared vocabularies. Religious words I would encounter in Mormon spaces would be virtually equivalent to those I encountered at my mother's nondenominational Christian church. I quickly learned, however, that although the words themselves may be the same, their definitions differed in important ways. Through active conversation with evangelical Christians, I came to understand that these subtle or implicit differences sometimes had large theological implications. One such moment was in attending a "small-group" Bible study with other Christian youth my same age. In discussing a passage from the New Testament, I spoke of my gratitude for Christ's atoning sacrifice, accomplished in the Garden of Gethsemane and on the cross. The pastor quickly interrupted me, clarifying for the Christian youth present that the concept of the Garden holding atoning significance was unique to Mormonism, and that the "biblical" understanding was to restrict the atonement to Christ's crucifixion alone. While my own theological understanding was expanded in that moment, I couldn't stop my cheeks from flushing with embarrassment. I felt that I had unintentionally spoken in a disruptive way and had once more highlighted my own sense of difference.

Besides family dynamics, school also became a place where the realities of an interfaith life became very clear to me. I had many friends of diverse faith backgrounds. I wanted to know what they believed, how they were raised, and what their personal religious or spiritual practice looked like. Through these early interfaith experiences, I became increasingly aware of the pluralistic world around me and had a newfound thirst for understanding it. Around the lunch table, my friends and I would discuss many topics relevant to our religious lives. I was fortunate to attend a school in Arizona, where my friends included Christians and Jews, Muslims and Hindus, Buddhists and atheists, and persons of other worldview backgrounds. We grew so interested in learning more about one another that, at a certain point, we decided to take our informal lunch table conversations into a more formal and structured space. Without really knowing at all what we were doing, we collectively decided to form an interfaith student club, an undertaking in my sophomore year of high school that proved to be an incredibly formative and highly educational experience—albeit in ways I didn't always anticipate.

The earliest iteration of our club's name was "Coexist," invoking a bumper sticker we often encountered. A few weeks later, we decided, upon further reflection, that simply "coexisting" was a poor goal to aim for when it came to navigating our diverse religious identities and practices. We were looking to cultivate shared understanding, as well as feelings of respect, cooperation, affirmation, tolerance, and mutual appreciation.

This was far easier said than done for teenagers lacking any formal training in religious studies or interfaith spaces. While we had the sponsorship of a faculty member, given the sensitivities around religion in public school spaces, she merely allowed us the opportunity to use her room and projector. She herself took a quiet background role. Any conversation or instruction about religion was ours to facilitate, spearhead, and determine for ourselves. Because of this, in our search for common ground at the beginning, we often attempted to highlight shared values, beliefs, or parallels between our traditions at the expense of really acknowledging significant differences. This sentiment of harmonization had the effect of over-emphasizing perceived similarities without properly contextualizing them in history, practice, or theology. The Christian Holy Trinity was rather immediately, and clumsily, compared to the Trimurti within Hinduism. Stories of miracles and healings in various traditions were often related to the stories of Jesus of Nazareth in the New Testament. As a result, the comparisons we made—though well meaning—could be rather superficial, if not cheap. Regrettably, some non-Christian students reported feeling othered in the process. In my own efforts to lean into my newfound interfaith reality, I found myself unintentionally establishing dynamics that had caused me distress when I had been their recipient in other contexts.

I wasn't fully to blame for these blunders, of course. My friends and I had been conditioned in ways we didn't immediately recognize. Our inherited lens of analysis and understanding was very much reflective of the kind of normative Protestantism that subtly permeates so much of American public life, culture, and outlook on religion today. We tended to approach traditions as monolithic bodies of specific beliefs that individuals assented to, not the internally diverse, living and breathing, messy, and varied realities they often are. Even in our arrangement of the club's schedule of topics, our approach tended to be exceptionally Christian-centric, a bias I definitely had to learn to overcome. In our scheduling, about half the year was devoted to covering some of the variety seen within the Christian world—allotting time for Catholicism, Orthodoxy, and multiple expressions of Protestantism, as well as Mormonism. The same exploration of diversity was not granted in a comparable way to

Islam, Judaism, Hinduism, or other faiths. They were treated as singular blocks that could be adequately covered in a lesson or two. This was one of the few times where our faculty sponsor explicitly counseled us in our approach, challenging us to consider the messaging to be found in such an arrangement. Once more, I felt embarrassed to have engaged in such an oversight, but I allowed the experience to deepen my resolve to further investigate the baggage I brought to the interfaith table.

Through this "on the ground" learning experience, I became more comfortable extending grace and patience to myself and others around me as we navigated these discussions together. Our most valuable moments of learning came when, having stumbled, we opened ourselves up for correction and introspection. Like exercise does for muscles, these moments stretched and strengthened my confidence. I was becoming more adept at generously and productively engaging in interfaith spaces. However, my school had given me a safe and supportive environment in which to internalize skills, values, and methods that I could bring home. Interfaith relationships within my family quickly improved. Feelings of anxiety and fragility were replaced by confidence and trust.

I entered interfaith spaces in an effort to make sense of my family situation and to learn about other people's religions. In interfaith spaces, I found invaluable tools with broad usefulness—tools related to communication, active listening, conflict resolution, peacemaking, and reciprocity. Acquiring them necessitated practice; and practice required a willingness to make mistakes, to learn from them, and to make corrections.

Part V

POWER DYNAMICS

Chapter 27

An Iyánifá's Missteps in the Land from Where Day Dawns

The Invisibility of First Nations, the Hypervisibility of Blackness, and the Need for Interreligious Justice

M. Ajisebo McElwaine Abimbola

Ironically, the theme of the 2009 Council for a Parliament of the World's Religions, held in Australia, was "Making a World of Difference: Hearing Each Other, Healing the World." The gathering was dedicated to the role of Indigenous Knowledge as the key to solving the world's environmental crises. Yet, my very first encounter in Australia had very different sensibilities. To my utter horror, upon arrival at the point of entry to Australia, many of the items in my carry-on backpack were impounded by Customs and Immigration officials. It was devastating!

The organizers had been deliberate in their efforts to foreground Indigenous voices in response to the climate crisis. My husband, Professor Wande Abimbola, Àwíṣẹ Àgbáyé (the Voice of Ifá in the World), was a keynote speaker. He and I organized several breakout sessions on Yorùbá religion.[1] We were eager to share rituals, knowledge, and discussion, in an exploration of the deep connections among the Indigenous people of the world.

The stories of these connections are told in the sacred, oral literary corpus of Ifá. One particular verse is so fundamental that it is widely used to close ceremonies. *Obi* (kola nut) is cast to confirm that rituals were completed to the satisfaction of the Òrìṣà (divinities). To prepare the *obi* (kola nuts) for this check-in, the diviner or priest sprinkles water on the *obi* and calls on Mother Earth three times, *Ilè mọ pé o*. Those present reply in unison: *A a pe ye*, meaning, "we do not want to go there." They then hold the *obi* in the palm of their right hand, raise and stretch their right arm until it is perpendicular to the body, and chant:

Ọtún mi àbá
Ní Ìwọnràn níbi ojúmọ́ tí í mọ́ ọn wá.

When I stretch out my right hand, I call upon *Ìwọnràn*, the place from where the day dawns [Australasia], to generate wonderful ideas.

The diviner then shifts the *obi* to their left hand, lifts and stretches out their left arm, and recites:

Òsì mi àṣẹ
Lágbàáigbò Ifẹkiibíti.

When I stretch my left hand, I am praying that those wonderful propositions should come to pass all over the land of Ifẹ̀ [Africa]).

With these four lines, Ifá not only certifies that there is an important solidarity between Black and Indigenous peoples across the globe, but also that this connection is steeped in geographical and astrophysical knowledge so accurate that it could only have been acquired through travel between the easternmost point on the horizon to the farthest point in the west.

I chanted that prayer in 2009 to invoke the Ancestors and the Òrìṣà to lend their support as my spouse, our then-eight-month-old son, Iroko, and I traveled nearly ten thousand miles for the Council for a Parliament of the World's Religions. Our purpose in coming to the Parliament was to make connections with other religious leaders, to build a network of spiritual comrades, to destigmatize Indigenous Africana religious traditions, and to showcase the beautiful relationship that Yorùbá and Yorùbá-descended religious traditions have with the natural world. We wanted to share what my spouse calls "Africa's special gift to the world": the immeasurably vast Ifá literary corpus, which is a repertoire of knowledge about how to live in harmony with the earth and its inhabitants. We wanted to demonstrate that the Yorùbá religious tradition—Ifá-Òrìṣà epistemology, ontology, theology, and literature with spiritual leaders, political figures, communities, and academicians—has a rightful place among the world's major religions.

As I prepared for the journey, I had become focused on the transformational potential of the two worship-oriented sessions we would lead at the Parliament and how powerful it would be for some of our Òrìṣà to be present in the room with us. This would organically lead to an embodied learning experience for participants. People would be able to *feel-know* what it means when we say that the Òrìṣà *come to be present with us*, to *share information,* to *intervene in the Spirit World on our behalf,* to *rearrange the Cosmos in our favor.* Performing rituals rather than describing them made sense.

My husband is well known for his poignant and masterful chanting voice. I knew that when the people heard him chant Ògún's *ìjálá* songs, they would weep and weep—for the songs of Ògún the Justice-Seeker are elegies not only for the hunters, warriors, judges, archers, and snake-charmers, but also for the uncountable numbers of lives that have been lost to war. When the Àwíṣẹ chants Ifá in ritual context, there is no doubt that what we are hearing is the Voice of Ancient Africa and Time Immemorial.

As priests, we are obliged to consider the possibility that we might trigger the *Orí* (inner head) of any individual present to manifest an Ancestor or a Divinity. Therefore, we took care to prepare the sacred items we would need if that were to occur: instructions for participants, chants, incantations, water and clear alcohol, *obi* (kola nut), *orogbo* (bitter kola), and *ataare* (alligator pepper).

We were fully cognizant of the fact that we would be inviting certain (carefully selected) Òrìṣà (divinities) to function as moderators and co-presenters during our sessions. The participants' own experiences would serve as discussant, while our interreligious community would be introduced to the kind of worship that happens when we sing the songs of the Òrìṣà, feed them their favorite foods, wear their favorite colors, and, most importantly, venerate them as they exist in the earthly world, in material form. We would bring to Melbourne objects from the natural world that had been *bequeathed* by the Òrìṣà; *consecrated*; and (in some cases) *created* by knowledgeable elderly people from the Òrìṣà community of my spiritual lineage in Ọyọ Town, Nigeria.

Of course, we packed *ikin Ifá* (sacred palm nuts with visible eyes that can see all of our Selves and their relations in Spirit form through all the cycles of time). And after seeking the support of appropriate entities, the following divinities were packed with great care in our luggage:

- *Èṣù Yangí* in his meteorite form;
- *Èṣù Èlɡ́bara* in clay form;
- *Ògún* as a small, ancient iron implement and a tiny, but disproportionately heavy, iron-wielding forest stone;
- *Ṣàngó's* thunderstone (soil molded electrically into the shape of a double-headed ax when compressed into rock by a bolt of lightning);
- *Oṣun* as a brass bell and a sacred yellowish stone from the fresh, flowing waters of the great Oṣogbo River;

- *Yemọja* in the form of a glowing semi-precious stone from the Òògùn River (River of Medicine).

We included two small pieces of bone extracted from the corpse of a female elephant who had passed on peacefully and allowed her skeleton to embody Obatála—plus Olókun and his children in the form of a giant conch shell, seashells, and cowries. And, we tucked in water gourds that live symbiotically with saltwater barnacles.

Despite the support of the Parliament's organizational team on site, and their prior efforts to alert authorities that people with unusual ways would be coming to Melbourne en masse, the customs officers who greeted us when we landed in Australia refused to allow our "possibly contaminated" divinities into their country. They went so far as to insist that there might be insects inside the *ikin Ifá*. They informed us that, by law, they would have to smash one to reveal its contents!

This group of White men in uniform and in positions of authority rough-handled every single item from each piece of our luggage as if they were handling junk. They seized our kola nuts—even though they do not have seeds, and are, therefore, not forbidden agricultural items. Sadly, they held no regard for the fact that some of the contents they were throwing about were breakable, or that they should be treated with great respect and honor. As they touched our shrine implements with disdain, my very being cringed. It was a spiritual assault.

After several hours of interrogating us and ransacking our belongings, the authorities advised us to be thankful that we had not been deported immediately for violation of agricultural codes. Our hosts from the Parliament, who had been waiting for us all day long without water to drink, without a chair to sit on, and with no idea of what had happened to us, were finally permitted to escort us to our hotel—albeit without our cherished divinities. Quite literally, the immigration authorities had placed our Òrìṣà in quarantine! They told us not to worry, though, because—as a courtesy to the Parliament—they would request special permission from their supervisor to hold our divinities in their "confiscated items" area, rather than destroying them immediately in accordance with usual protocol. The best we could hope for was that we might be able to retrieve our icons on our way out of Australia—and this proved to be the case.

Since that 2009 meeting of the Council for a Parliament of the World's Religions, my husband and I have continued to visit institutions of learning and community-based sites to share Yorùbá culture, ritual, and literature with spiritual leaders, political figures, communities, and academicians in our respective capacities as Àwíṣẹ Awo ni Àgbáyé and Asojú Èsìn ati Àsà Yorùbá. We joyfully participated in the 2015 Council for a Parliament of the Religions in Salt Lake City, Utah, and the 2018 Parliament in Tkaronto (Toronto), Canada.

Our experience in Melbourne in 2009 left us with the smallest grain of understanding of the spiritual pain that was added to the extermination project undertaken against Aboriginal Australians and Torres Strait Islander peoples and the "discrimination and intolerance against earth-based Indigenous spiritual and ceremonial traditions."[2] They have suffered through religious crusades (mass murders) condoned by the Vatican through the Doctrine of Discovery, spearheaded by the church and the British State, and enforced by representatives of government. This is a manifestation of the "cultural bomb," a term so perfectly coined by Ngugi wa Thiong'o. He explains that "the oppressed and the exploited of the earth maintain their defiance: liberty from theft."[3]

During the Melbourne convening of the Parliament of the World's Religions, participants had the opportunity to hear directly from Indigenous persons about these very matters. One significant vehicle was *An Indigenous Peoples' Statement to the World Delivered at The Parliament of the World's Religions Convened at Melbourne, Australia on the Traditional Lands of the Wurundjeri People of the Kulin Nation on December 9, 2009*. It asserted: "The principles of subjugation contained in [the *Inter Caetera* papal bull of 1493 and the Doctrine of Discovery] and other such documents, and in the religious texts and documents of other religions, have been and continue to be destructive to our ways of life (religions), cultures, and the survival of our Indigenous nations and peoples."[4] The collective of Indigenous people who composed this document called for:

- immediate action on climate change "and its far-reaching impacts on our Peoples and homelands";
- protection of "significant and sacred sites within their traditional homelands and territories";
- "protection of Sacred Places used for prayer and ceremonies" where "we Minister to the earth and heal her sacred soul";
- the strengthening of cultures and languages "by bringing together elder cultural and wisdom keepers and Indigenous youth";
- the "return of the bones of our ancestors and our sacred items";
- the "immediate support and implementation of the United Nations Declaration on the Rights of Indigenous Peoples"; and for the Pope and the Vatican to "publicly acknowledge and repudiate the papal decrees that legitimized the original activities that have evolved into

the dehumanizing Doctrine of Christian Discovery and dominion in laws and politics."[5]

That document made participants in the Melbourne parliament aware that they were meeting on the land of the Wurundjeri People of the Kulin Nation, yet more was needed. While interreligious dialogue requires open communication between individuals or representative groups, *interreligious justice* demands more. It is not enough to share time, space, and knowledge, make friends, and begin to see the humanity in those whom our Eurocentric socialization taught us to regard as Other. Let us not dialogue to the exclusion of action. The state violence enacted on our Yorùbá divinities in 2009 was bloodless and short-lived. Even still, it serves as a reminder of the cultural genocide enacted upon Aboriginal and Torres Strait Islander peoples through gruesome, widespread, and long-lasting violence, as was the enslavement and colonization of African peoples.

In working toward interreligious peace and justice in the world, we must not gloss over the enduring relationship between institutionalized anti-Blackness and settler colonialism. I find myself continuously in an insider/outside role; for although I am an Òrìṣà priest and an Iyánifá, I am also a White woman whose linguistic, cultural, and immediate ancestral background is European. In this context, I have realized that, in my zeal to provide Parliament participants with an "authentic" Òrìṣà experience, I mistakenly neglected to weigh my decisions against the authorities and principalities to whom I would be accountable in a colonial state—and with the oppressive "norms" of global settler colonialism, anti-Black racism, and White supremacy.

It is time for the wonderful propositions of the Black and Indigenous peoples of the world to come to pass without the interference of the White gaze, land grab, murder, kidnapping, and the cultural bomb. Therefore, as I reflect on the 2009 Parliament of the World's Religions, I offer some guidelines for hosts of future events:

1. Black and Indigenous people must be involved at the planning and organizational level where decisions are made about who will be invited/how proposals will be solicited, what the process will be/how community protocols will be respected, how the program itself will be designed, and what will be the follow-up.
2. Encourage participants to leave their most precious, sacred artifacts at home.
3. Treat as sacred all material objects brought to the event, unless instructed otherwise. Don't touch without permission, and only ask for that permission if absolutely necessary.

4. Set the tone for a global event by finding out what will be the entry point for guests, and alerting officials on site that leaders from around the world will be passing through their transit area. Prepare a visually appealing one-page handout to distribute to authorities at points of contact and be prepared to provide cultural competency training upon request.

5. Avoid compartmentalization. Let people tell you who they are. This is especially important for folks who were not born into the lineage or tradition and who have become spiritual kin and adopted family members.

6. Do not assume homogeneity of experience. For example, although Black and Indigenous people share a racialized historical experience of oppression, land theft, enslavement, and murder, there are significant differences that must not be overlooked. It is not correct or appropriate to assume that "Black" or "Indigenous" people are a monolith.

7. Tell the truth. Let people tell their own and their ancestors' stories. Have the difficult conversations. Do not ignore history. Heal. Let yourself be fully present, and let your own self heal too.

Postscript

In all of our travels since the Parliament, we have only experienced one other instance of religious discrimination similar to that which we experienced in Melbourne, Australia. Our reentry point was the airport in Miami, Florida. We were returning to the United States from an extended stay in Nigeria, during which we had been able to assemble many more *ikin Ifá* than we are usually able to find. Similar to what we had experienced in Australia, a U.S. Customs and Immigration officer was adamant that our *ikin* should not be permitted to enter the country because "it could be contaminated." After a long and fruitless discussion, my husband and I were permitted to enter the United States and to continue our journey to our home in Georgia. Our spiritually, intellectually, ancestrally, and economically valuable *ikin* remained in federal custody.

For most people who have grown up in industrialized nations without access to nature in her most raw form, the way that *Òrìṣà* (divinities in material form) work is unfathomable. It is difficult for our brains to grant agency to an item that would go in the "not living" column of a sixth-grade science worksheet. How can something be both "not living" and a living god at the same time? So, consider this. That huge bag of *ikin Ifá* that was confiscated at the Miami airport? Somehow, when we got home to Atlanta, *it was waiting for us on top of the dresser in our bedroom.*

Notes

1. The Ọ̀ọ̀ni of Ifẹ̀, Àrólé Odùduwa, Ọ̀ọ̀nirìṣà, Aláyélúwà Ọba Okùnadé Ṣíjúwadé, Olúbùṣe II, together with a cadre of Babalawos from all over West Africa, installed Wande Abimbola as Àwíṣẹ Àgbáyé in 1981. It was not until 2013 that the Ọ̀ọ̀ni of Ifẹ̀ installed the first three Asojú Èsìn ati Àsà Yorùbá (Ambassadors of Yoruba Religion & Culture). I was honored to be one of those three.

2. From "An Indigenous Peoples' Statement to the World Delivered at the Parliament of the World's Religions Convened at Melbourne, Australia, on the Traditional Lands of the Wurundjeri People of the Kulin Nation," Melbourne, Australia, December 9, 2009, http://www.nativeweb.org/people/Indigenous-Peoples-PWR-12-10-09.pdf.

3. Ngugi wa Thiong'o, *Decolonising the Mind: The Politics of Language in African Literature* (Nairobi: East African Educational Publishers, 1986), 2.

4. "An Indigenous Peoples' Statement to the World."

5. "An Indigenous Peoples' Statement to the World."

Chapter 28

CASES OF COVERING AND UNCOVERING
At the Border of Interreligious Missteps and Racism

BILAL ANSARI

Sometimes, the line between an interreligious misstep and racism is painfully narrow, as the incidents recounted here will demonstrate. In one case, something should have been *covered*, but wasn't; in another, something was *uncovered*, as it should have been; in a third, a mistake was made in an attempt to *recover* after a hate incident.

Case 1: Covering the Stations/Uncovering Bigotry

In 1999, after two years of volunteering as a lay religious leader in urban correctional institutions, I, a newly minted prison chaplain, agreed to a paid contract. My first assignment was in a prison in rural Connecticut. I was on-boarded and welcomed by my site supervisor (a Catholic nun with a PhD from Yale) and my regional supervisor (a Protestant reverend with a DMin) who worked at a women's prison on the same compound. The director of religious and spiritual life was a Black reverend, who retired in a year. I then spent most of my decade of service (1999–2009) under the supervision of a Catholic priest.

This prison was hidden from public sight by forest, situated on state land with a wonderful lake view, only a mile from a beautiful beach on Long Island Sound. My office on the prison grounds, which I shared with a Protestant chaplain, was located inside a chapel with a white steeple. In typical Catholic fashion, the "Stations of the Cross" markers were permanent fixtures at intervals on three of its interior walls. In the minds of the officers and in the imagination of the administration, this was a Christian place. As a Muslim, I was considered an outsider. Yet, before my arrival, it had been decided that this Christian place would be used for Muslim *salat*—ritual prayer.

155

To my surprise, when my supervisor's religious community of sisters learned that I would be arriving and that Muslims would pray regularly in the chapel, they knitted covers to be hung over the Stations of the Cross. The chapel clerk or Muslim worshipers would cover the Stations just before each of our five daily prayer services, since—according to our creed and faith tradition—we cannot prostrate in a room where graven images are displayed. Afterwards, we would remove covers and store them until the next prayer-time. It was a fine routine—until the unfortunate events of September 11, 2001.

Immediately after 9/11, the warden wrote a powerful letter. At every roll call for the next six weeks, he or his major read it out loud to make clear that negative behavior toward Muslims was not going to be tolerated. This letter talked about what happened to the Japanese who had to endure being put into internment camps at the outbreak of World War II. He gave a history of how America has responded in a negative way toward other Americans in past moments like this present one. In the aftermath of that attack, the administration asked me to lead the prison community vigil, reflecting their commitment to diversity and inclusion. The warden asked me to be present—visible as his colleague—for every roll call. I continued to lead the Muslim prisoners in prayer in a chapel designed for worship in the Catholic tradition. This early administration worked actively to disabuse any ideas that I—one of the Muslims here in America—was a foreign invader, and to cut down the backlash that was known to be coming.

Before September 11, 2001, I had a good working relationship with the senior prison administrators. Most of them were transfers who made the commute from my hometown of New Haven. Most of them had spent a good portion of their careers in that city; they had lived experience and urban understanding of what diversity and inclusion really meant. After September 11, however, many of those officers were transferred to other venues. The new leadership was mostly from the local rural area. With that change, a hostile institutional culture was uncovered. Many people in that region viewed racial diversity as an urban incursion taking away their good union jobs. The prison now had an administration characterized by an "insiders versus outsiders" mindset—and I was the most marginalized outsider.

The prisons I worked in, like most in the United States, were paramilitary operations. Many of the correction officers would now be doing tours in Iraq and Afghanistan where they would be killing, in their minds, the enemies who just attacked the United States of America. At roll call and in the canteen, that attitude of "looking for the enemy among us" was thick in the atmosphere. I would be asked for my identification card, as if I was an inmate. In the minds of those corrections officers, I was a third-degree criminal, an outsider from New Haven, a Black male, and a hostile Muslim invader. Everyone knew that a backlash against Muslims was inevitable. To be Muslim was to be impugned with collective guilt. You had to prove you were not one of the terrorist attackers. In truth, I was simply attempting to take care of my growing family as a young father and union job member, like everyone else. The level of anxiety and stress was intense, due to daily fighting for equitable treatment from the state of Connecticut's industrial prison complex. It took its toll on my mental health. It felt like I was in a perpetual war. I won a few battles; but ultimately, I lost the war. The collateral damage included the dissolution of my marriage.

When the backlash came, I went from leading the community vigil after 9/11 to being called "Bin Laden" while walking across the yard toward the chapel. In response to the 9/11 attack, the more narrow-minded members of the prison administration grew increasingly hostile. Some of them resorted to subterfuge! Time after time, I would arrive to prepare the worship space for Muslim prayer, only to find that the coverings for the Stations of the Cross had been stolen and trashed. The nuns would knit a new set. I would put them to use. We Muslims would pray. We would store the Stations of the Cross coverlets. Members of the prison staff would steal and trash them. The nuns would knit a new set. Something had to give!

One of the earlier administrators (before he was transferred) had pitched a solution to my supervisor. "Let's hang the Stations of the Cross markers on hooks," he'd said. This made a lot of sense. The Muslim community could take them down easily when it was our prayer time, and we could put them back up just as easily. I thought it was an elegant and equitable solution. The supervising chaplain didn't like it one bit! It would compromise the integrity of the Christian chapel; she insisted on covers.

One morning, when I arrived to lead prayer on a *Jum'ah* day, I discovered that replacement coverings for the Stations of the Cross markers had not yet arrived. So, I gathered the Muslim community together in the main compound and led prayer there! That turned out to be a security violation. It was also an attention-getter. The prison administrators now realized that something needed to be done. Again, prison administrators themselves recommended hanging the Stations of the Cross markers on hooks, and again, the supervising chaplain immediately rejected that idea. On the day we prayed on the main compound, administrators declared that the Stations of the Cross would be nailed to the wall, but all of them would have to be placed on the chapel's back wall. The supervising chaplain was on vacation when that happened. She returned to find the integrity of the Christian chapel completely unsettled. She felt betrayed. She felt I had undermined her authority.

Shortly after the Stations of the Cross matter was settled, the supervising chaplain was abruptly transferred to another institution. She left us in a huff—and that set off a chain of retaliatory attacks on me by other members of the prison staff. They smashed pictures of my Islamic art. They surveilled my office. They tampered with my computer. They played an audio file called "Jihad or Terrorism." They suspended me for five days without pay as they investigated "suspicious material" on my computer. They placed yellow tape around my office and closed it off. They carried my computer out, covered in a red bag. Someone slashed my tires. My mother, to encourage me during this time, gave me my fourth-grade class picture to remind me how I was one of the first to desegregate my all-White elementary school. These officers went into my office and targeted this photo of me: they painted over my face with White-Out and scribbled "Nigger" above and below my head in red ink. I requested a transfer. As a chaplain, I never prayed in that chapel ever again.

In retrospect, it had always been an awkward space and place for me to be in. I was now four years into my professional chaplaincy sojourn. In those four years, my Protestant regional supervising chaplain on the same compound did not once perform a site visit nor attempt to intervene or reconcile. The one Muslim supervising adviser came out on the behest of the director (a Catholic priest) to write me up on something he claimed to have witnessed but had not actually seen. Rather, he was told by my supervising chaplain that I had allowed inmates to lead themselves in prayers. So, he wrote me up as if he witnessed it. How dare I draw a comparison between our inmate-led Muslim *salat* and the gospel choir's praise/worship service that Christian chaplains allowed inmates to lead! I, a young minister, failed to fully understand the complexity and structures of power that I was up against—the influence of the Catholic diocese as a lobby versus the marginal position of Muslims within the state of Connecticut.

I believe the failure of top leadership to create a truly interfaith environment played a key factor in the uncovering of the hostility the prison staff had against me. Supervising chaplains, Protestants, Catholics, and fellow Muslims could have come together to intervene for greater interfaith cohesion; they could have shown the second wave of administrators what it meant to be truly inclusive. Instead, there was insistence on covers, instead of support for uncovering a greater sense of interfaith community. From above and below, I was regarded as just another outsider, invading their space.

Case 2: Covering/Uncovering an Incident

In 2011, I was the new chaplain at a prestigious college. It was homecoming weekend. Many Black students were among the alums who came back for the celebration. During the festivities, a Black female resident advisor (RA) returned to her dorm, looking forward to unwinding with some of the students. When she got to her room, she was confronted by a shocking sight. Scrawled on her door, in bold black permanent marker, were the words "all niggers must die!"

Word spread fast that there had been "an incident." The institution, whose president had been in that position for only a year, was eager to cover up its stench. A predominantly White college since 1793, it had just opened a new office to oversee institutional diversity, inclusion, and equity. The administrators downplayed the severity of the incident. But, as more students became curious about what had truly happened, the less the administrators could keep quiet.

As the night progressed, a meeting was called to address the public about the occurrence. A large group of students, many of them Black, gathered in a nearby multicultural center. The college's president chose to stay home. In his place, he sent the college's new senior vice president and the dean. When they spoke to the crowd, they simply said that "something nasty was put up" and "it was nothing serious." They said it wasn't anything life threatening. They admitted that something had been written, but stressed that the college administration was refusing to "give life to those words"—and then refused to say what the words were. They appeared to be ignoring just how nasty the incident really was. The students could tell something serious was up; this explanation felt too watered down.

The more the administration denied the seriousness, the more they they offended the female Black victim in the room (the RA whose door had been desecrated). Eventually, she burst into tears. This was a turning point in the conversation, for sure. The crowd demanded to know: "If the words you refuse to repeat aren't painful, then why is she sobbing like this?" Backed against a wall, the administrators fled to an adjacent room and called the university president. They said, "Listen! We've got a crowd of students here. They want to know the details. Can we tell them? And they want you here!" The president responded, "I'm not leaving my home; but you can tell them the details." The administrators returned to the gathering place and did just that: they told the students what really happened, what really had been written on the dorm-room door that night.

A silence fell over the crowd and spread through the building. The students were in shock. As an administrator myself, as a Muslim chaplain, a Black man, I was hearing these words for the first time. Warm tears immediately flowed down my cheeks. I looked around as I tried to hold myself together. We were experiencing a collective uncovering of past trauma in this place. I imagined that the new vice president must have felt it himself. He had been a student here in the 1970s, and he wished to protect us all from the lash and impact of those words. The gathering of Black alumni, students, and staff issued a deep sob as they grieved over the impact of such harsh words. Soon they were engulfed in anger. They wanted answers! Why didn't the president think it was important to be here for this discussion? Why was this hatred downplayed? They insisted the president come and address the issue in person, but he refused. The students immediately left the multicultural center and assembled outside. They decided to take matters into their own hands.

After brief consultation with me, two female leaders of the Black Student Union settled on a plan: to march past the president's house in double file. The police department was just down the street from it. I convinced the students not to occupy the president's residence. I explained: we should occupy the police station to insist that investigation and documentation of this hate incident should begin immediately. The students organized themselves into two lines and began the walk, chanting and calling others to join them in their cause. We got the president's attention! We could see him and his family peering through a window, watching us march past their home, chanting, as we made our way to the police station.

Quickly, the protest group of fifty students turned into a crowd of more than five hundred students. Not even one of them would leave without a report being filed. This incident needed to be addressed, documented, and investigated. The two Black female leaders of the Black Student Union entered and exited the police station with raised hands, elated to have a report on file.

Meanwhile, once the crowd reached the police station, the president became willing to leave his residence. He made his way to the multicultural center. A large group of alumni and students met with him and other administrators until the early hours of the morning. After that group dispersed, its leaders met with the university president until 3:00 a.m. It was agreed a community forum would be called at 10 a.m.

At 8:00 that morning, I received a telephone call from the college president. "I need you in my office at 9:00 a.m.," he said firmly. It was eight o'clock in the morning. I'd been up most of the night. He repeated, "I need you in my office at 9:00 a.m. I need you in my office. Please be here at 9 a.m." That's it, I thought. I'm done. It has not been ninety days since I began my new job at this college—and I am about to be fired! My God, I thought, how do these racial problems follow me? I'm just four years away from all the struggle I thought I'd covered already in my prison ministry. Yet, here I am again! As a Muslim chaplain, I have to shepherd others through racial problems—this time, at an elite private institution.

There was a crisp chill in the air that November morning in New England. I remember that vividly. When I arrived at the president's office, I discovered that his conference room on the fourth floor was packed with senior administrators sitting around a long table. I paused and stared out the window at the campus chapel steeple. Then I entered the room. I quietly found a place to sit in the back. The president went around the room and asked, "Okay, what are we going to do at this forum?" He was referring to a public meeting that would happen in the afternoon. Everyone wanted to know how the college was going to respond to what had now been reported as a hate crime.

The president asked each person around the table for their opinion. Then, he turned toward me to say, "And you. I know you know what to do. You are here because I want to hear your opinion on what you think that we should do." I responded, "Sir, if I were you, I would tell everyone in this room to go with you to this forum; and I would ask everybody in this room to take pads and pens with them. I would tell them that, when they get to the forum, they should just listen and take notes. That forum is going to be emotional. It's going to be heated at times; but the students need to know that you are listening. The campus needs to know that you hear them, and that you are taking their concerns seriously. Listen attentively! You let them know that this is what we're here to do. Tell them, 'We're not here to do anything else other than to hear you and listen. And then collectively, we will come back together, and we will give a thoughtful response.'"

And after I said that, the president said, "Well, I heard what everybody has to say. And," he continued, pointing to me, "we are going to do what he says to do. We are going to this forum, and we are all going to listen." I can remember holding my breath until I got outside. Then I let out a huge exhale; and I thanked God!

I went to the community forum for the first hour. Students began to vent. When it got heated—when students started to curse and swear—I went up to the podium and I spoke: "Dear beloved students, I am Black. I am in pain. I am hurt. I'm devastated about how this all went about," I said. "But we come from a tradition of Black people who have fought for civil rights, for the human dignity of all. And our leaders have done it in a dignified way, despite the pain, despite the hurt. So, I'm asking you, in the face of this hate, that we respond with love. Don't let the hate take your heart. Do not be consumed by hate; but let us all respond with love."

I put the microphone down, I left the room and walked out, absolutely exhausted emotionally. I was walking toward the chapel, on my way to my car. The president of the college ran out, yelling my name, "Bilal! Bilal! Bilal!" I was in the middle of the street. I turned back to meet him at the corner. He said, "I just want to say, you know, thank you for that. Thank you for everything, Bilal." And he stretched out his arms and gave me a big hug. Then he ran back to the forum. I walked past the chapel to my car, and thanked God again.

Case 3: Uncovering Our Mistake

During the week that followed, the chaplains' office tried to figure out how to respond in a pastoral way in the face of such a racist attack. My colleagues—a Presbyterian minister, a Jewish cantor, and a Catholic priest—decided to take the students on a service trip. The previous April, a series of violent tornadoes wreaked havoc on a Black community in Tuscaloosa, Alabama. We could help rebuild a community in the Deep South while reflecting on our own need for recovery. Each of the new homes we were helping to construct would include a "safety room" designed to endure the storm's highest winds. We planned to work at the Habitat for Humanity site all day, then gather in the evening to process the experience theologically, spiritually, and morally. We would end with a trip to the Birmingham Museum and the 16th Street Baptist Church. We would seek to answer the question *Why are we all here?* from our own religious traditions. We would cover whatever came up from our students, so we thought. We had no idea about what would be uncovered.

In hindsight, we failed, as a team of interfaith chaplains, to build time ahead of this trip among ourselves to talk candidly and honestly about the racial implications of the project. We were all very comfortable as we boasted about our ability to make "interfaith" a very meaningful experience. We turned interfaith into a verb among ourselves. We spoke of it as "interfaith-ing." But, the role of race and faith? That we never really covered. Or, we covered it up so as not to have such difficult conversations. We occupied ourselves with making a place where all could belong and feel welcomed. We never contemplated our troubled past with our religion in America, and what our religious institutions have historically done to cause racial harm. The students on this trip brought those questions forward. Some of their questions were like strong storm winds! We counselors were not prepared as an interfaith team to address them.

We chaplains had covered our logistics planning: airplane tickets, shuttle service, restaurant reservations, faith community services, lodging, food prep and clean up, and historic location tours. What I failed to calculate was how the racial event on campus would bring up my people's racial history in the Deep South. My grandfather's brother was lynched in the Deep South. Why did I fail to plan for the images I would conjure of bodies swinging from the poplar trees? How did I not expect for someone to call me a terrorist on the Habitat job site? How could I not anticipate that, at the Habitat worksite, some White volunteers would tell me I need to work harder? I knew how smart our students were. Yet, I did not expect them to ask hard questions about the steepled church we slept in: its position on slavery, civil war, and the civil rights movement. All my interfaith colleagues were White males. I did not know whether they had worked through their fragility, whether they acknowledged and understood their privilege, or whether they understood why it was important to be an anti-racist.

As a team of chaplains, we failed to cover this in our pre-interfaith trip planning process because we were expert interfaith-ers! As a team of chaplains, we agreed on the scope of the project, but we failed to uncover and engage in those deep racial and religious conversations among ourselves beforehand. Understandably, during the trip, a lot of fragility came up. As staff, we tried to explain away the reality that the students were experiencing, often for the first time. As an advisory team, we were not really prepared to listen to the racial harm ourselves. We were there, doing interfaith service work in the Deep South. We looked at "interfaith" as an action to do, instead of looking deeply at the intersection of our identities of race, socio-economic class, instead of uncovering the historical harms. The moral injury was uncovered in the student exchange.

We visited the Birmingham Museum at the end of the service project before returning to campus. At the museum, many of the White students just wanted to rush through, then get to the meal and lake house afterwards. This upset many of the Black students. They did not like being rushed when they were experiencing their racial history heavily and needed to unpack and process that. We did not anticipate what the marginalized students would need. Each site visit checked a "tourism" box, but racial attentiveness was lost.

The painful incident on homecoming weekend had been the reason for the trip and for this week of painful discussions. It had ended with a very unsatisfying visit to a museum. We had not allowed for time to deeply uncover the meanings of that site visit, to reflect on our purpose as faith leaders, or to uncover what had been enriching. We had intended the trip to be a powerful experience. Instead, students and administrators alike returned to campus with unreconciled racial and religious questions. We ourselves were not prepared for that. We did not do the necessary work beforehand. We did a lot of logistical planning: transportation, food shopping, cooking. All of those things were covered; but "racial attentiveness" was the safety room we, the interfaith team, should have built. We covered the bodies, but not the souls.

A Last Word

In the prison, on campus, and during the interfaith community service trip, things were covered; things should have been covered, but were not; and things were uncovered, as they should have been. During an attempt to recover, a serious mistake was made. What do these stories lead you to discover about the sometimes painfully narrow line between interreligious missteps and racism?

Chapter 29

By What Authority?

A Spiritual Caregiver-in-Training and the Problem of Power

Danielle J. Buhuro

I, an ordained clergyperson of the United Church of Christ, am the ACPE certified educator/CPE supervisor at a level I trauma medical center on the north side of Chicago.[1] This is the story of an enthusiastic, passionate young seminary student in a CPE program I once supervised. I will call him Douglas. During orientation, Douglas expressed three goals: to improve his active listening skills, to gain a consistent prayer and meditation life, and to increase his pastoral confidence. While I valued all of his personal goals, an incident during his first week of visiting patients convinced me that my priority should be helping him achieve his third goal—more pastoral confidence

In Douglas's first verbatim (a detailed report on a visit with a patient) to his fellow students, he explained that he was finding it difficult to enter into a patient's room and provide the patient with pastoral care. I invited Douglas to reflect on why he felt this encounter was difficult for him. Initially, Douglas thought the encounter was difficult because the patient was on contact isolation, thus staff were required to dress in disposable protective clothing before entering the room. Douglas thought he was having a reaction to the inconvenient task of putting on a gown, mask, and gloves. After establishing trust, I invited Douglas to reflect on why entering the room of a patient on contact isolation is difficult.

During an individual supervision meeting near the beginning of the unit, Douglas informed me that he had thought intently about this difficult task. I liked Douglas's persistence in thinking about this issue. I felt drawn to him because I liked how much he stated he valued the learning process. His strong desire to learn reciprocated my strong desire to journey with him in his reflections. Our supervisory-student relationship was like a beautiful dance, where we moved about gracefully, in tune with each other. Douglas believed his inability to enter rooms of patients on contact isolation was related to his personal history. Douglas informed me that his parents had always taught him to be respectful of other people's space, resisting the urge to be intrusive. Thus, Douglas expressed an inability to walk into *any* patient's room regardless of whether the patient is on contact isolation or not. Furthermore, he found it even more grueling to enter a room if the door was closed, causing him to knock on the door first, wait for an affirmative response, then push the door open.

I invited Douglas to bring this concern before the entire group and solicit feedback from his peers. I chose this as my supervisory intervention for two reasons. First, I observed Douglas remaining quiet during group sessions. I wondered if he found trouble asserting himself in group conversations—especially when most of the others were extroverts. At the same time, I wondered if he was resisting being challenged by his peers so that he could avoid addressing his growing edges. I also wondered whether Douglas's difficulty in entering patients' rooms was experienced as a difficulty as well by other members of the group. Thus, Douglas's challenge could be a learning moment for others.

Douglas shared his struggle with his peers during a group session. His peers were supportive and empathic. Two members of the group shared Douglas's struggle. Hearing his peers share their similar struggles assured Douglas that he was not alone in his feelings. One of Douglas's peers also challenged him to reflect on what was behind his fear of entering patients' rooms. This extended unit of CPE is congregation-based. Students complete some of their program hours in their home parish. One of Douglas's peers asked him if he experienced the same scare when he worked at church. After careful reflection, Douglas responded about how his experience at church is different from his experience at the hospital. Douglas stated how much he liked doing ministry at church because his parishioners looked to him for guidance and direction.

I experienced an "aha" moment. I began to wonder if Douglas's pastoral growing edge was going into spaces establishing his pastoral authority rather than being in spaces where authority was given to him. By mid-unit, I raised my wondering with Douglas. After careful reflection, he was able to make connections about this growing edge and his personal history. Douglas spoke about being the youngest child in his family. Murray Bowen's Family Systems Theory and Birth Order Theory helped him see how much he enjoyed the privilege of an older sibling and family members taking care of him throughout his life. Douglas acknowledged how this dynamic had negatively impacted his pastoral authority: he only feels comfortable in ministerial settings where, in essence, he will be cared for, nurtured, and the automatic recipient of power. This dynamic also impeded Douglas's ability to enter group conversations. He preferred waiting for his peers to stop talking rather than interrupting them or adding his voice to join in with them.

Who's Your Daddy? Transactional Analysis, Power, Identity, and the Spiritual Care Context

This power dynamic that Douglas referenced centers on the parent-adult-child emphasis of transactional analysis. Douglas learned that, when functioning as Christian pastor, he found himself placed on a pedestal by his parishioners—where he was seen as a parent who related to the parishioners as children. On the other hand, this parental authority is nonexistent in the spiritual care and chaplaincy field. Under the surface, the element that Douglas struggled with is that the chaplain is not seen as the parent in the spiritual care encounter. Rather, the patient or client in the encounter functions as the authority, guiding the encounter while the chaplain responds to the needs and desires outlined and driven by the patient. In some sense, the chaplain must initiate proving or gaining authority because, unlike the parish minister, authority is not automatically bestowed. Another learning is that, unlike the parish ministry context where many Christian pastors function as parent to parishioners functioning as children, the chaplain and the patient both ascribe to an equal distribution of power, relating to each other as adult to adult.

The parent-child, top-down authoritative structure existent in many Christian churches is birthed from the complicated hierarchal characteristic existent in the foundation of some Christian ideology. Black liberation theology (popularized by James Cone) and womanist liberation theology (popularized by Katie Cannon, Jacqueline Grant, Delores Williams, and others) highlight an empathic, loving, nurturing and liberating side of God who is inevitably Emmanuel ("God with us") and stands on the side of the oppressed. Less progressive and more conservative, evangelical and right-wing Christian theologies promote a Christian doctrine that sees God as an authoritative, sin-punishing, heterosexual male figure concerned only with spiritual and eschatological matters. In the spiritual care context, we discover that this perspective is not held by many people who grace the doors of a health-care institution.

In a multicultural, interreligious spiritual care context—where many patients may be Muslims, Buddhists, humanists, and atheists—the evangelical conservative Christian pastor is challenged to experience a larger worldview outside of his limited perspective. These were difficult ministry learnings for Douglas to adjust to. In some sense, Douglas had to come to grips with the inappropriateness of attitudes of Christian privilege and superiority in the multireligious spiritual care context. Many Christian clergy grapple with this ministry misstep when they try their hands at chaplaincy.

Another ministry misstep that many Christian clergy must address is gaining self-awareness of how power carried or shifted in the spiritual care encounter is also based on race, gender, sexual orientation, class, and other categories. A reoccurring theme I, a Black woman, witness with many of my White, male Christian CPE students is their ease in walking in pastoral authority when they enter chaplaincy training. On the other hand, in many of my Black students—especially among those who are female, LGBTQIA+, or differently abled—I witness the opposite: many of them tend to desire to demonstrate humility and submissiveness. They struggle with walking in their pastoral authority, lowering themselves to the role of child in relationship to others. I contend that so much of our American society continues (both consciously and unconsciously) to enact the Carl Linneaus human taxonomy study, ranking White heterosexual, able-bodied Christian males at the top of a hierarchical structure while all others fall into lower categories of value, worth, and dignity. Linneaus's taxonomy informs our present-day theology, psychology, sociology, and anthropology.

My supervisory strategy entailed encouraging Douglas to make more use of the clinical method of learning. Initially, Douglas averaged visiting only about five patients per eight-hour shift that he worked. I invited Douglas to trust the process and push himself to make more patient visits during his daily shift. My thought was the more Douglas enters patients' rooms and practices being in a space where he is not immediately bestowed authority and has to work for it or share it equally with another, the more comfortable and confident he will feel. I invited Douglas to reflect on and write about specific techniques chaplains use to employ their pastoral authority when they visit patients. I also encouraged Douglas to reflect on and address how racism, sexism, and other -isms or dynamics had impacted the visit. I encouraged Douglas to speak with his peers about his progress. Again, because I value the benefit of a group learning experience, throughout the rest of the unit, I invited Douglas's peers to comment on his progress toward his goal, while I also encouraged him to challenge his peers.

A New Kind of Authority

By the end of the unit, Douglas had grown dramatically. He learned to trust himself when entering a patient's room. He learned that his pastoral authority can be established in any environment—whether it's a hospital room or church pulpit. His challenging his peers caused them to gain trust in him. He learned more than how to enter a patient's room. He learned how to initiate patient engagement. Once Douglas established his pastoral authority and, at the same time, respected the authority of the patient, he became very comfortable with visiting patients. Once Douglas became aware of his White male privilege, he began to experience a shift in his spiritual care encounters. Most pivotal and rewarding, Douglas learned that his Christian faith does not have to be at the center of the moment. The number of patient visits he now makes each day has almost tripled! Now, another growing edge has developed for Douglas: he needs to learn how to *exit* a patient's room.

Notes

1. CPE stands for "clinical pastoral education," a program of experiential learning for spiritual caregivers in training. ACPE is the administrative and accrediting organization. See http://acpe.edu.

Chapter 30

TESTING PERCEPTIONS
Interreligious Engagement with Gen Z

MAGGIE GOLDBERGER

As I slipped into the back pew, the congregation was already standing for the Gospel Acclamation. I had come straight from a long shift at a nearby abortion clinic where I volunteered on Saturdays as an abortion doula. I was usually able to squeeze in a quick meal before the 45-minute commute that got me home just in time for Saturday evening Catholic Mass. This week, however, appointments had run late. I hadn't eaten, and I had just barely made it in time to receive Communion. I tried not to dwell on the posters in the church's bathroom stalls promoting a local anti-choice crisis pregnancy center whose annual fundraiser I had protested with friends and NARAL coworkers a few weeks previously. I let my mind wander to the burritos I would enjoy with my girlfriend later that evening, before getting together with my roommates to plan our annual Passover seder. The priest began his sermon. He excitedly told the congregation that a local interfaith group he had been instrumental in starting was pushing for legislation to allow undocumented immigrants to apply for driver's licenses.

"We're meeting right here in the church tomorrow evening! We're working with a few other congregations nearby; but I would love to have a big group come out to represent our parish." The issue was close to the hearts of our parish's large immigrant population, and one that I was firmly in support of. Despite this, I knew that there was no way I would be attending the following evening's meeting. I had no problem blending into the background of a crowded Mass, but I had long wondered if there was a place for someone like me in interfaith organizations.

Multiple Religious Belonging

I grew up as part of a rapidly expanding group of young people for whom first experiences of interfaith engagement happened at home, navigating our own multigenerational interfaith families. Children of interfaith families learn at a young age how to navigate both the joys and difficulties that arise when two or more religious worlds are thrown into close contact. In my little interfaith bubble, Santa Claus and menorahs just belonged together; statues of the Virgin Mary gazed out the window of a suburban house packed with guests eating a deli spread after sitting shiva, and grandparents tried in vain to keep Jesus and Easter eggs out of Passover seders. I had attended enough O'Brien bat mitzvahs and Silverstein First Communion parties to know that many families in my community, including my own, had struck their own unique balance of what was permissible and what was beyond the pale, what foods could be eaten, and which prayers could be uttered.

My perceptions, of my own faith and others, were put to the test the first time I encountered an interfaith political organization as a teenager in my hometown. A friend and I had come across the group through a demonstration that they had staged in protest of the Iraq War in a downtown plaza close to our school. We joined in the demonstration and soon struck up a conversation with a friendly young man. He excitedly told us about a small local interfaith group that he was involved in starting up. "All our members represent different congregations and religious traditions in town," he explained; "Are you guys religious? What religion are you guys coming from?"

I hadn't expected the question. "I'm Catholic," I said, referring to the church I attended each week with my family.

"I'm Catholic, too," my friend chimed in; "we're both Catholic and we're both Jewish," she explained.

Confusion clouded his once cheery face. "How does that work?" he asked.

"What do you mean?" I asked back. It struck me then (so comfortable I was in my little interfaith family bubble) as the stupidest question I had ever heard.

"We just . . . do both," my friend added. Clearly, she too felt this was a bizarre and ridiculous line of questioning into what was, to us, the most natural thing in the world.

"But what do your parents tell you about God? How do you talk about Jesus at home?" The very idea of having such a structured conversation about the Lord over dinner obviously struck both of us as so ridiculous that we couldn't even fathom an answer. Was he right? Were our families strange or bizarre? I wondered how I or my friend could ever participate in a group like the one he was involved in; how would we identify ourselves in such a multidenominational setting; with whom would we ally ourselves, and who would we erase from our own narrative?

Political Divisions and Diversity

When I went to college, that memory stuck with me, and, although I was drawn to interfaith celebrations, like the innovative Holi-Purim celebration my college hosted each year, I was wary of explicitly interfaith organizations. They seemed to be built around a model of faith and engagement that didn't match up with my own, or with the faith experiences of most of my peers.

My relationship to my own faith was evolving as well, and I saw my friends and classmates react to the religious communities in which we had been raised with frustration, anger, despair, and alienation. I watched my friends—some with joy, others with despair—leave behind churches that did not affirm their queer and trans identities, and where they would not be able to participate openly or authentically. I watched others quit positions with campus Jewish groups and disaffiliate with community synagogues and Jewish organizations when they felt that these sites had become hostile and unwelcoming communities where their activism surrounding Palestine had them labelled as "self-hating Jews."

In the small Minnesota town where I went to college, the need for interfaith cooperation was powerfully clear. Racial and religious tensions rippled in our rural community, home to long-time White and Indigenous communities as well as recently arrived migrants from Mexico and Somalia, each bringing with them their own traditions, languages, religions, and lifeways.

As a religion major, I had begun working for an initiative of my college's religion department to research, document, and build bridges among Minnesota's diverse religious communities. Through my work with the project, I had visited churches, mosques, synagogues, temples, and sacred Indigenous lands—photographing rituals, eating delicious foods, and recording the personal stories of congregants and devotees. It was a more comfortable model of interfaith engagement for me, because my role, more often than not, was "visitor" or "recorder." My personal identity was, I told myself, irrelevant or invisible.

During my work on this project, I watched as Trump's Islamophobic campaign rhetoric transformed from racist talking points into national policy. Racial tensions and mistrust were on the rise in our sharply divided rural community. A local mosque with which we had established a partnership invited us to an interfaith *iftar* cohosted with local Christian congregations. The event was held in the mosque's gymnasium; basketball hoops were folded into the wall to make room for a dozen folding tables oriented toward a small stage. As we filed into the auditorium, the room was filled with community members of all ages, young and old, families and children. "Please write your name and what congregation you're coming from on a nametag," we were reminded, as people began to find their seats. I wrote the name of my college.

A group of young members of the mosque, all in their twenties, greeted us, and began a presentation on the history of the mosque and basic information about Islam, clarifying common misconceptions and familiarizing their largely Christian audience with the basics of Islamic belief and practice. Each presenter, all young, active members of the mosque in their early twenties, shared a bit about their relationship to Islam, and how it fit in with their American identity. Of course, their presentation didn't encapsulate the nuances or internal diversity of Islamic practice across the world, but that wasn't the goal. It was informative, easy to understand, and geared directly at the fears and concerns many White Christian community members had raised over the years. "Each of us will be joining a table for our *iftar* meal, so feel free to ask us any more questions!" one of the presenters announced.

Joining me at my table was a young woman I'll call "Joanna" (not her real name). Joanna and I began chatting, and quickly learned we had a lot in common. She was a recent graduate of a nearby university that the pro-choice group I led on campus had done a lot of organizing with. We realized quickly that we knew a few people in common, and bemoaned experiences of feeling that our activist identities were not always welcomed in our faith communities, and that our religious identities were not always welcomed in our activist communities. Among the mosque representatives that evening, she was the only convert and the only White Muslim. She shared with our curious tablemates her story of discovering Islam in college, after being raised in a nonreligious household, and making the decision to become a Muslim. She discussed the difficulties her conversion had caused in her relationship with her bewildered family, learning to deal with Islamophobia as an adult, and, ultimately, the meaning and joy she had found in her newly adopted faith. The evening, so far, was shaping up to be everything I had hoped it would be. Everyone at our table began to share their own personal stories of faith identity and belief; for a moment the event felt grounded, building a genuine and trusting encounter between individuals rather than representatives of larger faith traditions.

As our meal was wrapping up, she oriented us to the prayer service that would be starting up soon and informed us of some basic etiquette for entering the prayer hall, explaining that men and women would be asked to separate, with men praying in the front of the room and women at the back. "Don't you think that's sexist? As a woman, doesn't that upset you to have to pray in the back of the room?" an older Christian woman at our table asked her pointedly. Joanna looked visibly uncomfortable. "It's not the practice of every mosque. Some mosques I've attended in the past separate women onto the left and right sides of the room, or women have a prayer hall or balcony of their own," she explained. "But you didn't answer my questions. That still sounds unequal to me," the woman insisted. "Why would you join a religion that doesn't treat women equally?"

"In some denominations of Judaism, men and women pray separately as well," I chimed in, thinking of a recent site visit I had done to an Ortho-dox synagogue; "I've visited many synagogues where women have told me how much they actually find the gender separation to be a powerful force for building community."

Joanna smiled appreciatively. "That's an interesting way of looking at it," she added, before directing the conversation toward elements of Islamic practice that she had found particularly empowering as a woman.

I had shared the story about Jewish gender-segregation in hopes of de-escalating the situation, which I feared was undoing the progress I believed had been made in breaking down many of the harmful percep-tions of Islam that were circulating in our local community. What I had not shared with the group was that I had been so viscerally upset by being forced to participate in a recent Passover service from behind an opaque curtain, with the majority of the room and service entirely hidden from my view, that I had held back tears of rage. While I didn't doubt the women who told me they found the *mechitza* (partition) empowering, I knew that it was far from the case for many. I thought back to my conversation with Joanna at the beginning of the evening about feeling a constant push and pull between our political and religious commitments, and our desires to effect change in both. The way the event had been organized, Joanna had been expected to speak, not just for herself, but on behalf of a unified and coherent vision of Islam. Although the picture presented to Chris-tian community members of Islam might have been messier, I wondered what more we all could have gained from a conversation where all parties could truly speak for themselves, rather than having us speak as repre-sentatives of an uncomplicated image of Christianity, Islam, and Judaism in conversation.

A few weeks later, I found myself thinking again of the uncomfort-able end to our *iftar* meal as I sat in another congregation's rec room—this time a Lutheran church in St. Paul—where a group of Twin Cities Uni-tarian, mainline Protestant, and Reform Jewish clergy had organized an interfaith gathering before leading a large group to lobby on behalf of reproductive rights at the Minnesota state capitol. "A lot of people are surprised when they see that there are Christians and people of faith who support choice," a minister said to the assembled crowds; "they think we're all like the Catholics." Much of the audience laughed appreciatively, but I shrunk in my seat, feeling suddenly both unwelcome and misunderstood. It wasn't the first, or the last time, that Catholics had been the butt of jokes at pro-choice organizing meetings and interfaith gatherings I had attended. It also wasn't the first time that I had heard such broad assumptions being parroted about "which religions" should participate in certain movements—who was assumed to be an ally and who was assumed to be hostile to the cause.

It was interfaith organizing at its laziest, led entirely by clergy representing denominational bodies that were easily politically aligned with the movement, but who excluded some of St. Paul's largest religious communities, likely dubbed as "conservative" because of the official teachings of clergy and institutions. I thought of the large numbers of Catholic patients who sought care, and the Catholic health care workers who treated them at the local abortion clinic where I volunteered on the weekends. I thought of passionate Muslim organizers like Joanna who, despite Islam's comparatively strong teachings in favor of reproductive choice, were not represented because, seemingly no local imams had wanted to join a religious coalition for such a contentious political issue. I thought of the many abortion doulas I knew who practiced earth-based pagan, Afro-Caribbean, and unaffiliated spiritual healing traditions who were never given a platform in interfaith meetings on choice because their spiritual lives happened outside the walls of strictly defined "congregations." I thought too of the fearless young Jewish activists I knew whose religious faith had made them fierce advocates for choice, who had been alienated from their rabbis and congregations over their activism for Palestinian liberation and would not be invited to join in the day's events as representatives of Reform Judaism.

Transforming Interfaith Spaces for a New Generation

Much has been written on the uniqueness of Gen Z's religious character. Although sometimes characterized as America's least religious generation, members of Gen Z are not wholly disengaging with religion. Rather, they are engaging with religion and spirituality in new ways. Disaffiliation rates are high among this generation, with many leaving behind organized congregations and denominations in favor of individual spiritual practices; additionally, many are embracing dual or multiple religious identities.[1] Even among those who continue to identify with more mainstream religious and denominational groups, internal divisions over issues of gender, sexuality, and major political flashpoint issues have divided congregations in ways that are often exacerbated along generational lines.[2] While I believe that the political need for interfaith movement building is urgent, I have often wondered if there is a place for me, and other young people like me, in interfaith organizations structured around a model of faith that does not resonate with many of my peers.

As more young people begin to identify with multiple religious and spiritual traditions, as rates of disaffiliation and political conflict within religious denominations continue to rise, and as these trends continue to be most heavily concentrated among the current generation of teens and young adults, how can interfaith organizations adapt creatively to meet a new generation of spiritually driven activists and movement builders? Orienting interfaith gatherings around an understanding of diversity inherent to religious traditions, and refusing to paint large traditions with a single brush, will be a great start. However, to rise to this moment, organizations need to re-think at a fundamental level the ways that they recruit and build their membership and leadership. Many organizations have already taken concrete steps in responding to a changing religious landscape by appointing community activists and laypeople to leadership roles rather than relying on ordained clergy and by re-imagining the boundaries of what would define membership in a religious community—looking beyond traditionally defined congregations. Not only do such transformations reflect the changing religious trends of a new generation, they make room for the internal diversity of identities and experiences that has always marked American religious communities—making interfaith spaces more productive and honest sites of action and encounter for people of all ages.

Notes

1. Daniel A. Cox, "Generation Z and the Future of Faith in America," *Survey Center on American Life* (March 24, 2022), www.americansurveycenter.org; Zaina Qureshi, "Generation Z Is Remixing Religion," *Sojourners*, March 9, 2022, www.sojo.net.

2. Qureshi, "Generation Z Is Remixing Religion."

Chapter 31

LISTENING TO THE BUDDHISTS
IN OUR BACKYARD
Recentering the Marginalized, Welcoming the Unknown

CHENXING HAN AND ANDREW HOUSIAUX

Nervous and excited, we piled into the Suburban that would serve as our behemoth of a ride for the next week of temple visits and drove the twenty-five minutes to Chua Tuong Van, a Vietnamese Buddhist temple in Lowell, Massachusetts. With its yellow vinyl siding, white trim, and red roof, this building might be mistaken for a residential home, were it not for the stone lions and Quan Am statue at the entrance, the golden dharma wheel and colorful dragons adorning the rooftop, the large marble sign with marigold letters announcing the temple name and address. Dr. Tham Tran, the temple's youth group leader, greeted us with a warm smile at the front door.

"Welcome," she exclaimed, ushering us in from the cold. "You can call me Tham. Please take off your shoes here. Thank you for bringing these oranges! We can offer them to the Buddha." We followed her through the reception room to the expansive main hall. The students gasped upon seeing the elaborate altar area flanked by golden parasols and bronze bells, filled with offerings of polished fruit and vibrant flowers, and crowned by a gold-robed seated Buddha statue. The wall behind the statue was entirely covered by a painted mural: deer and rabbits grazing on lush foliage, an azure lake with gray mountains in the distance, a majestic bodhi tree towering over this nature scene. The mural extended to the lofty ceiling, which had been transformed into a summer-blue sky with cottony clouds.

"Shall we bow together?" Tham asked. She demonstrated how to make a full-body prostration, and we followed suit in respectful imitation. Tham then gathered us into a circle to lead a mindful breathing practice based on the writings of Thich Nhat Hanh. The abbot of the temple,

Thich Tham Hy, then delivered a dharma talk in Vietnamese that Tham translated. For the remainder of the morning, the two of them patiently answered our many questions.

After inviting us to sit at the long table in the reception room, Ven. Hy poured us each fragrant cups of jasmine tea. One of our students sighed with nostalgia. The tea reminded her of her grandmother's home in Japan. By this point, we had learned that Ven. Hy was Tham's uncle. Sitting before this brown-robed monk and his niece, we felt ourselves an extension of their family. The student who spoke of her Buddhist grandmother spotted a miniature Zen garden on a dresser by the dining table. Admiring the bamboo rake in the sand box, she asked, "Wow, where did you get this?" Ven. Hy didn't miss a beat. "Amazon!" Hearty laughter all around. We shared more in common than we'd thought.

Strangers made kin, in the span of a few hours. You can see it in the photos: we are beaming, delighted by these new connections.

Whose Buddhism?

So began "Listening to the Buddhists in Our Backyard" (L2BB), an immersive, experiential study of Buddhism with six high school seniors at Phillips Academy, a boarding school in Andover, Massachusetts. The project emerged as a creative partnership between the two of us, a high school religious studies teacher with a background in experiential education (Andy), and a writer, educator, and advocate for the Asian American Buddhist community (Chenxing). For all of spring term 2022—the final ten weeks of these students' secondary school education—we focused on learning about the tremendous diversity of Buddhism in the Merrimack Valley, an area north of Boston within a fifteen-mile radius of our campus. This part of Massachusetts is home to a range of Buddhist temples established by Khmer, Vietnamese, Thai, Lao, and Chinese immigrant communities.

The eight of us—six students, two teachers—grew up in multiple parts of the United States, as well as in Brazil, China, France, and Japan. We came from a diversity of faith backgrounds—Catholicism, atheism, Protestant Christianity—and varying levels of exposure to various sects of Buddhism. Over the course of the spring, we visited Khmer, Thai, Vietnamese, Lao, Chinese, and Nichiren Buddhist temples in the Merrimack Valley, as well as an insight meditation center and a Tibetan Buddhist temple in the Cambridge, Massachusetts, area. We spoke with a religiously diverse group of divinity students, many of them practicing Buddhists.

In short, L2BB was a locus for intra- and interreligious encounter. As coteachers, we conceived of this project in response to what we consider a major, widespread mistake: the teaching of Buddhism (and especially

American Buddhism) in ways that are completely divorced from living contexts.

Asian Americans make up over two-thirds of American Buddhists.[1] However, as Allison Truitt emphasizes in her recent book, *Pure Land in the Making: Vietnamese Buddhism in the US Gulf South*, pedagogically limited approaches to the study of Buddhism contribute to the ongoing erasure of these communities: "I realized [that] Vietnamese Buddhists were overlooked in multiple ways. . . . Buddhism as taught to U.S. students emphasized the ancient past, not the actual practices of contemporary Buddhist communities just a thirty-minute drive away."[2] During our visit to Lumbini Buddhist Temple in Lawrence, Massachusetts, a Vietnamese American monk recalled the one day in ninth-grade world history when his class studied Buddhism; he saw little of his own community's experience reflected in that day's lesson plan.

Too often, the story of American Buddhism is told through White protagonists: Kerouac and the Beats, Thoreau and the Transcendentalists, contemporary secular mindfulness teachers. Too often, Buddhism is located solely in textbooks, in ancient history, in Asian countries, or in doctrine and philosophy. The implication is that living Buddhism can only be accessed through a study abroad program in Asia, or that "authentic" American Buddhism can only be found in White convert meditation centers.

What message does this send to the Asian American Buddhist individuals and sanghas in our own neighborhoods? To our Jodo Shinshu students, whose temples are over a hundred years old, whose family members survived the incarceration camps of World War II? Or to our students who grew up engaging with Buddhist rituals under the guidance of relatives who immigrated from Bangladesh, Burma, Cambodia, China, Korea, India, Laos, Nepal, Sri Lanka, Taiwan, Thailand, Vietnam, and elsewhere in Asia where Buddhism is practiced? What message does this send to our students of Asian heritage raised in non-Buddhist households, who are keen to learn more about Buddhism but are confused by the erasure of Asians and Asian Americans from convert-Buddhist spaces, classroom lesson plans, and media representations?

A Pedagogy of Openness, Wonder, and Relational Accountability

In response to these questions, we made three significant pedagogical shifts when designing our program and choosing the center of gravity for our study of Buddhism: from past to present; from texts to communities; and from Asia to America. We centered the lives and experiences of our present-day Asian American Buddhist neighbors—the very people who comprise the majority of American Buddhists yet remain marginalized in mainstream media and educational institutions.

Listening to the diverse group of monastics and laypeople in the Merrimack Valley—and immersing ourselves in the social, physical, and sensory environments of the temples they've built—was foundational to our learning. Our students fully engaged the sights, smells, sounds, textures, and tastes that come with inhabiting Buddhist spaces. Just as it has been for the vast majority of the world's Buddhists across time and space, they encountered Buddhism through all their senses, in community—and not just through printed words on a page.

While a range of factors had to come together for this program to happen, we wouldn't be writing this chapter if we didn't believe that L2BB holds insights for other educational and religious contexts. It is true that L2BB came to fruition only after years of effort. It emerged from conversations between the two of us after the publication of Chenxing's first book, *Be the Refuge: Raising the Voices of Asian American Buddhists*, whose journey from first interview to publication spanned nine years.[3] Our six students were part of a larger program called "The Workshop," which Andy and other faculty spent several years advocating for and developing at their high school. Students in the Workshop were able to drop their usual five or six classes and choose from one of four interdisciplinary, collaborative, faculty-mentored learning projects. Freed from the typical high school schedule of forty-five-minute classes, our students were able to visit local temples for an entire morning, followed by a two-hour debriefing session at a local café.

Even if the precise structure of L2BB may not be replicable, the pedagogical spirit certainly is. What is possible when intra- and interfaith engagements are grounded in openness, wonder, and relational accountability? Far more than an assessment by a single authority on how well we've done, certainly. (Indeed, none of the Workshop students received grades for the spring term.) As one of our students, Olivia Yang, wrote in an article for the international online journal *Buddhistdoor Global*: "All of the wonderful people we visited were generous enough to share their wisdom and open their doors to us without asking for anything in return. . . . [M]y peers and I have been overwhelmed by a profound empathy and kindness that has redirected our academic, social, and emotional trajectories."[4]

See, Think, Wonder

In preparation for that first temple visit to Chua Tuong Van, we studied Don Farber's *Visions of Buddhist Life*. Examining this collection of photographs featuring Buddhists from around the world, we returned repeatedly to a straightforward set of questions: What do you see? What does it make you think? What do you wonder?

This thinking routine from Harvard's Project Zero (known as "See, Think, Wonder") trained us to distinguish observation from inference, to attend closely to our sensory experience without immediately grasping for semantic meaning. Each day we practiced this slow looking, spending several minutes viewing these photographs in silence before articulating what we saw, what it made us think, and what we found ourselves wondering. This lay the groundwork for us to become more thoughtful observers and students of our local Buddhist communities. Like her peers, Olivia connected this practice with Buddhist teachings on impermanence (*anicca* in the Buddhist liturgical language of Pali) and not-self (*anattā*) as she connected how "engaging with Buddhism through physical, bodied experiences has helped [her] to reimagine what it means to be a Buddhist in a world that is constantly being rewritten. . . . The acknowledgment of impermanence in all its forms—in the retelling of history, in the understanding of the self—is essential to developing the flexibility needed to build practices of kindness and understanding."[5]

See, Think, Wonder—observing with the senses, reflecting on these observations, and articulating questions that arose from our witnessing and contemplation—thus became a way to cultivate deeper compassion. When we paid attention well, when we observed slowly and took things in, we could respond to our environment with an open-hearted and broad-minded curiosity. As we prepared for our visits, the students began to develop questions about the history of the temples and about the lives of the people we were going to meet. After a few visits, they discovered that even simpler questions—"What is this?" "Who comes here?"—often led to richer answers. By relinquishing our attachment to the questions we wanted to ask, we made more room for the questions our hosts wanted to answer, for the stories they wanted to tell.

Be Comfortable Saying "I Don't Know"

As teachers who were experimenting with an adaptive and emergent curriculum, we made plenty of mistakes over the course of this project. In the very early planning stages, we imagined temple visits in Boston, not fully aware of the diversity of local communities in our own backyard of the Merrimack Valley. We planned a boatload of readings on the usual topics—the Four Noble Truths, the Eightfold Path—before replacing them with orienting texts such as Carol Stratton's *What's What in a Wat*, which would help us navigate the primarily Southeast Asian, Theravada

Buddhists spaces we would be visiting.[6] We underestimated how overwhelming it would be to visit so many Buddhist communities in the span of eight consecutive days. We questioned our skillfulness in addressing complicated interpersonal dynamics between the students, as well as moments of tension during temple visits (when an elder's views on sexuality or mental illness clashed with our own, for example).

When faced with the discomfort of working through these mistakes as best we could, we found grounding in eight words that the students had committed to the whiteboard from the get-go:

GROUP NORMZ
Be comfortable saying "I don't know"

These words guided us all spring. As the social pressure to appear smart receded and the wish to learn together grew, the students embraced this norm more and more. As teachers, we also stepped back from dispensing knowledge or providing an immediate response to student inquiries. At the end of the term, one student reflected: "The best thing you did as teachers was not answering our questions. It made us dig. It made us curious. It was the first time in my high school career that I *wanted* to work this hard—because if I didn't, I'd be letting down my fellow students, as well as the incredibly wise and compassionate people who gave us so much, without asking for anything in return."

Over the course of the project, our students' curiosity took them back to Chua Tuong Van several more times to engage with the youth programming there. In the process, they read Dr. Tran's research about identity and cultural preservation among second-generation Vietnamese youth.[7] They learned about the temple's classes on traditional dance and Vietnamese language. They respectfully bowed to the Buddha, then hugged Micky the temple cat with gleeful abandon (there's a selfie to prove it). They also noticed how the temple offered English-language services in addition to daily programming for the Vietnamese community. Their vision of Buddhism became more expansive—and more accurate—than would have been the case if they had just read texts, focused solely on Buddhist philosophy, or studied Buddhist history. They saw the Buddha's teachings as they were lived and embodied in practice: as deeply communal and interdependent in nature.

Who Is the Teacher? Who Is the Student?

After these immersive, interdependent experiences, the students sought to share their learning in ways that would engage the broader public and embody central themes and values that had emerged over the term. They designed and hosted two events: an online conference and an in-person symposium. The students crafted and led a Land and Lineage Acknowledgment, adapted from the Five Earth Touchings ceremony of the Plum Village community, which they learned about at Chua Tuong Van. They invited us to offer gratitude to the land and its ancestors; to our own religious and spiritual lineages; and to the parents, mentors, and teachers who have facilitated our learning and becoming. Recognizing the futility of trying to convey everything they learned, the students focused on three broad themes that emerged from the visits to the temples: *dāna* (generosity), youth groups, and adaptation to U.S. culture (described by one monastic as "mixing without dissolving"). To be precise, they didn't just *focus* on these three themes, but *enacted* them in wholehearted, embodied fashion.

Afterward, many attendees asked us if we had written the script, made the slides, and created the website that serves as a living archive for their work to date: ListenToLocalBuddhists.org. Not at all, we happily informed them. This was all the students' doing. We just facilitated the process and gave feedback when requested.

"I feel like a glorified lab rat!" exclaimed one of our students, who arrived at several revelations about her mother's relationship to Catholicism and her own conflicted experience of the religion over the course of L2BB. We nodded in agreement, an eight-headed anthropologist, a den of curious lab rats conducting an experiment with no clear end date. In Olivia's words:

> It's daunting, but there's also a freedom in incompleteness. I'm beginning to find that one of the most important parts of learning is in the humility of knowing nothing. I can see it now: what I know now is vast compared to where I first started just a few weeks ago. And yet, at the same time, I know that I know nothing.
>
> Buddhism embraces this humility and ceaseless diligence as a fundamental feature of life itself. The recognition of ignorance and the reconciliation of change exist in constant juxtaposition with one another. To me, the cultivation of generosity hinges on this delicate fulcrum. As I make decisions about the self and the community I want to envision, leaning *into* change will be profoundly valuable.[8]

Who is the teacher? Who is the student? Who is transformed in learning? The short answer is: *everyone*—if we recognize our fundamental interdependence, if we remember the joy and freedom of not knowing.

L2BB welcomes us into more nuanced and inclusive understandings—not just of American Buddhism but of intra- and interreligious diversity more broadly.

American Buddhism is not a country club but a vast family tree. Some branches are distant from others. Many branches have been overlooked. But all the members of this family tree share common roots. And the fruits of the tree are meant to benefit not just the family, but anyone and everyone seeking refuge and nourishment. You, too, are welcome here. We hope you'll stay awhile.

Notes

1. Pew Research Center, "Asian Americans: A Mosaic of Faiths," Washington, DC, July 19, 2012, 33.

2. Allison Truitt, *Pure Land in the Making: Vietnamese Buddhism in the US Gulf South* (Seattle: University of Washington Press, 2021), x.

3. Chenxing Han, *Be the Refuge: Raising the Voices of Asian American Buddhists* (Berkeley, CA: North Atlantic Books, 2021).

4. Olivia Yang, "Young Voices: What to Do with Impermanence," *Buddhistdoor Global* (blog) (July 1, 2022), www.buddhistdoor.net.

5. Yang, "Young Voices."

6. Carol Stratton, *What's What in a Wat: Thai Buddhist Temples: Their Purpose and Design: A Handbook* (Chiang Mai: Silkworm Books, 2010).

7. Tham Tran and Elizabeth Bifuh-Ambe, "Ethnic Identity among Second-Generation Vietnamese American Adolescents," *Journal of Ethnic and Cultural Studies* 8, no. 2 (2021): 167–86.

8. Yang, "Young Voices."

Chapter 32

Pathways for Leadership
Uplifting Women's Voices and Challenging Male Misconduct

Cassandra Lawrence and Wendy Goldberg

For Hagar, Sarah, Tamar, Dinah, Deborah, Vashti, Esther, Phoebe, Rahab, and the many women from those times through today who are left unnamed or cut out of our religious, cultural, and interfaith histories.

It is the first thread in our tapestry of connections. In August 2018, both of us—eager for a safe space to discuss how multifaith communities can cultivate a culture of inclusivity—attended a global gathering for grassroots activists and interfaith peacebuilders focused on skill building, networking, and organizing. While we didn't actually meet each other there, this conference set a series of events into motion that would bring us together over the question of whether the interfaith movement was willing to hold an interfaith leader accountable for his harassment and abuse of women in pursuit of that safe space.

Cassandra: On the last day of this gathering, a few of my friends and I were invited to a conversation with some college-aged volunteers who had been sexually harassed by one particular interfaith leader and wanted to know how to proceed.[1] In this circle, we quickly learned that the man in question, a gatekeeper in the interfaith movement, had a reputation for creating hostile work environments in interfaith spaces, especially for young women. He was well connected, but, primarily, worked independently. He had raised funds for many organizations. Unfortunately, there was no known protocol for how to proceed, so we left the conversation thinking nothing could be done. Given this man's reputation, who would believe a group of unknown young women?

A few days later, I learned that the interfaith leader in question was an ordained United Methodist pastor. As a United Methodist myself, I knew that our denomination had an accountability mechanism for clergy misconduct. In comparison, the interfaith movement didn't have a path for accountability. I was a trusted member of both the interfaith community and the United Methodist Church—the perfect platform from which to support the women directly harmed by him.

I, myself, was starting my second year of seminary. My decision to earn a master of divinity degree, in pursuit of ordination in the United Methodist Church, had been influenced by meeting religious and traditional leaders in our country and worldwide who were working together to address injustice, conflict, and poverty in collaboration with human rights-based peacebuilders. Interfaith justice and engagement are my calling. I had been working in interreligious engagement at the national, local, and international levels as an independent consultant for five years, during which I had built a diverse web of friends and colleagues I could trust as we started this accountability process.

Wendy: In 2006, I was president of the Reform Jewish congregation in Omaha, Nebraska. Our search for a parcel of land on which to build our new facility gave birth to an audacious experiment: Tri-Faith Initiative. Its mission was to bring together in permanent residency a synagogue, church, mosque, and interfaith center on a 38-acre campus in America's heartland. As a founding board member of Tri-Faith, I helped grow this unprecedented interfaith initiative for a decade. Leading communities that understand the benefits of building cultures of belonging was the opportunity of a lifetime. So, in January 2019, I eagerly joined the Tri-Faith staff.

On February 4, 2019, five weeks into my position as associate director, I received an email in the wee hours of the night from a colleague expressing concern about the health and reputation of our organization and the well-being of all women who work there. The email alleged immoral behaviors by our executive director that violated fundamental values we hold as an organization: sexual harassment, stalking, violation of restraining orders, emotional manipulation, and sexual assault. She stated:

> I am putting aside my fears to tell you my story out of concern for all the young women who do and will work for the organization and all the women who have already been victims. I express firmly that I do believe my safety and well-being are at risk in doing this. . . .
>
> This is my story, and there are dozens of others who've been sexually harassed, intimidated, and assaulted by him. A group,

including myself and four others, have filed formal complaints with the West Ohio Conference of the United Methodist Church, but the immoral behavior doesn't stop with us.[2]

Tri-Faith had a zero-tolerance policy for sexual misconduct. Therefore, the executive director was put on leave immediately; after an investigation, our relationship with this individual was severed. However, as a new interfaith leader, I was frustrated that there were no clear channels of accountability or path to addressing the related questions. How could we protect our organization? How much, if anything, should the women in our organization know about the situation?

Cassandra: That February 4 email was written by one of the women who was in the August 2018 conversation—a woman who was now working with a group to seek accountability. By the time news of our work reached Wendy, I had spoken directly with a dozen women who had been harassed, assaulted, groomed, or abused by this man. He had used his public role as clergy and an interfaith leader to manipulate and abuse women and eventually threaten them into silence.

I had learned that few women, if any, felt they could come forward. Either they were scared of him, or thought no one would believe them, or felt that interfaith work, their organization, and their funding were too important to risk angering him or his allies. (He had a reputation for cutting people off who offended him or who dared to hold him accountable.)

We didn't know whom to trust in this process. When women in interfaith organizations did come forward, those same organizations would publicly thank this man for his great work while quietly letting him go. His reputation was proving more important than the stories of these women or the hostile work environments he left in his wake.

Wendy: Nearly nine months later, on November 2, 2019, while attending a training designed for leaders committed to countering anti-Muslim discrimination in their communities, I received an alarming call from a community therapist who had heard that "someone was in Omaha investigating further allegations" about our former executive director. I told her that I was aware of another woman who was gathering names; I could share her contact information. As I looked for it, I realized that she was sitting next to me, registering people for the training.

As I approached Cassandra Lawrence, I wasn't sure whether she was the problem or the solution! Was she investigating, advocating, or both? I wasn't sure whether I could trust her, either. I wasn't sure who I could trust in the tangled mess this man had left.

Cassandra: I didn't expect to become an advocate for women in the interfaith movement. I studied religion, ethnic conflict, the Middle East, mediation, and dialogue. I had expected my career to focus on bridging our religious and cultural divides. It was through my re-education on the history of racism in our country that I started to relearn how gender, specifically White Christian womanhood, was instrumentalized to inflict violence on enslaved peoples and the religious other.

As I became involved more deeply in racial justice work, I saw how even "well-intentioned" groups and institutions knowingly and unknowingly uphold these dangerous power dynamics. So, when I realized that I, too, believed that, perhaps, nothing could be done about this man's behavior because of his position and power and because there were no accountability measures, I remembered these lessons from racial justice work. I remembered that there had been no accountability measures for Black people because the White establishment didn't consider them worthy of protection—except in their value as property. The experience of sexual harassment in interfaith spaces is not the same as the centuries of enslavement, violence, and racism inflicted on our Black siblings. Still, racial justice work provides essential lessons for looking at institutions more broadly. I understood from racial justice work just how far institutions, including religious institutions, would go to protect themselves and their power brokers.

This isn't just about White Christian men. These beliefs and relationship patterns are internalized—cultivating self-hatred and policing others within marginalized identities. It has cultivated colorism and its equivalent in interfaith spaces that exclude Indigenous, Dharmic, and interfaith/interspiritual communities. In our North American context, this cultivation is fostered by White and Christian supremacist ideologies and theologies within our interfaith spaces. Our interfaith movement—however much we think it is populated by the kindest, most open-minded, and most compassionate of society—is not immune from White Christian supremacy. Our interfaith movement is not so fragile that it shouldn't be held accountable for protecting against abuse and harassment.

White Christian supremacy cultivates a notion of biblical womanhood that denigrates women in other religious, racial, and cultural communities and only allows women to borrow power, if given any at all. Men and women are only allowed into those elite power circles if they continue to uphold the power centers that are at once unconquerable and yet fragile to any critique.

By the time I was becoming an advocate for this group of women, I had been speaking about and working on addressing racism, religious intolerance, and Christian supremacy even within our interfaith movement. This advocacy work changed me deeply. I experienced that, while I could speak politely and follow whatever rules there may have been about reporting harassment, I was largely treated with suspicion. Many others who came forward with us were treated with hostility. The newness of this experience showed me just how rarely I am treated with suspicion. I knew from racial justice work that the experience of being treated with suspicion is far too common for my Black, Brown, Indigenous, and Muslim siblings.

I felt my need to be taken seriously while continuing to be the nice Christian woman who gets along with everyone. When Wendy told me that, when she met me, she was not certain whether I was the problem or the solution, I could feel that need to be pleasant and appeasing bubble back up. There was never any doubt about the need to advocate for these women, but it put me squarely in conflict with my public reputation as a "pleasant woman."

Cassandra and Wendy: In April 2021, we participated in a virtual convening to discuss sexual harassment in interfaith spaces and to explore how to give intentional support to survivors. Some attendees had experienced sexual harassment; others had not—including some of the very leaders who need to support creating pathways to accountability. We're glad this meeting happened. Yet, one meeting doesn't change reality. Unfortunately, far too many people have stories of experiencing sexual harassment by leaders entrusted to lead. The work to name and address harassment and to create cultures of care and accountability must continue.

We have found strength—with each other and with other women who are interfaith and religious leaders—in supporting one another more intentionally while creating a community of accountability. Our circles of care and knowledge help us identify issues and fortify our solidarity while we find ways to support those hurt by sexual harassment and discrimination. We discuss the emotional and physical consequences of the trauma of these experiences and the profound impacts. We support one another as we speak up when we see wrongdoing and support all affected by these situations. Our circles of care have named missteps and mistakes of the interfaith movement, both in private and publicly. Here are some of our collective insights.

The story and events that brought us together are not unique. There are abusers among us whose names are passed along the whisper networks, warning interns, volunteers, and new staff to protect themselves. In public, some of the names of people who are abusive are treated as sacred talismans, signaling membership within an elite circle of male privilege, leading to the highest religious authorities and funding streams. Knowing these men can guarantee entry to top global meetings. These men are far too often seen as beyond accountability, because to connect the secrets whispered to the public persona is to guarantee loss of access to that cadre of relationships. In a field built on relationships, we are told we cannot risk losing or threatening one of these elite if we want to keep our professional and organizational status.

Each of us and the others we know have attended meetings where the all-male panel is seen as normal and desirable. When women are on panels, too often they are invited at the last minute and chastised for speaking equally to the men. We have attended meetings where women's contributions are categorized only within the stereotypes of virgin, mother, and deviant or designated as secretaries, caterers, and childcare workers, withdrawing our agency and dignity. We have attended meetings where women are told to cover up, to be more religious and quiet, to pray more, and speak less. Sometimes we're told the space is only for people who are ordained or hold some religious authority; yet, there seems to be an ever-growing list of excuses for exclusion of ordained women. Some people wield their positions of religious authority abusively. They harm, harass, and discriminate against the vulnerable among us. When women are Black or Brown, are Muslim, or of a Dharmic or Indigenous religion, their exclusion is even starker.

The whisper network is never fast enough nor broad enough to protect the vulnerable. It creates the impression that it is up to us as individuals to protect ourselves, because these elite men's reputations, and interfaith engagement, more broadly, are more important than our individual dignity and safety. The whisper networks are never sufficient because they rest on fighting through the shame and doubt to speak to an even closer confidant. Responsibility rests on close confidants to reach out to one another to warn others. Interfaith networks and organizations are presumed not strong enough to withstand scrutiny or accountability.

Interfaith leaders are often unaccountable to any particular agency. Clear channels of accountability are nearly nonexistent in an industry largely led by volunteers, organizations with a small staff, and a cadre of individual leaders who are selected by their religious communities, or self-appointed, to engage in interfaith work. This lack of clear channels means we don't know whom to trust when seeking support after being harmed. This isolation can be as painful as the abuse, in a space where connection and bridges are held so highly. Keeping these secrets and subverting public accountability measures with nondisclosure agreements eat away at the very foundation we seek to create in interfaith engagement.

Accountability channels and codes of conduct are only as strong as the people who know and follow them. Too often, accountability channels are hidden behind layers of shame and doubt, mixed with a deep desire by the survivor not to harm the interfaith spaces we love—a desire reinforced through implicit and explicit narratives of fragility. The silence of others tells us that our silence is the preferred response to abuse—and if we can't stay silent, we should probably leave.

Our dignity is not political. When we and countless other women—Black, Brown, Muslim, Indigenous, Dharmic, LGBTQIA+, and others—attempt conversations about experiences in interfaith spaces of gender harassment, abuse, discrimination, and racism, we are told "it's too political," that it doesn't have anything to do with interfaith engagement, or that it will damage the movement. We ask people to divide our intersectional identities leaving integral parts of ourselves outside this sacred work. We are told explicitly and implicitly that our experiences aren't important. We are inviting our faith communities to remember that justice is intimately connected with wholeness, healing, and belonging. When we pursue these ideals, we create the very pluralism we strive toward in our movement.

It is time to build transparent survivor-centered accountability and create spaces for abuse to be known, for healing, repentance, and justice to exist together finally. Shutting down conversations about sexual harassment and discrimination does not stop the abuse from happening. It simply means that we can't see our common struggle for women's leadership, equity, and dignity that already exists across religious worldviews. Accountability measures and codes of conduct are baseline measures. We must amplify our collective narratives of women's dignity and leadership. We are told that the differences in how women are able to hold leadership reflect different religious worldviews. Yet, when we start digging, we discover groups within *every* religious community supporting survivors of sexual harassment and abuse. They are working to hold accountable the leaders who committed the abuse and or covered it up.

These circles uplift each other, celebrate each other's wins, especially when they're cut from the official record, support each other in negotiating for a place at the table, and work together to bring others to every table. This network of faith-rooted survivor support and advocacy groups is leading the way for interfaith spaces to support survivors and transform our culture of discrimination and silence.

We are working to create a movement of interfaith relationships based on one another's full humanity. We are learning the names of those who were erased from public records, who were silenced, and who were loud. We are finding the history of women who built the interfaith movement, who are building the interfaith movement. We are challenging the idea that the interfaith relationships we are building should be based on access to power and funding. We are learning to build relationships based on long-ings for trust, healing, and justice. We are striving to build an interfaith community capable of integrating the full humanity of women, and thus embracing the fullness of humanity.

Notes

1. According to the U.S. Equal Employment Opportunity Commission, "Harassment can include 'sexual harassment' or unwelcome sexual advances, requests for sexual favors, and other verbal or physical harassment of a sexual nature," https://www.eeoc.gov/sexual-harassment.

2. Used with the author's permission.

Chapter 33

CURRICULAR CONUNDRUMS
Best Intentions, Diversity-Equity-Inclusion, and the Classroom

Vrajvihari Sharan

Recently, a student with a Hindu background came to me with suicidal ideation, having been inadvertently outed on social media by a classmate. Their presumption was that because Hinduism was a religion, it did not accept homosexuality. They were certain that their family would disown and defund them.[1] Complicating the matter further were things this student had learned about Hinduism through their university coursework: that their ancestors—and perhaps even their own parents—practiced religiously mandated, caste-based oppression of Dalits; that their formerly favorite festival of Holī had its origins in uncivilized orgies; and that their ancestors conformed to the usual Hindu-heathen trope of being polytheist worshipers of cows and idols. In short, this student was sitting in the office of the director for Dharmic life and Hindu spiritual advisor at a Jesuit university, wracked with shame, declaring vehemently a profound hatred of Hinduism!

The fire, in this case, had been ignited by the immature action of the student's peer. However, it had been fueled by outdated information—and, in my experience, that happens all too frequently. Approximately 40 percent of all my student care interactions as a university spiritual care provider result directly from trauma experienced in the classroom at the hands of the well-meaning instructor who is trying their best to embody their institution's latest expectations around "diversity, equity, and inclusion" (DEI). Our Catholic university is invested in improving provisions for both mental wellness and DEI; so, my colleagues are usually aware of the signs of trauma that are experienced generally by young adults. Yet, evidently, they have blind spots when it comes to recognizing transgenerational historical trauma and its correlates as experienced by students of Dharmic backgrounds in their classrooms.

I also serve as an adjunct professor in the department of theology and religion and the department of linguistics. I relish the opportunity to participate in knowledge transmission, which requires me to equip myself with the tools to carry out this task within ever-changing contexts. However, from aligning pedagogical strategies with the latest research on young-adult psychology, updating content to better reflect developments in my discipline and those that intersect it, to being aware of the current events that affect different constituents in my classroom—the task of the instructor now demands more dynamic responses to ever-increasing layers than it did even five years ago. This constant barrage of intellectual upgrades must take place no longer at surface-mail speeds; it has to outpace the immediacy of tweets and other social media.

Still, if one were to search for resources and assistance as an instructor, there are increased opportunities for professional development around these issues. I also see dozens of students per week in my other role as spiritual care provider, for reasons that members of my vocation are trained well to deal with. Yet, aside from dealing with emotional, psychological, and interpersonal well-being, spiritual care providers operating in institutions of higher education are having to face an additional area of need for which the discipline of spiritual care provision does not prepare them: managing the effects of the transgenerational transmission of historical trauma while living amidst the frameworks set up to benefit those who perpetrated the majority of said trauma. The effects of historic trauma as experienced directly by these students as descendants of the original trauma recipients are exacerbated when surrounded by the institutions and frameworks which, though popularly recognized as having harmful pasts, have not addressed their roles in the lesser known atrocities committed overseas. Though there is much to be said on this topic, here I focus on survey courses, particularly in world religions, and the effects I have seen on students today.

The Problem of the "World Religions" Paradigm

In countries with Anglophone Protestant heritage such as the United States and the United Kingdom, as well as in other European empires, the 1960s witnessed paradigm shifts on numerous fronts. Direct imperialism was on the decline, and new means of establishing political and economic strongholds in former colonies and territories were being hashed together; immigration policies were being debated and reformed, the United States and other civil rights movements were reaching their crescendo, and countries were rushing to establish themselves as superpowers, or make allies thereof. Amidst these and other profound changes came the push to reform curricula in order better to reflect the needs of the people of the day. Spearheaded by phenomenologists, the move to include "world religions" in religious studies introductory survey courses was seen as a breakthrough for underrepresented constituents. Since Ninian Smart's pioneering efforts with the Shap Working Party on World Religions in Education (1969), numerous scholars have proposed reformulations or replacement frameworks.[2] Yet, the world religions paradigm continues to dominate national curricula, with non-Christian religions and spiritual traditions presented at high-speed after a comparatively thorough grounding in (liberal Western) Christianity is given.

For better or worse, national curricula followed in foreign countries (mostly former colonies and territories) are based wholly on outdated curricula either from the colonial period or in the nascent period of independence and educational reform committees. Rather than embark on critical analysis, the pressures of the time led to various innovations to ensure that new generations of students understood the centrality of the new national identity, encoded throughout their studies. Apart from government schools, private schools in former colonies are predominantly those established in colonial times by churches and missionary societies. In South Asia, few can equal the prestige of Catholic schools.

Concurrently, a significant shift was under way in the Roman Catholic Church: the Second Vatican Council. *Nostra Aetate* (1965) declared that the church "rejects nothing that is true and holy in other religions," which is well received and promoted, but should be understood in the fuller context—namely, "[the church] regards with sincere reverence those ways of conduct and of life, those precepts and teachings which, though differing in many aspects from the ones she holds and sets forth, nonetheless often reflect a ray of that Truth which enlightens all men. Indeed, she proclaims, and ever must proclaim Christ 'the way, the truth, and the life' (John 14:6), in whom men may find the fullness of religious life, in whom God has reconciled all things to Himself." Accordingly, the already pejorative "*a ray of truth*" that is to serve as the basis of cordial relations (toleration *not* equity) must nevertheless only be those that reflect Catholic perceptions of "truth." This is of vital importance, for in former colonies around the world, Catholic institutes of higher education are most highly regarded for reasons that can be directly attributed to abundant resources, student grants, and alumni professional networks (established in the colonial era) in comparison with the comparatively new domestic schools. When Catholic schools include a "world religions" course, it is often after eight or more years of primary education in which theology entails catechisms and in-depth study of Catholic morals, ethics, and values—against which a cursory study of the world's religions will necessarily present them as comparatively deficient, exotic yet deviant traditions insofar as depth is sacrificed for breadth.

The Original Purpose of Anglophone Education
among Non-Christian Peoples

Undergirding the establishment of English education in India was the notion that it would both create a class of "native" administrators for the empire embodying Christian/post-Christian British values and bring the best of Western advancements to the sub-continent without engaging in Christian proselytization.[3] However, the same ideologues who publicly championed this apparently secular English-language education privately celebrated the conversion of "heathens" by means of an educational method that sanitized native languages of their spiritual dimensions. For spiritual traditions such as the Dharmas, which are wholly dependent upon transmission of stories and histories through the languages they were created in, this was effectively the death knell.

A case in point is highlighted by Suzanne Owen: "While the World Religions paradigm was brought in to allow the inclusion of non-Christian religions in education, it has instead remodeled them according to liberal Western Protestant Christian values emphasizing theological categories."[4] She discusses how the idea of mutually exclusive religions—which are described in frameworks of political geography and ethnicity—is prevalent in Anglophone Christian theory, and not in Dharmic traditions. For multi-Dharmic societies in South/Southeast Asia, the historic common pluralism had never involved such strict territorial boundaries; yet as more and more people graduate from educational institutions with outdated curricula, religious nationalisms deign to segregate along so-called historical, national, ethnic, and political lines, even "Hindu" and Buddhist Dharmas, for example, which have in fact interacted comparatively freely.

The Classroom of Now

The theoretical inconsistencies of the world religions paradigm are familiar throughout contemporary Western religious studies. Its worst outcome lies in "representation burden"—the oft-cited trauma that undergraduates from minority backgrounds are forced to experience daily in the classrooms of higher educational institutions here in the United States and in Anglophone institutions across the world. Some instructors continue to attempt to validate their own outdated presumptions of a spiritual tradition by singling out a representative student, simply on the basis of a student's name or ethnicity, and soliciting their views. This insufficient method traumatizes minority students by making them the objects of an inquisition in front of their peers by a person of power and privilege. Furthermore, it fails to account for the lack of traditional formation (either intellectually or spiritually) of the student in question, given that their parents likely emigrated as part of the highly skilled immigration policies enacted in the 1960s.

"Highly skilled" is a euphemism for people who sought economic betterment through an English education and performed well in disciplines that were useful in the United States (mostly science-based), which meant they would, by default, be distanced from any traditional formation at home or in their communities. If they did associate with a religion, it meant they were doing so on the terms laid out by colonial, political thinkers, which by default leaves one prone to the messaging of religious nationalists that operates within the parameters set thereby. Most minority students experience ridicule on many grounds in American schools, religion being one of the numerous traits that are targeted—along with color, physiology, language, ethnicity, nationality, immigration status, ability, gender, sexuality, presumptions of caste, and so on. However, none is so easy to denounce or change (as the case may be) as one's religion. When a student first arrives, independent of family, to their university and seeks to rise to the challenges to their community/social formation laid to them by peers, or proselytizing groups on campus, the search to find answers inevitably leads to religious studies courses.

Elective courses that could provide answers for minority students at my institution require completion of three credits in either Bible studies or an introduction to theology and religious studies course under a suitably fashionable pseudonym. Such courses are mandatory for all undergraduates regardless of major in Jesuit institutions. As pressures for DEI increase, the stock method for already stretched faculty has been to strive to be inclusive by inserting a few weeks of broadened perspectives on a given topic, if not an outright survey, nevertheless based on the world religions paradigm with few, if any, recalibrations to answer the valid issues highlighted by scholars of the field. This approach is also being adopted in history, sociology, anthropology, law, business, medicine, and all other academic disciplines, in social justice circles, and in the university administrations themselves, with even worse consequences, as they have extremely compact curricular or policy spaces to insert them, which results in colonial generalizations being mistakenly construed as affirming contemporary minority experience.

Concluding Thoughts

What became of the student I mentioned at the outset? My work consisted of first working with the student (and additional professional resources) to address their suicidal ideation, and then we moved to the foregrounded causes. As our conversations continued, I found out that they belonged to a family that embraced Śaiva Dharma—a monotheistic spiritual path; and that their particular tradition was Liṅgāyata—which is anti-caste, anti-imperialist, and features empowered women spiritual leaders who fought the patriarchy of the Mīmāṁsaka (Vedic ritualism) kingdom within which they lived nearly a millennium ago. We worked through the foreign and Indian calibrations of "Hinduism" as a British-sanitized world religion; we trundled through the gloriously disorienting Dharmas of South Asia, encountering dozens of sexual orientations and genders, and pluralist epistemologies. A chief moment came with the realization that the teachings on *kāma* (desire) from before the Common Era include descriptions of same-gender marriage. With this, the student could finally feel a sense of comfort in a few of their identities: ethnic, linguistic, spiritual, gender, and sexual. Even with the problems inherent in ancient approaches to these issues, that they exist in the depth they do at all was welcome news to this student. They finally reclaimed their Śaiva identity. Not only did that allow this student to come out to their parents; it also enabled work with their parents and the ossified presumptions they inherited through their own Anglophone educations in India.

Moreover, accessing the student's Śaiva heritage allowed them to confront a significant issue—the politicization of Hinduism. Being able to finally understand its origins, the student could see that by contrast, Śaiva traditions existed along various ethical spectra. Adherents of Balinese Āgama Śiva (before the contrived category of Balinese Hinduism was created in the 1950s) dine on pork that is blessed before God, which to a Śaiva brought up as an Indian adherent of Hinduism would be thoroughly incomprehensible. Such Hindus should be vegetarian, so says the foreign and domestic Orientalists' trope. One needs to conform, lest they forgo the ability to claim the identity in a world in which one's Hindu identity is the only Dharmic identity that is congruous in discussions of equal rights. If one is not vegetarian, one is automatically either wayward, or simply, not Hindu—and this particular student was required to defend their meat-eating stance to both "Hindus" and members of other religions and those of none. Many of the student's Hindu peers had simply opted to denounce any connection to spirituality as a result of similar pressures.

The academic reassessment and reframing of Dharmic spiritual traditions and other First Nation traditions from Asia and across the world will be a gargantuan undertaking. Not only will it challenge Western perceptions, it will necessitate the agitation of the foundations upon which national, ethnic, linguistic, cultural, and "religious" identities are built in former colonies—and that will be met with understandable resistance by

English-educated members of the present-day Dharmic societies. As well, it will necessitate the recalibration of financial systems that resource such initiatives, since most research funding now comes from foundations linked to worldviews established in the 1960s. Without such a reassessment, contemporary scholarship on "Hinduism"—in fact, on the world's religions in general—will definitely continue to achieve Orientalist goals.

Notes

1. Hinduism *is* a world religion insofar as it is a product of the World Religions categorizations. Buddha, Jaina, and Sikh Dharmas are distinct. "Hinduism" became a label for everything else. In the late 1800s and early 1900s, political and newly indoctrinated "religious" leaders produced by South Asian educational institutions took it upon themselves to define this religion (generally along the lines expected by the British theologians who would later ratify this understanding). If one were to seek a more representative understanding of the spiritual traditions of South Asia, one would encounter approximately seven hundred First Nations spiritualities. Among them are Kirat Mundhum, Saranā Dharma, and the traditions of the Kalash, Sentinelese, and so on; monotheist traditions (Śaiva, Śākta, Vaiṣṇava, Smārta); philosophical traditions that are either theist or nontheist (Yoga, Sāṅkhya, Vedānta, Nyāya, Vaiśeṣika, Pūrvamīmāṁsā). Then comes Sanātana Dharma (or, "Hinduism"), which was formalized in the 1800s and thus has the religious identity phenomena that are intelligible to all Anglophone academies. None of the historical traditions have completely impervious boundaries: some Vedānta practitioners inculcate Vaiṣṇava devotion; Śaiva adepts include many lines of Yogic adepts; Kirat Mundhum has a place for Śiva; and Kāśmīrī Śāktas fuse Sāṅkhya and Vedāntic principles.

2. The Shap Working Party on World Religions in Education—formed by Ninian Smart, Geoffrey Parrinder, and F. H. Hillard in 1969—attempted to assimilate instruction about world religions into the British national curriculum. With the best of intentions, it nevertheless interpreted non-Christian religions through a liberal, Western, Protestant lens. For more, see Suzanne Owen, "The World Religions Paradigm: Time for a Change," *Arts and Humanities in Higher Education* 10, no. 3 (July 2011): 253–68.

3. Vrajvihari Sharan, "Diversity, Decolonization, and Autochthonous Voices: Hinduism's Dilemma for Interreligious Studies," in *The Georgetown Companion to Interreligious Studies*, ed. Lucinda Mosher (Washington, DC: Georgetown University Press, 2022), 255–66.

4. Owen, "The World Religions Paradigm," 258.

Chapter 34

ANTISEMITISM AND ISRAEL
Tales from the Interreligious Dialogical Mine Field

C. DENISE YARBROUGH

The public square, including the realm of social media, is polarized and bellicose, and those of us who have dedicated our lives to building bridges across religious and cultural difference navigate particularly toxic territory, none more explosive than the Israeli/Palestinian conflict. When the topic of Israel arises among students, social media memes reign and the discourse becomes hostile. As the director of religious and spiritual life at the University of Rochester, and as an active member of interfaith organizations within the Rochester community, I live this new reality and have learned a few lessons along the way.

In early February 2022, I got a call from my Hillel director. Knowing that she was doing a workshop on antisemitism on Zoom that evening, I picked up the call with some trepidation. "How did the workshop go?" I asked. "It was a disaster. I ended it early. The SJP [Students for Justice in Palestine] sent a bunch of students who had a completely different agenda, wanting to debate issues about Israel and apartheid, and when I repeatedly told them that was not the purpose of this training, they kept on pushing. I muted them and finally had to end the workshop." My heart sank. I dreaded what was to come. Sure enough, later that evening the campus newspaper ran an article with the headline "Student Voices Silenced at a Medallion Program Workshop." The headline was changed by the next morning to "Medallion Program Ends Abruptly after Moderator–Student Conflict."[1] The Instagram accounts of the president of the student government and of the SJP club blew up with outraged posts about the aborted workshop. Jewish students took to social media in defense of the Hillel director. The Israeli/Palestine conflict was once again wreaking havoc with our mission to promote interreligious cooperation, intercultural understanding, and civil discourse.

Flashback to May of 2021, during the conflict between Israel and Gaza. The president of the Student Government had posted numerous anti-Israel memes on his Instagram account. Jewish students reported those posts to Hillel and filed numerous bias incident reports. The president of the Student Association spoke with the Bias Report Response Team, and with the Hillel director, who tried to take an "educative" approach, explaining to him why his strident posts about Israel were perceived as antisemitic speech by Jewish students. He was very clear that he felt called to be an activist for the Palestinian cause and that what he posted was protected political speech and not antisemitism. He did not moderate his social media posts over the summer and into the next academic year. He attended the workshop in February in solidarity with SJP peers, and took to social media immediately thereafter.

In the ensuing weeks, the controversy raged on. A Hillel student wrote an op-ed for the *Campus Times* entitled, "Don't You Dare Tell Me What Antisemitism Is," directed to those who took issue with the definition being offered in the workshop. In that op-ed, the student—expressing sympathy with the plight of Palestinians, while affirming his support of Israel—wrote:

> These are all of the things that leaders of liberal movements of all stripes request—that they be allowed to have the ultimate authority on prejudice against them.
>
> I don't feel that me or my people have been granted that authority. I am terrified every time someone tries to create a forum to discuss antisemitism, because I know it is a coin flip away from turning into another room full of anti-Zionists yelling that they aren't antisemitic bookended by comments that make my stomach turn.[2]

Meanwhile, SJP students and their supporters lodged complaints about the Hillel director with the dean of students and the dean of the college. They also filed formal reports through the Bias Incident Reporting system, asking that she be fired, accusing her of silencing students of color, and complaining about the Jewish student's op-ed.[3] Jewish students filed bias incident reports about the behavior of the SJP students at the workshop and their subsequent social media posts on Instagram. On February 21, the president of the SJP wrote a formal letter of complaint to the Bias Report Response Team, copying me, in which she accused the Hillel director of giving her name to an Israeli newspaper, which published an article about "Antisemitic Zoombombing" on American campuses, quoting our Hillel director with reference to the incident with her workshop.[4]

The student accused the Hillel director of putting her in danger by giving her name to the Israeli newspaper. In fact, the paper had contacted the Hillel director directly. She had talked briefly with them about the incident and had referred them to the *Campus Times* article, in which that student was quoted by name.[5]

The student reported that she feared being placed on "the Canary Blacklist of Pro-Palestine Activists," which would make it difficult for her to get employment back home. After being named in the Israeli newspaper, she quickly made all her social media accounts private and closed her LinkedIn account. Her fear was not unfounded, although the very fact that she is president of the University of Rochester branch of Students for Justice in Palestine, a national advocacy organization present on many American college campuses, could have put her in a vulnerable position long before this incident erupted.[6]

The deans and the Bias Report Response Team consulted me for input as they responded to the complaints from the workshop. I mentioned the difficult and nuanced nature of any discussion of antisemitism when criticism of Israel is involved. The definition of antisemitism that our Hillel director used is one that is widely accepted by the Jewish community. However, to define antisemitism in such a way as to include any anti-Zionist speech, or any use of the words "apartheid," "settler colonialism," or "ethnic cleansing" with reference to Israel's occupation of Palestinian territories, invites considerable opposition among people who support the Palestinian cause, including scholars and many American Jews.[7] Our Hillel director was offering this definition of antisemitism as a nonnegotiable given, at least for the purposes of that workshop, in order to educate potential allies about how the Jewish community receives and hears criticisms of Israel and to explain why the Jewish community believes such comments to be antisemitic. The SJP students wanted to debate the definition, specifically referring to an Amnesty International report that had just been released.

The intersection of race and religion/ethnicity with respect to the Israeli/Palestinian conflict is a source of considerable tension for the Jewish and African American communities in our highly polarized culture. In Rochester, we experienced this tension both in the local community and on our campus. In May 2021, Jewish citizens in the town of Brighton (a Rochester suburb) confronted a local councilwoman, who is African American and a vocal supporter of the Palestinian cause. In response to the Israel/Gaza conflict that month, she made some strong public statements supporting Palestinian rights and critical of Israel. Her Jewish constituents were strident in their criticism of her public statements, calling them antisemitic. She was again confronted by her Jewish constituents in February 2022, within weeks of the controversial workshop on antisemitism on campus, when she made public statements on a local NPR radio program in which she expressed support for Palestinians and compared the oppression they experience under Israeli occupation to oppression that African Americans have experienced in American culture for generations.[8] She, like many African Americans, perceives American Jews as enjoying White privilege. However, the Jewish community points to the rhetoric of White nationalists, who make statements like "Jews will not replace us," as evidence that they do not enjoy such privilege.

This racial tension plays out on college campuses in peculiar ways. Jewish students interested in social justice or anti-racism work find themselves unwelcome in student clubs that focus on those issues because they are presumed by many of their peers to support Israel—a "racist," "apartheid," "settler colonial state"—and, therefore, are deemed incapable of being true allies in anti-racism or social justice work. Students supporting Palestine do not accept the premise that their criticisms of Israel are antisemitic. They say they are engaging in protected political speech. The SJP students attended the workshop on antisemitism intentionally to debate a definition of antisemitism that prohibits certain criticism of Israel. With respect to racism, they perceive the Jewish community to be a privileged White community that is constructing a broad definition of antisemitism to silence "students of color" who are challenging Israel's occupation of Palestinian territories.

This controversy did not just involve students and student affairs staff at the university. Members of the university's board of trustees, along with alumni donors and some parents of Jewish students, were pressuring university officials to support the Hillel director and the message of her workshop. They were concerned about a pattern of antisemitism on campus, harking back to the student Instagram posts from May 2021 and the subsequent attempts to disrupt the February 2022 workshop. That there were powerful people weighing in on this controversy in favor of the Hillel director and the Jewish students, while the Palestinian student and her peers had no comparable community or influential advocates, concerned those of us trying to mediate the controversy. Again, the specter of White privilege arose in the face of the Palestinian students' accusations of bias against students of color, even as we understood the reality that Jews don't always benefit from that perceived privilege. We were trying to care for all our students at once, but were satisfying none of them.

Meanwhile, I was invited by an affiliated university mental health organization to offer a workshop on religious diversity for their employees. They specifically asked that this workshop address antisemitism. For that part of my presentation, I used some of the slides that my Hillel director had used in her workshop. I was clear when presenting that they were not my slides, that they offered a Jewish perspective on what constitutes antisemitism, and that there would be some Jews and scholars who would disagree with some parts of the definition.

At the time of the workshop, I received very positive feedback from the participants. I learned some seven weeks later that some person(s) who attended the workshop filed a complaint against me, alleging a violation of the university's Policy against Discrimination and Harassment, arising out of my discussion of the definition of antisemitism. The fact that I "distanced myself" from the definition suggested to the complainant(s) that I did not embrace the definition. In their eyes, that was evidence of antisemitic animus on my part.

While the complaint about me personally was dismissed, the Bias Report Response Team ultimately determined that an Alternative Resolution to the complaint against the Hillel director would be appropriate. This would entail creating opportunities on campus for "sustained and meaningful dialogues about Israel and Palestine, as well as sustained and meaningful dialogues about antisemitism." The memorandum continued:

> The Alternative Resolution will offer additional education and a community conversation on the Israeli/Palestinian conflict. Moving forward, a multi-pronged approach to addressing this subject matter will be taken into consideration. The College will be working closely with the Institutional Office of Equity and Inclusion, our colleagues across the University, and with student organizations to plan for upcoming conversations and academic talks to allow our university community opportunities to converse and engage in open dialogue.[9]

The Hillel director and I agreed that this "resolution" would not satisfy the Palestinian student and her allies. By the time the resolution was offered, the semester was well advanced. There was no time to plan an appropriate event before the end of the semester. The Palestinian student graduated this year. She will never participate in any of the proposed dialogues. On May 30, another bias incident report was submitted anonymously. The report characterized the college as "a racist place for Islamophobic, colonial White supremacists to enjoy their basic liberties at the expense of brown and black students asking for basic human rights in and outside America." The reporter indicated that they did not want to be contacted.

Learnings

What can we learn from these incidents? First, that critical interreligious encounters today are deeply intersectional. Everyone involved in this controversy came into it carrying racial, religious, ethnic, geo-political and personal baggage. Each of us responded to it from our own positions of privilege or lack thereof. The racial reckoning that is happening in this country, both with respect to the enslavement of Africans and the treatment of Indigenous peoples living on this land when it was founded and settled, intersects with the realities of the ongoing occupation of Palestinian territories by Israel. Many people struggle to balance support for Jews and Israel with support for Palestinians living under an oppressive military occupation. Those wanting to support Palestinians while honoring their relationships with the Jewish community walk a delicate tightrope, fearful of saying the wrong thing and lapsing into language that will be deemed antisemitic or, if we are too careful, appearing blind to the realities of Palestinian struggles.

Second, it is extremely difficult on a college campus to manage the volatility of this issue. American Jewish college students struggle to construct their Jewish identity, while figuring out how the State of Israel plays into that identity, if at all, and how they will articulate for themselves what it means to support Israel, even if they are critical of the occupation. They struggle with how to be Jewish in this highly polarized world in which the Israeli/Palestinian conflict frequently intrudes, creating conflicts that threaten their sense of security and safety and subject them to antisemitic rhetoric and threats. Palestinian students and their allies struggle to have their stories heard in an American culture that knows the Israeli Jewish narrative best. They also struggle to be heard when these conflicts erupt, in part because they simply do not have the influential allies and communal resources that are available to the Jewish students. They perceive themselves as experiencing the marginalization and discrimination that comes with being persons of color in America today.

Third, as an institution the university must wrestle with how it manages the considerable challenges of rising antisemitism in contemporary culture while also promoting robust and civil discourse about a controversial international conflict. The university strives to provide a safe space for Jewish students, faculty, and staff while also welcoming international students, including some from Palestine. The Palestinian students believed that the university endorsed the definition of antisemitism offered at the leadership workshop. They further believed that their voices were silenced, and their perspectives discounted.

Interreligious dialogue on our campus will not solve the intractable Israeli/Palestinian conflict. The university is a microcosm of our larger community, with controversies here paralleling those in the local community, the nation, and the world. If we are to achieve our purpose as an educational institution, we must help our students find constructive, intersectional approaches to identity in which divergent voices can be heard—and avoid canceling. They must learn to reflect and respond to one another as human beings, rather than reacting to a one-dimensional caricature of their own making. As Diana Eck so famously said, "Diversity is a given. Pluralism is an achievement."[10] At the University of Rochester, with respect to the Israeli/Palestinian conflict, we're living with diversity and striving toward pluralism.

Notes

1. Alyssa Koh, "Medallion Program Workshop Ends Abruptly after Student-Moderator Conflict," *Campus Times,* February 2, 2022. www.campustimes.org.

2. Ethan Busch, "Don't You Dare Tell Me What Antisemitism Is," *Campus Times*, February 13, 2022. www.campustimes.org.

3. What they did not know was that she is not a university employee. She is employed by the Hillel organization to serve students on the university campus. When they were informed of that, they nonetheless wanted some disciplinary action to be taken.

4. Dion J. Pierre, "University Lecture by Israeli Chemist Latest Target of Antisemitic 'Zoombombing' at Campus Events," *the algemeiner,* February 15, 2022. www.algemeiner.com.

5. Alyssa Koh, "Medallion Program."

6. For Students for Justice in Palestine's self-description, see https://www.nationalsjp.org.

7. Indeed, Amnesty International released a report in February 2022 in which it documented the ways in which Israel is an "apartheid" state. See also Chris McGreal, "When Desmond Tutu Stood Up for the Rights of Palestinians, He Could Not Be Ignored," *The Guardian,* December 30, 2021.

8. Evan Dawson, Megan Mack, and Emmarae Stein, "Discussing the Motivations Bringing Black Americans to the Palestinian Cause," on WXXI *Connections*, February 15, 2022. www.wxxi.org. One week later, the station ran a separate program devoted to antisemitism, in response to significant pushback from the local Jewish community about the program on February 15. That program aired February 22, 2022.

9. Internal letter from Bias Report Response Team to Hillel director, March 24, 2022.

10. See "What Is Pluralism," the first drop-down menu at pluralism.org.

Afterword

Mahan Mirza

Last week, I participated in a workshop with students from Pakistan on Muhammad Iqbal's *Reconstruction of Religious Thought in Islam*.[1] We met in an idyllic cottage in Virginia, about an hour from Washington, DC. When I told the participants about my past involvement in a program to advance scientific literacy for madrasa graduates, titled "madrasa discourses," they told me that they were familiar with the project.[2] They added, to my dismay, that in their circles the program had come to be known derisively as "madrasa disco."

How did this happen? We had been very careful to manage the program's image, well aware that outreach to institutions of traditional Islamic learning with U.S. dollars, led by professors at a Catholic university, would raise eyebrows. A rhetorical blow to our image came from an unexpected quarter: the inclusion of American college students in the summer and winter intensives that we organized in Nepal and Qatar. Friendships quickly developed, smiling mixed-gender selfies followed; and lo! a serious intellectual program transformed—in the eyes of would-be critics—from "discourses" to "disco."

Hindsight is 20/20. Perhaps a strict social media policy, clearly spelled out and explained in advance, might have helped to keep the conversation focused on substance rather than style. Live and learn. That is precisely why reflection on both successes and failures is so important: so that we can learn from our mistakes and do better next time. The natural sciences know this lesson well. As an undergraduate student in mechanical engineering, I worked as a research assistant in a materials science lab. Every experiment in that lab advanced science, regardless of whether a hypothesis was confirmed or not. Failed results in science provide valuable data points for roads not to be traveled.

If failure is success in science, why not so in the humanities? Perhaps we should learn to value our mistakes as much as we value our successes. This volume opens up an important conversation in this direction. The stories here offer a rich library of case studies in what went wrong. The lessons are invaluable. Even when things don't go perfectly well, we must

207

remember that all is not lost. Our experiences are lampposts, lighting the way for future experiences and future generations. We might recall George Santayana's famous line, "Those who cannot remember the past are condemned to repeat it."

Our experience in "madrasa discourses," as maligned as it might be in some circles, has been transformative for its core participants. Our very first guest instructor in the inaugural summer intensive commented that it was the most meaningful teaching experience of his career.[3] And just today, I received an email from another student in Pakistan seeking to join the program. There are always going to be sincere souls who look deeper, who not only act out of the goodness of their hearts, but also attribute to others the best of intentions.

As we take this opportunity to reflect on the many missteps along the journey, let us rejoice in the courage to act, ponder the wisdom that accompanies nonaction, forgive others for their trespasses, forgive ourselves for our follies, commit to doing better next time, and embrace the blessing of second chances, knowing well that if we choose to walk, we will slip again, and that is just how things should be.

Notes

1. Muhammad Iqbal, *The Reconstruction of Religious Thought in Islam* (Palo Alto, CA: Stanford University Press, 2013).

2. Mahan Mirza, "Scientific Literacy for Madrasa Graduates: A Project for Religious Renewal at the University of Notre Dame," in *The Maydan*, September 18, 2018.

3. Mahan Mirza, "Deed over Idea: Toward a Shared Caliphate," in *The Routledge Handbook of Religious Literacy, Pluralism, and Global Engagement* (London: Routledge, 2021), 83.

Editors and Contributors

Editors

Lucinda Mosher, ThD, is director of the Master of Arts in Interreligious Studies program at Hartford International University for Religion and Peace, senior editor of the *Journal of Interreligious Studies*, rapporteur of the Building Bridges Seminar, and secretary of the Episcopal Church's Standing Commission on Ecumenical and Interreligious Relations. She is the author or editor of more than twenty books, including *The Georgetown Companion to Interreligious Studies* (2022).

Elinor J. Pierce, MTS, is research director at The Pluralism Project at Harvard University. She is also a consultant and independent filmmaker, whose most recent documentary—about the Tri-Faith Initiative in Omaha, Nebraska—is currently in production. She is the author of *Pluralism in Practice* (Orbis Books, 2023).

Rabbi Or N. Rose is the founding director of the Betty Ann Greenbaum Miller Center for Interreligious Learning & Leadership of Hebrew College. A publisher of the *Journal of Interreligious Studies* and a prolific author and editor of scholarly and popular works in the fields of Jewish spirituality and interreligious studies, his recent works include the coedited volumes *Words to Live By: Sacred Sources for Interreligious Engagement* (2018) and *Rabbi Zalman Schachter-Shalomi: Essential Teachings* (2020).

Contributors

M. Ajisebo McElwaine Abimbola, a practicing priest of Ifá-Olókun, Ògún, and Ẹgbẹ-Ogba, is a co-founder of Ifá Heritage Institute in Ọyọ, Nigeria. She is a PhD candidate in curriculum and instruction at Boston College, and a teaching fellow in its African and African diaspora studies department.

Bilal Ansari, DMin, is Assistant Vice President for Campus Engagement at Williams College; concurrently, he is associate professor of Practice and co-director of the Master of Arts in Chaplaincy program at Hartford International University for Religion and Peace.

Preeta Banerjee, PhD, is the Hindu chaplain at Tufts University.

Rabbi Daniel Berman, JD, has served Temple Reyim in Newton, Massachusetts, since 2013.

Rev. Danielle J. Buhuro, DMin, a United Church of Christ clergyperson, is executive director and lead CPE supervisor of Sankofa CPE Center, LLC.

Rev. Francis X. Clooney, SJ, PhD, is Parkman Professor of Divinity and professor of Comparative Theology at Harvard Divinity School and president of Catholic Theological Society of America. His books include *Learning Interreligiously in the Text, in the World* (2018).

Lexi Gewertz, MTS, is chief operating officer at Re-Imagining Migration in Boston, Massachusetts.

Wendy Goldberg, MA, is a founding board member and the executive director of the Tri-Faith Initiative in Omaha, Nebraska.

Maggie Goldberger, MTS, a recent graduate of Harvard Divinity School, is a former research associate for The Pluralism Project at Harvard University and a current doctoral student in religions of the Americas at the University of Chicago.

Jack Gordon is a documentary filmmaker and host of the radio show/podcast series *Interfaith-ish,* in Takoma Park, Maryland.

Rev. David D. Grafton, PhD, a Lutheran pastor, is professor of Islamic studies and Christian-Muslim relations at Hartford International University for Religion and Peace. He is the author of *More Than a Cup of Tea: A Generation of Lutheran-Muslim Relationships* (2019).

Hans Gustafson, PhD, is director of the Jay Phillips Center for Interreligious Studies in the College of Arts and Sciences at the University of St. Thomas in St. Paul, Minnesota, and author of *Everyday Wisdom: Interreligious Studies in a Pluralistic World* (2023).

Chenxing Han, MA, is the author of *Be the Refuge: Raising the Voices of Asian America Buddhists* (2021) and *one long listening: a memoir of grief, friendship, and spiritual care* (2023).

REV. SOREN M. HESSLER, PhD, a United Methodist clergyperson, is director of recruitment and admissions at Vanderbilt Divinity School and a member of the *Journal of Interreligious Studies* advisory board.

REV. WAKOH SHANNON HICKEY, PhD, a Sōtō Zen priest, is a board-certified hospice chaplain in Napa, California, and author of *Mind Cure: How Meditation Became Medicine* (2019).

ANDREW HOUSIAUX, MTS, is the Currie Family Director of the Tang Institute at Phillips Academy Andover, where he also teaches philosophy and religious studies and is co-teacher of *Listening to the Buddhists in Our Backyard*.

RABBI NANCY FUCHS KREIMER, PhD, associate professor emeritus of religious studies at the Reconstructionist Rabbinical College, was the founding director of its department of multifaith studies and initiatives.

YEHEZKEL LANDAU, DMIN, is an educator, leadership trainer, author, and consultant working to improve Jewish-Christian-Muslim relations and promote Israeli-Palestinian peacebuilding.

REV. CASSANDRA LAWRENCE, MDIV, is a provisional deacon in the United Methodist Church, working on issues of interfaith and racial justice.

REV. CHRISTOPHER M. LEIGHTON, EDD, a Presbyterian clergyperson, now retired, was founding executive director at The Institute for Islamic, Christian, Jewish Studies, Towson, Maryland.

KATHRYN MARY LOHRE, MDIV, is the executive for ecumenical and interreligious relations & theological discernment in the Evangelical Lutheran Church in America office of the presiding bishop and former co-chair of the "Shoulder to Shoulder Campaign: Standing with American Muslims, Advancing American Values."

JEFFERY D. LONG, PhD, is the Carl W. Zeigler Professor of Religion, Philosophy, and Asian Studies at Elizabethtown College. He is the author of *Hinduism in America: A Convergence of Worlds* (2020).

CHAPLAIN AIDA MANSOOR, MS, MARS, is the director of field education at Hartford International University for Religion and Peace.

Rabbi Rachel S. Mikva, PhD, serves as the Herman E. Schaalman Chair in Jewish Studies and senior faculty fellow of the InterReligious Institute at Chicago Theological Seminary.

Mahan Mirza, PhD, is executive director of the Ansari Institute for Global Engagement with Religion, at the University of Notre Dame (Indiana), where he is also a teaching professor of Islam and science at its Keough School of Global Affairs.

Nisa Muhammad, DMin, is assistant dean for religious life at Howard University, where she is advisor to Youth Justice Advocates, the Muslim Students Association, and the Chess Club.

Anthony Cruz Pantojas, MATS, MALS, and PhD candidate in cultural studies at Universidad Ana G. Méndez-Gurabo, is the Humanist chaplain at Tufts University and a graduate student in anti-racist curatorial studies whose writing has appeared in numerous public and scholarly outlets, including *The Journal of Contemplative Inquiry* and *The Journal of Interreligious Studies.*

Eboo Patel, PhD, is founder and president of Interfaith America and author of several books on interfaith leadership. An Ashoka Fellow, he served on President Obama's inaugural Faith Council.

Jennifer Howe Peace, PhD, is a senior researcher at Jonathan M. Tisch College of Civic Life at Tufts University and a senior advisor to The Pluralism Project at Harvard University. She is a co-editor of *Interreligious/Interfaith Studies: Defining a New Field* (2018).

Hussein Rashid, PhD, is the founder of *islamicate*, L3C—a consultancy focusing on religious literacy. He is the executive producer of the documentary *American Muslims* and the animated *New York Times* op-doc "The Secret History of Muslims in the US."

Heather Miller Rubens, PhD, is executive director at the Institute for Islamic, Christian, and Jewish Studies in Towson, Maryland.

Vrajvihari Sharan, PhD, is director for Dharmic Life, the Hindu spiritual advisor, and adjunct professor in the departments of linguistics and Asian studies at Georgetown University.

Rev. Marcia Moret Sietstra, DMin, former senior pastor of Spirit of Peace United Church of Christ in Sioux Falls, is the co-founder of South Dakota Faith in Public Life.-

Nikky-Guninder Kaur Singh, PhD, a renowned scholar of Sikh sacred literature, is the Crawford Professor and chair of the department of religious studies at Colby College in Waterville, Maine.

Bin Song, PhD (philosophy), PhD (religious studies), is assistant professor of philosophy and religion at Washington College in Chestertown, Maryland, and the 2023 recipient of its Award for Distinguished Teaching. He is a past-president of North American Paul Tillich Society and the current co-chair of the American Academy of Religion's Confucian Traditions Unit.

Jon M. Sweeney is the author of many books, including *The Pope Who Quit* (2012); coauthor and editor of *Jesus Wasn't Killed by the Jews* (2020); and co-director of The Lux Center for Catholic-Jewish Studies at Sacred Heart Seminary and School of Theology in Franklin, Wisconsin.

Jaxon Washburn, MTS, is a recent graduate of Harvard Divinity School and a former research associate for The Pluralism Project at Harvard University.

Rev. C. Denise Yarbrough, DMin, is director of religious and spiritual life at the University of Rochester, canon for Ecumenical and Interreligious Relations for the Episcopal Diocese of Rochester, and a member of the Standing Commission on Ecumenical and Interreligious Relations for the Episcopal Church.

Index